AWS SOLUTION ARCHITECT ASSOCIATE & AWS CLOUD PRACTITIONER CERTIFICATIONS 2019

The Next Level Guide

Charles Clifford

CONTENTS

PREFACE

Over a career, a lot of time and effort is spent in collecting enough knowledge so that no matter what use case is presented the solution architect will feel like they know what to do. Within that same window of time the evolving methods, technologies and techniques that life presents to the solution architect are continually moving beyond their knowing.

No worries, at the same time, there is a part of the solution architect that just knows in the moment how to walk the walk, carefully over treacherous terrain. When you understand a use case and are present with whatever technology is actually happening in the moment there is a different mode of knowing. This manuscript contains field notes of such moments with Amazon Web Services (AWS) resources and services.

In its most basic expressions, this manuscript is like a dictionary of terms intended for a practitioner new to the AWS cloud. In its more complete expressions, this manuscript is like an encyclopedia of AWS resources and services intended for the AWS cloud architect.

This guidebook can no more make the reader an AWS Solution Architect Associate than buying a guitar does a musician make. If we learn a scale that does not mean that we can play a song. There is no substitute in life for hands-on experiences, and that rule certainly applies to AWS. This guide aspires to help bring a person who is new to working with the AWS cloud into the next level as an AWS certified Cloud Practitioner. From that level, this guide aspires to help a Cloud Practitioner enter into the next level as an AWS certified Solution Architect Associate.

For those familiar with the 2019 AWS Academy Cloud Foundation (CF) and Cloud Architecture (CA) classes, they will recognize their topics scattered throughout this manuscript's table of contents. This same set of readers will also immediately recognize their coherent integration into a single thesis that accurately presents both the CF and the CA materials in whole as well as in part.

These same folks will also see where this manuscript dives deeply into each of those explicit CF and CA topics as well as into their related implicit topics which underlay that unified thesis. The depth of exploration and explanation present in this manuscript is not feasible in a classroom context, since few buyers have the large blocks of time required to be in such a class. So pace yourself as you read through this guide. Each chapter contains big chunks of information which take time to digest and assimilate. It is advised that you not rush through the content.

This manuscript has value to the reader because it functions as a compact source of important information that we need to learn about all of the AWS services and resources covered in both the CF and CA certifications, as well as dozens of other related and important AWS services that are not at present covered in either the AWS Academy CF or CA class.

It is anticipated that, by learning the details of each AWS resource/service, and by contemplating how their features and functions complement each other, the reader will be able to see and imagine the countless ways in which AWS resources and services can be combined, can be integrated, together into a working solution. The scope of their plug-n-play possibilities is, without exaggerating, mind boggling, to be sure. Therefore, rarely in this manuscript, are such hypothetical solutions described. Instead, the intent is to describe only the common-place combinations of resources and services that are direct, one-on-one, links.

By describing the common-place links (that you will likely encounter in the real world) the hope is that the reader will be empowered to create chains of links and do so using their own powers of imagination. Once you learn the important facts about an AWS resource or service, and then put out that same level of effort with the next AWS service, you start to see, through a process akin to osmosis, how the parts fit together to form the whole, link by link into a chain of desired length. For example, given high availability of secured URL content as a business requirement, numerous 'off-the-shelf' AWS resources and services can be quickly, consistently, and securely integrated into a valuable utility highly available in the Internet marketplace.

Until that time when you can see each part clearly and how/where/when/why that part is needed, one has no other option than to dive deeply into each resource/service, learn what can be known through research, memorize its features and functions, and gain hands-on experience with the resource/service. Ideally, the reader will also be applying and refining those understandings in the field, in the real world, in the AWS cloud. It will be those personal experiences that connect of your understanding of an AWS resource/service with the real-world use cases that will produce within you a deeper, commanding, knowledge of AWS; a form of knowledge that is based on your personal experiences of your failures as well as your successes.

The coverage by this manuscript addresses those topics required to be understood by a 2019 AWS certified Cloud Practitioner. Moreover, the scope of this manuscript is thankfully limited to that required to attain the 2019 certification as an AWS Solution Architect Associate. The 2 sections of this manuscript that explain the CF curriculum and the CA curriculum describe which AWS resources and services map to each. This manuscript goes beyond those resources and services covered in the CF and CA curriculums to provide the reader with coverage of new high-value AWS products and services. For example, Docker container services, software engineering services, data analytic services, etc.

Unless you are a techno-geek, the information contained in this manuscript will be dreadfully dull and boring to you. No apologies to the reader are, or can be, offered by this writer for the lack of tragedy or comedy in this manuscript. On rare occasion, given good cause, a diagram is introduced to help the reader see some certain thing.

The vocabulary, the grammar, the rhetoric used in this manuscript functions just like an ETL (extraction-transformation-load) statement, whose purpose is to upload raw data directly into the readers' frontal lobe. The technique is pure brute-force but is always only executed at a pace that the individual reader sets for themselves. Given an AWS resource or service, a formula/algorithm is loosely adhered to while writing about it. There is an introduction that clearly explains what the AWS resource/service is, as well as where and when it is useful. Next, at depth and breath, the AWS resource/service is described in all its practical details, how it is used, and why it is used in certain ways, and where applicable investigates that AWS resource/service from cradle to grave. Over the course of dissecting an AWS resource/service in that manner, engineering principles and generally accepted best practices are introduced at specific places/contexts.

Things not contained herein

The concern of this writer is to transmit knowledge as efficiently and effectively as this media permits, to use this medium to broadcast connectionless communication. As such, the writer's duty is to ensure the quality and correctness of the information contained in each packet placed inside the channel. Beyond that act there is nothing the writer claims as their own concern. This writer is not concerned if packets are lost in transmission or are corrupted in transit or discarded upon arrival.

Though the writer has a strong personal preference for AWS over Azure or GCP, this manuscript is devoid of 'sunshine, lollypops and rainbows' rhetoric intended to cultivate garden path fantasies by, or to promote magical thinking on the part of, the consumer. Therefore, there are no sales pitches herein about any AWS resource or services covered in this manuscript. For purpose of full disclosure, this author has not been compensated by any party to create this manuscript – it's all funded from my dime.

This manuscript explains the what, when, where, how and why about an AWS resource/service. The reader is advised to use this manuscript as a first step on longer journey with each AWS resource and service that interests you. Contemplate the nature of that beast, find out the tricks the resource/service can – for a fee - perform at your command and learn how to operate a herd of them as in a digital circus that amuses you.

The only handholding the manuscript provides is a perspective in which information content is structured into distinct but related parts of a whole, where each part is readily accessible, in its appropriate 2019 setting and easily consumed by the reader. The structure supports a process that is akin to eating an elephant a bite at a time but in this case is the elephant is digital, i.e., is the 2019 AWS products and categories.

For a given AWS product that is part of the AWS Solution Architect Associate certification, any question about it is fair game within the certification exam. There are volumes of certification exam questions available to the public. Therefore, this manuscript does not contain a single, not even 1, question.

The purpose of an examine is to help you evaluate your personal understanding of a topic. That purpose is not shared by this writer, the goal of that purpose is not a concern of this writer. Based on their own experiences, the writer advices the reader to find, to contemplate and know the answer to, as many AWS certification examine questions as proves of benefit to the reader.

INTRODUCTION

El Guapote "Jeffe, would you say that I have a plethora?" From the film 'The Three Amigos"

I might not have the superior intellect of the in-famous El Guapote, but perhaps there is something to be said in praise for the motto 'too much is never enough.' When you look into the 2019 AWS products (i.e., its services and resources) you can see that AWS continues to be very busy releasing new products. Yes, today, AWS has a plethora of product offerings. And, the January 2019 reorganization of AWS services and resources into 23 categories

Analytics	Application Integration	AR & VR	AWS Cost Management
Blockchain	Business Applications	Compute	Customer Engagement
Database	Developer Tools	End User Computing	Game Tech
Internet of Things	Machine Learning	Management & Governance	Media Services
Migration & Transfer	Mobile	Networking & Content Delivery	Robotics
Satellite	Security, Identity & Compliance	Storage	

Table #1: AWS Product Categories, Jan. 2019

Behind the scene, that reorganization has had a profoundly disruptive effect on all of the AWS certification books published before 2019. The pre-2019 AWS certification classes and materials reflect the past and still present AWS cloud architecture. The past and still present AWS products support the 'roll-your-own-service' approach, e.g. you create an Internet-based solution using EC2 instances, EBS, EIN, EIP, VPC, etc.

The present and future foundation of AWS cloud architecture is 'serverless,' e.g., AWS Lambda, Amazon Kinesis, Amazon SNS & SQS, Amazon DynamoDB, Amazon S3, as well as other core serverless services. The present and future AWS cloud architecture is more of an 'avoid-rollin'-your-own-service' approach that allows a client to focus on the computations and the data. In the serverless environment there is little need to focus on EC2 instances, EBS, EIN, EIP, VPC, etc. These past and still present AWS products are under the covers of the serverless services, are transparent to the present and future AWS customer.

By integrating the past with the still present as well as the future AWS cloud architectures, this manuscript harmonizes the dissonance introduced into pre-2019 AWS training materials (by the 2019 reorganization of AWS product categories). Here in this manuscript is the complete 2019 Cloud Foundation (CF) curriculum fully integrated with the complete 2019 Cloud Architect (CA) curriculum.

There is no practical benefit to be gained by learning the cloud foundation if you do not apply that knowledge and dev/op an AWS cloud solution. It is not possible to architect a viable AWS cloud solution unless you have commanding knowledge of AWS resources and services. Taken together, these assertions appear to be like the classic chicken-egg argument. In truth, the individual has to make efforts in both dimensions, during all moments. That is what system engineering is all about, in its most basic expression, on the ground or in the clouds.

2019 AWS CLOUD FOUNDATION (CF) CURRICULUM

The pre-2019 Cloud Architect curriculum had 3 portions, 2 of which were tightly coupled to the past and present 'roll-your-own-service' AWS cloud architecture. Those 2 parts have been re-assembled by the AWS Academy into the new 2019 Cloud Foundation curriculum:

1. Cloud concepts
2. Highlights of AWS core services
3. AWS cloud security
4. Introduction to cloud architecting
5. AWS cloud billing and support services
6. To be successful in the AWS Academy CF class, AWS recommends that the person:
7. Be familiar with cloud computing concepts;
8. Have working knowledge of distributed systems;
9. Be familiar with general networking concepts, and
10. Have working knowledge of multi-tier architectures.

Consequently, there are very few of us who do satisfy their pre-requisites. So, unless you have paid all of the required dues, it is not advised to raise your personal expectations of quick success at fully comprehending the CF materials.

The term 'working knowledge' is a polite way of saying that the reader has already made enough mistakes with a product that they can exclude a bunch of futile gestures, and knows what to do, and can do what needs to be done to build and operate a cloud solution.

This writer does not assume that the reader has paid those dues. This writer understands that we all start from the same line, at which at one point in time we had made zero progress from that line. So, at the back of this manuscript is an appendix that covers the back-ground information needed to understand cloud resources and services provided by any cloud vendor. That appendix is written for all of us mere mortals.

When you have paid those significant dues, the AWS cloud starts looking really good, compared to its cloud competitors. You will find most things you need are on a shelf and are largely plug-n-play components. You will quickly come to appreciate that many of the AWS back-office teams eat a lot of dog-food, i.e., many technologies and tools are invented by AWS which are then used internally by AWS teams before they are released to the general public.

The AWS services and resources available to the public are the same set of services which AWS needs to deploy and operate its infrastructure, its cloud. It pays AWS to make those tools as efficient and simple, as easy to use, as feasible. We, the AWS consumers, benefit from the solutions that AWS creates to solve AWS's internal cloud infrastructure construction and operation challenges.

The shared AWS culture's aspiration to solve the plethora of problems with cloud architecture is the good cause for AWS Serverless Applications. Solving that challenge internally created a suite of AWS services: DynamoDB, Lambda, SNS, Kinesis, etc.. Today, for a fee, we as AWS consumers can leverage those services in a secure, performant efficient, and hopefully cost effective, manner.

CF Highlights of AWS Core Services

AWS identifies the following resources and services, listed below in no particular order, as 'core:'

1. AWS Management Console
2. Amazon Elastic Compute Cloud (Amazon EC2)
3. Elastic Block Store (EBS)
4. Amazon Virtual Private Cloud (VPC)
5. AWS Identity and Access Management (IAM)
6. AWS Organizations
7. AWS Security Groups
8. AWS Cost Explorer
9. AWS Trusted Advisor
10. AWS CloudTrail
11. AWS Config
12. Amazon CloudFormation
13. Amazon Simple Storage Service (S3)
14. Amazon Glacier
15. Amazon Elastic File System (EFS)
16. AWS Lambda
17. Amazon Relational Database Systems (RDS)
18. Amazon Aurora
19. Amazon DynamoDB
20. Amazon Redshift
21. AWS Elastic Beanstalk
22. Amazon Route 53
23. Amazon CloudFront
24. Elastic Load Balancing (ELB)
25. Amazon CloudWatch
26. Auto Scaling
27. AWS Technical Support Plans
28. AWS Command Line Interface (CLI)
29. AWS Software Development Kits (SDKs)

Please refer to the table of contents for the locations in this manuscript where those AWS resources and services are covered. In this manuscript, the coverage of the core AWS resources and services (excluding the AWS CLI and SDKs) goes beyond the scope of the CF material and covers the scope defined in the CA materials. It is important to note that neither the CF or the CA certification exams delve into either the AWS CLI or the AWS SDKs. That is not to suggest however that a cloud architect is not expected to be able to use the AWS CLI or the AWS SDK.

2019 AWS CLOUD ARCHITECTURE (CA) CURRICULUM

The new 2019 Cloud Architect (CA) curriculum covers the services that are the 'serverless' AWS cloud architecture, but more importantly CA has a primary focus on principles, best practices and design patterns for developing and operating solutions that are based on the past, the present and future, AWS cloud architectures.

The cloud architect understands which AWS service has built-in auto-scaling, built-in high availability, built-in fault tolerance, and how/when/where to use them in a solution. The cloud architect understands at which layer of the solution/application/use-case which AWS services can be used to support security, auto-scaling, high availability, and fault tolerance.

It is around the exploration of the design patterns best suited to TCP/IP and HTTPS based systems that the plethora of AWS resources and services are based. And, the best practices for those design patterns, and the architecture principles on which both are founded, are the primary focus of the new 2019 Cloud Architect curriculum.

Best practices, design patterns, and architecture principles are hard-won guidelines, that are un-wise to ignore, and very foolish to violate. They are no more 'shoulds' than is the act of prudently applying the brakes of a moving vehicle. Best practices, design patterns, and architecture principles are not opinions. They are the common sense required when in the cloud. They are our benefactors, our allies and trusted comrades.

The re-categorization of Cloud Architect curriculum is so dramatic and widespread in scope that the pre-2019 content is not nearly adequate to be used to gain the 2019 AWS Solution Cloud Architect Associate certification. The reason for this sorry state of affairs was not the result of anything that the authors ofthose material had done or had failed to do.

In the chapters that follow is the information collected to fill in the gaps that exist between the per-2019 materials and the significantly expanded 2019 materials. Fortunately, not all AWS products are covered in either the 2019 Cloud Foundation or the 2019 Cloud Architect curriculum.

Analytics	Application Integration	~~AR & VR~~	AWS Cost Management
~~Blockchain~~	~~Business Applications~~	Compute	*Customer Engagement*
Database	Developer Tools	~~End User Computing~~	~~Game Tech~~
~~Internet of Things~~	~~Machine Learning~~	Management & Governance	*Media Services*
Migration & Transfer	*Mobile*	Networking & Content Delivery	~~Robotics~~
~~Satellite~~	Security, Identity & Compliance	Storage	

Table #2: AWS Product Categories - Solution Architect Associate Certification, Jan. 2019

The 2019 organization of the old familiar AWS services and resources with new product offerings blends together the well-known with the unfamiliar, the unknown, in ways previously unattainable, inconceivable. This manuscript is made in the re-incarnated AWS image circa Q1 2019.

To be clear, there is very little information present in this manuscript that is not also present in the volumes of documentation published by AWS and freely available to all inquiring minds that have the luxury of time to make such endless journeys. But, to not waste your time while on that endless journey, you need to know what to look for, which requires that you already know what exists inside the AWS libraries and also requires that you already know why, when and where, to use said AWS resource/service, i.e., recognize the design patterns inherent in the use case and understand which best practices are relevant, and where/when/why/how to apply them. This manuscript intends to remedy that disadvantage.

This manuscript is a library, is a collection, of dense concentrations of information about AWS services and resources but only to the extent that the AWS resource/service is germane to attaining certification as an AWS Solution Architect Associate, as of February 2019. This manuscript is a well-organized report of the facts, of just the facts, about AWS resources or services that are the AWS cloud, as well as their best practices and design patterns.

There are > 80 separate AWS resources and services included in AWS Solution Architect Associate certification, all of which are covered in this manuscript. Please refer to the table of content for the topics, AWS resources and services, covered in this manuscript. Go ahead and add them up, and you'll quickly see that there really are a plethora of AWS products.

The new 2019 Cloud Architect curriculum explores the following topics:

- Designing a virtual private cloud.
- Designing for high availability.
- Approaches for automating an infrastructure.
- Approaches for decoupling an infrastructure.
- Designing web-scale storage.
- The Well-Architected Framework.
- The Well-Architected Framework Pillar 1: Operational Excellence.
- The Well-Architected Framework Pillar 2: Security.

- The Well-Architected Framework Pillar 3: Reliability.
- The Well-Architected Framework Pillar 4: Performance Efficiency.
- The Well-Architected Framework discussion with Pillar 5: Cost-Optimization.
- Design patterns for large-scale cloud architectures.
- Trouble-shooting AWS solutions

As is evident, the structure of the table of content of this manuscript reflects the CA topics of study and has been superimposed on the CF curriculum.

To be successful in the AWS Academy CA class, AWS recommends that the person:

- Earned AWS certification as Cloud Practitioner;
- Be familiar with cloud computing concepts;
- Have working knowledge of distributed systems;
- Be familiar with general networking concepts, and
- Have working knowledge of multi-tier architectures.

CLOUD ARCHITECTURE AND DISTRIBUTED SYSTEMS

'The first principle is that you must not fool yourself - and you are the easiest person to fool'
Richard Feynman

Unlike a cloud, cloud architecture does not materialize out of thin-air: it is rooted, not by sky hooks, but in the lineage of terrestrial computing, to which we all owe a deep debt of gratitude in particular to Eric Von Neumann and Alan Turing. As they demonstrated, our notions of a computing machine can limit our creativity, while other notions can extend our creativity with the machines.

One notion, that a system is a temporary construction, was not alien to Mr. VN or Mr. T. But most IT people in most places, most of the time, most often want a system to be permanent. The common belief is that the more permanent the system the longer the paycheck cycle will be. It is difficult to change a belief, one based in fact or in fiction.

In the cloud, everything you can do (for free or for a fee) is temporary. There are countless things you can do in the cloud, more things to do, more quickly, than you probably can do on-premise. A cloud-based solution is like a cloud in the sky: you look up at that sky and you see that cloud. Look up into that same sky sometime later and that cloud has changed or might not be there at all, and where either outcome does not affect your perspective of things.

The temporary nature of a cloud-based application/system triggers notions about the cloud that make anxious (and therefore alienate) most people, most of the time, in most places. Most people, most of the time, in most place, have a deep aversion to the inherent temporary nature of the stuff that we form attachments to. In truth, in time, it all goes bye-bye even me-myself-and-i.

This writer's vision of the cloud is as if it were a green field. If you prefer, a garden of which you are its gardener. As in terrestrial life, a green field is temporary. All fields have their four seasons, and green is only one of those. A field is green only as long as it is able to acquire, preserve, and grow capital profitably. All applications/systems have a profitability shelf-life: no system is permanent; all systems are temporary, move on, follow the money, i.e., don't beat a dead horse, instead pull the plug ... then plug it back in and see if it restarts and ...

The 2019 Cloud IT Paradigm: Simpler Friendlier Cloud

In the past decade:

- The storage and management of information, and
- The hardware and network supporting computations

have become arbitraged commodity services in the cloud.

To understand the cloud, is to understand:

- Virtual Network;
- Virtual Machines;
- Storage;
- Security, and
- Cost Model.

Every cloud solution overlays those dimensions. The layers above these just get more and more complex, and therefore more difficult to understand. In short order, for most people the cloud becomes too abstract/difficult to understand/ master, and therefore meets with high resistance. People fear what they do not understand. People do not like things that are complex and difficult to understand.

It is said that the tell of genius is the ability to keep things simple, but not so simple that only a simpleton can comprehend the response to the business requirements. So, to make things simpler, to make them friendlier, there is the advent of the Serverless Applications in the cloud.

For a serverless application you dev/ops a stateless function/container that automates a single event in your business process model (BPM), in your use case. That function/ container is source code, managed, configured, built, tested, continuously integrated, deployed. Given that function/container, it is AWS's responsibility to devops the infrastructure able to support your computation and information. Each time an instance of that function/container runs you are charged a fee.

Why Offer a Cloud Utility? Follow the $

The business motivation that gave birth to 'cloud computing' aimed to off-load the immense and rapidly growing CAPEX and OPEX (the costs of owning, developing, and operating computing resources).

Imagine a collection of boards, whereon there are board members who are simultaneously on 1-N of those boards, and who wish to decrease/eliminate CAPEX and OPEX for IT related stuff within their dominion(s). Furthermore, imagine that the quality of the IT related stuff is poor. Now, what if IT hardware resources, software services, and ops folks, could become a virtual OPEX, consumed at commodity prices, as an arbitrage?

Hence, AWS, Azure, and GCP. In a marketplace, a cloud resource/service utility is priced as an arbitraged 'commodity.' As in the case of mineral resources, in a physical dominion, there may be 0:1 and only 1 cloud 'commodity service utility' present.

Why Consume a Cloud Utility? Follow the $

If you are on the ground, why go into the clouds or become a hybrid?

- Eliminate/reduce the CAPEX of in-house IT infrastructure
- Outsourced IT infrastructure: computing, networking, and storage resources.
- Eliminate/reduce the OPEX of in-house IT staff;
- Outsourced IT staff: human operators of computing, networking, and storage resources.

Cost benefit analysis:

- What are the lift-to-the-cloud-refactoring charges plus the on-going cloud OPEX (the new operating expenses) over 3 years?

The CAPEX and OPEX savings are worthwhile, more often than not.

Cloud implementation and operation maps best to greenfield, as well as short-term IT ventures. At least 99% of on-site systems were never built to be dynamically provisioned at runtime, whether operated on-site or off-site. Few on-site natives are welcoming to cloud evangelists.

3 DevOps Models

Public cloud

- Off-site, shared IT infrastructure and its management are provisioned to the public, on a pay-as-you-use fee-basis.

Private cloud

- Exclusive contracted use of IT infrastructure and its management are provisioned to a single entity.
- IT infrastructure and its management may be on-

site and or off-site.

Hybrid cloud

- A combination of private cloud and public cloud.

3 Cloud Service Models

The usual 3 cloud service models are:

1. Infrastructure-as-a-Service (IaaS);
2. Platform-as-a-Service (PaaS), and
3. Software-as-a-Service (SaaS),

Each service model can be seen from 2 viewpoints:

- The cloud vendor
- The user/buyer

The role of the Architect is to see and understand the service model from both viewpoints.

Infrastructure-as-a-Service (IaaS)

The cloud vendor:

- Provisions virtual computing and virtual storage resources, typically dynamically on-demand, in real-time (like clean water from a faucet);
- Operates the physical computing and storage resources.

The user/buyer:

- Co-manages the virtual computing resources and virtual storage resources;
- Dashboard of metering metrics of virtual resources consumed;
- Contracted to some flavor of an IaaS pay-per-use paradigm.

Platform-as-a-Service (PaaS)

The cloud vendor:

- Provides the development tools, the application programming interfaces (APIs), software;
- libraries and management of the application services;
- Operates the infrastructure: physical servers, oper-

ating system, network, and storage resources.

The user/buyer:

- Uses the cloud vendor's proprietary development tools, application programming interfaces (APIs), as well as software libraries, thereby hardwiring their system to their chosen vendor platform;
- Dashboard of metering metrics of IaaS and PaaS resources consumed;
- Contracted to some flavor of an IaaS and PaaS pay-per-use paradigm.

Software-as-a-Service (SaaS)

A public-facing web-based application, accessed from most anywhere, anytime, over the Internet, by using a browser. Of course, the generic internet browser is device independent, and can be run on smartphones, tablets, etc.. An ephemeral, very thin (minimal), client runs in the browser. An ultra-lite application, if required, is installed on a user's device. Authentication, authorization, validation, etc., requirements vary widely.

The cloud vendor:

- Operates and manages the IaaS, the PaaS, and the SaaS public-facing application.

The user/buyer:

- Uses the cloud vendor's proprietary , or open source non-proprietary, development tools, application programming interfaces (APIs), as well as software libraries, to implement their web-based service;
- Dashboard of metering metrics of IaaS, PaaS, and SaaS resources consumed;
- Contracted to some flavor of an IaaS ,PaaS, and SaaS pay-per-use paradigm.

It is difficult to turn a profit when all things done by a SaaS are being done by arbitraged commodity resources/services counterfeits and knock-offs of last year's model.

Is that a cloud in the blue sky, or smoke?

Variety is the spice of life, on the land and sea, and in the clouds. The divergence in SaaS makes it extremely difficult to list the characteristics of cloud solutions.

Few cloud solutions embody all of these characteristics, but many claims to do so:

- Outsourced IT operating staff;
- The provisioning of infrastructure is fully automated;
- Easy access from heterogenous internet browsers;
- Horizontal scaling, dynamically in real-time, fully automated;
- Vertical scaling, dynamically in real-time, fully automated;
- Improved performance of infrastructure
- Reduced operating expenses, as well as reduced capital expenses;
- Contracted Service Level Agreements (SLAs);

Resource Limits as Guard-rails

As Darwin demonstrated, when the agenda is long-term resource limits are a good thing. In terms of a cyber-attack that intentionally consumes fee-based AWS resources and services, effective limits on AWS resources and services acts as a boundary that constrains the depth and breadth of the money-sink-hole produced by the attack.

Think of a virtual network in the cloud as a nice new suburb. Underneath the driveways and the foundations of the pretty residences (adorned with cute UIs) are holes opening up outside of every ones' perceptions. One moment, the earth opens up and consumes the real properties. The thing about a crashing virtual environment is that the components are most often cycled-up into their failed states, over and over again and again, as they fall part by part into the ever-widening hole that can well become the whole system. The AWS account has to pay the bill for resource and services consumed during a cyber-attack (and possibly also pay to clean-up the resulting mess to the resident society). Learn to love your resource and service limits. They are our friends in difficult times, as well as in the good times.

In a system, particularly in a system distributed through space and/or time, its attach horizon is weighted by the capital expense required to ensure that its operations are both viable as well as robust. In every system, there are 1:N price points at which operations detracts intolerably from the profitability of the BPM. For every system in the AWS cloud, AWS resource and service limits need to be set in at least 1 of the N price points which when crossed trash profits. Your task is to find those 1:N price points for each bundle of AWS resources and services you operate in the AWS cloud.

AWS Cloud Adoption Framework

In the course of their labors helping thousands of clients, AWS Professional Services developed the ***AWS Cloud Adoption Framework (AWS CAF)***. The CAF is a body of guidelines and best practices that help you expand into the AWS cloud successfully, and to build viable and robust solutions in the AWS cloud.

The AWS CAF has six (6) perspectives, or areas of focus:

Business – how to align the cloud solution and the business process model (BPM);

People – what cloud computing skills are needed by personnel, and how to upgrade them to those skills.

Governance – how to modify (as needed) business processes to ensure that they are compliant when executed in the cloud.

Platform – what design patterns, best practices, and tools are needed to optimize the use of AWS resources and services.

Security – how to define and implement the required security, governance and risk management required by the BPM.

Operations – guidance about how to provision and manage operational services in the AWS cloud.

For more information about the AWS CAF visit the link http://bit.ly/AWSCAF.

Serverless Application Framework

Given, the:

- Complexity of dev/op cloud-based systems and applications;
- Complexity of dev/op cloud vendor resources and services;
- Unsuitability of on-site systems/applications for the clouds;
- Difficulty of understanding complex things;

The adoption of cloud resources and services has been slow and limited to isolated pockets. To facilitate adoption of the AWS cloud platform, Amazon created an easy to dev/op proprietary framework that is well-suited to green-field Serverless Applications in the cloud. The Serverless Application framework hides all of the lower-level details and tasks from view and automates most dev/ops activities that previously required a person to accomplish.

A Strategy for the Clouds

The market strategy adopted by AWS is very similar to that used by Microsoft in 1990s. Microsoft made it easier to dev/ops green-field Windows NT systems and applications. Making it easier to use a complex tool, by hiding many of the details, created the next future IT environment, in which Microsoft came to dominance.

In addition to Amazon, Microsoft and Google have the same cloud market strategy.

AWS Well-Architected Framework

The purpose of the AWS Well-Architected Framework is to raise and increase awareness of the principles and best practices - relevant to security, cost optimization and performance efficiency – that all cloud architects must understand to devops viable and robust cloud solutions.

Developing a viable and robust cloud solution requires of the AWS Well-Architected Framework that it help you think critically about what you are considering doing, so that you can be successful in your endeavors. Admittedly, outside of a very small handful of software houses (i.e., AWS, Microsoft, etc.), you will rarely if ever encounter any IT project where there is any significant level of critical thinking occurring across the IT project team.

This writer is a strong advocate of the AWS Well-Architected Framework. In fact, the writer made certain that this manuscript's physical organization continually inundates the reader in that framework. There are 5 pillars of the AWS Well-Architected Framework:

1. Operational Excellence;
2. Security;
3. Reliability;
4. Performance efficiency, and
5. Cost optimization

This manuscript drills deeply into the AWS resources and services that support each 'pillar,' and correlates the relevant AWS resources and services to each pillar. Within each pillar are located all corresponding Cloud Foundation content as well. A review of the table of content displays how the structure of this manuscript is dictated by these 5 pillars. It is advised that the reader focus of one pillar at a time and work their way from pillar to the next, and then between each pillar.

Well-Architected Design Principles

'In theory, there is no difference between the theory and practice. In practice there is.'

Yogi Berra

So, how does one create a pillar of cloud architecture? First, grab hold of a sky hook, or a left-handed screwdriver, either will do fine, next, ...

A system architecture is based in its design principles,

which AWS defines as follows:

- Stop guessing about your present (and future) resource/service capacity requirements (and their costs);
- Test the production system at scale in a duplicate environment (before the production solution is provisioned in the real-world production environment);
- Automate process (rise above manual process that depend on particular persons) to make wise and prudent experimentation feasible;
- Allow for the evolution of your systems and their architecture (stop serving and feeding the (big ball of mud) machines, and ensure that the machines serve the BPM as the BPM evolves in response to, and exploits the, marketplace);
- Use data to drive system architecture (discover the critically important material facts always present in that small corner of the universe from which the use case arises, without which the solution is not viable or robust),i.e., base decisions on quantitative measurements of known and accepted facts, and
- Improve team skills through 'game days' (a game day is a premediated disaster event (usually announced ahead of time) during which the team and the solution are 'exercised' and evaluated in regard to their ability to recover and continue operating their portion(s) of the BPM. These events provide objective measurements of performance and procedures, with the intention of making improvements as may be needed).

Permanent vs Temporary

The cloud resource or service is temporary, just like clouds in nature, they come and go with the wind. When a resource is needed it is spun up on demand or on schedule, and when it is no longer needed it is terminated. Though a business application may run for years in the cloud, and be highly complex, the underlying infrastructure is not owned by the client, is not managed by the client, is a disposable commodity to the client, is a necessary evil to satisfy the greater good.

When the writer began to build business systems there were no separate disciplines in IT – as there were not enough people capable of doing the work. If you ran the IT project you likely had to assemble the PCs, install operating systems, write programs, create databases, etc.. As the field divided into specializations, you could afford to take your hands out of all the slices of the pie and delegate large chunks of the system to others. The next step was to let go of the hardware/network and learn to love the 'back-office' which was on-premise somewhere and often around the globe. For the past decade the next step that too many find too hard to take is to let go of the on-premise back-office and learn to love the cloud.

There illusion that on-premise solutions are permanent is very appealing and comforting to most folks. Most IT staff exist to serve the machines – the application and systems are both emotional as well as paycheck totems to them. To maintain that illusion of transcendent relationship between IT staff and machines/system, most IT organizations have instinctive emotional needs to keep those machines on-premise. To replace the on-premise machines with cloud resources managed by the cloud utility results in lost IT staff jobs and results in much smaller IT organizations.

It is not the technical challenges of cloud computing that is retarding its rate of adoption, it is the instinctive emotional baggage that is holding it back from reaching its stride. When the temporary nature of life is accepted there is no fear of about being capable of continually delivering results, there is no desire to coast of past efforts.

AWS NETWORKING

The AWS cloud offers these foundation utilities:

1. AWS Networking;
2. AWS Computing;
3. AWS Storage, and
4. AWS Identity.

Not everyone in IT has a personal interest in networking, or in virtual computers, in information storage systems, or system identity. In an on-premise environment, each of those spaces is in itself a comfortable niche within which a career can be well spent happily ignorant of the other three subject areas. The cloud does not offer us that luxury.

In the cloud, even when running serverless applications, a solid understanding of networking, of virtual computers, of information storage, and of system security are a must have. It is not expected that one's understanding be equal to that of a subject matter expert in all 4 subject areas, but there is a need to refrain from interjecting anti-patterns into those dimensions of a system. The more anti-patterns that are present in the system the less the system is a solution. Certain anti-patterns are notorious and can ruin a system, therefore we have design principles and best practices intended to stop them from being carelessly injected into the system.

Though it can be well argued that Security is the most important dimension of a system solution to master, networking is the foundation to which all other AWS resources and services attach and on which all are dependent. So, this manuscript begins with the network stuff. After networking, it is recommended that computing and storage be studied next, in that order. After those 3 are understood, study security and learn how all AWS resources and services fit together securely.

AWS Networking Resources and Services

The AWS Networking resources and services include:

1. AWS Data Centers (Locations)
2. AWS Regions
3. AWS Availability Zones
4. AWS Edge Locations
5. Amazon Virtual Private Cloud (VPC) and Subnets
6. AWS Account's default VPC
7. VPC Routing, Network ACL, and Security Group
8. Dynamic Host Configuration Protocol (DHCP),
9. AWS Elastic IP Address (EIP),
10. AWS Elastic Network Interface (ENI),
11. VPC Log Flows,
12. VPC Endpoint,
13. VPC Peering,
14. AWS Internet Gateway (IGW),
15. Virtual Private Gateways (VPGs),
16. Customer Gateway (CGW),
17. AWS Direct Connect,
18. AWS VPN CloudHub,
19. AWS NAT Instance & AWS NAT Gateway,
20. AWS Egress-only Internet Gateway

AWS Data Center (Location)

The physical foundation of the AWS cloud infrastructure are the data centers. ***A data center is a location where the actual physical data exists.*** AWS has a global footprint, and in various regions around the planet AWS has built clusters of data centers. AWS conforms its' data centers to a set of criteria. Each data center (location):

Is evaluated for environmental risk that are mitigated;

Has redundant design that 'anticipates and tolerates failures' while maintaining service levels;

Has critical system components are deployed in an N+1 configuration, where they are backed up across multiple Availability Zones (AZs), with sufficient capacity to load balance network traffic across the remaining AZs.

Continually monitors resource and service infrastructure usage to support availability commitment and requirements;

The physical address of a data center is not disclosed and all access to them is restricted;

In case of failure, has automated processes that move AWS customer data traffic away from the affected AZ;

Typically houses 50,000 to 80,000 physical servers.

None is a cold site, all are online (accessible from the Internet) and serving customers, and

Uses multiple custom Original Design Manufacturer (ODM) network equipment.

AWS Region

An AWS Location is composed of Regions. The AWS Cloud infrastructure is built around Regions and Availability Zones.

At present, around the world, there is one Local Region, 18 geographic Regions, with plans for 4 more Regions: Bahrain, Hong Kong SAR, Sweden, and a second AWS GovCloud Region in the US. The isolated GovCloud (US) Region is designed to allow US government agencies and customers to move sensitive workloads into the cloud by addressing their specific regulatory and compliance requirements.

Resources in one Region are not automatically replicated to other Regions. When data is stored in one Region it is not replicated outside that Region. AWS never moves customer resources or data out of the Region the customer placed them in. It is the responsibility of the AWS customer to replicate data across Regions, based on the customers' business requirements.

Each Region is:

- A separate geographic area;
- ***Completely independent*** of and designed to be completely ***isolated from the other Regions***.
- ***Composed of multiple Availability Zones (AZs).***

The two main benefits of the AWS Region are:

1. Regions allow you to ***operate application that conform to specific laws and regulations*** in specific parts of the world, and
2. Regions allow you to ***place AWS resources in the area closest to the end users*** who access those resources.

An AWS customer can deploy their application in multiple Regions. AWS products and services are available by Region, so you may not see all Regions available for a given service.

Certification test hint – vocabulary and rhetoric are clues into the meaning of a statement or thought. When the word 'disaster' is present in an AWS certification test question the best interpretation: an entire Region is lost.

AWS Availability Zone (AZ)

Each AWS Region contains 2 or more AZs. Each AZ is:

1. Physically isolated (typically within a metro area);
2. Located in a low-risk-flood-zone;
3. Uses discrete uninterruptable power supply (UPS) and on-site backup generators, where available each is fed via different power grids from independent utilities;
4. ***AZs in a Region are connected through low-latency links***, and
5. Redundantly connected to multiple Tier-1 transit providers.

AWS Edge Location

An Edge Location is where end users access AWS services. Among AWS 114 points of presence around the globe, there are 103 Edge Locations and 11 regional Edge Caches in 56 cities, across 24 countries (in North America, South America,

Europe, Asia and Australia).

The ***requests for Amazon Route 53 and Amazon CloudFront are automatically routed by AWS to the nearest Edge Location.*** In addition, the Edge Locations also offer AWS Shield and AWS Web Application Firewall (WAF) services.

Regional Edge Caches are used by CloudFront to store content that is not frequently accessed to warrant remaining in an Edge Location. The Regional Edge Cache is used by CloudFront to provide content without having to fetch that content from its origin server.

AWS Virtual Private Cloud (VPC)

An AWS VPC is a logically isolated section of an AWS Region, is a virtual network that contains 1-N subnets, where each subnet exists within an AWS Availability Zone (AZ). You can create multiple VPCs in the same Region.

AWS does not advertise your VPC network to the Internet. AWS does not charge a fee for a VPC, however there are fees for use of most AWS resources and services connected to the VPC.

A major advantage of AWS VPC is that you can connect your cloud resources to on-premise data centers by using a Virtual Private Network (VPN) connections.

AWS ***VPC supports both IPv4 and IPv6*** IP addresses. However, the support provided by AWS for IPv6 is distinctly different from and not as rich as the support available with IPv4.

At a minimum, ***an AWS VPC is a subnet defined by a CIDR block of IP addresses.*** To create an AWS VPC, you must provide a CIDR block which defines a range of private IP addresses. You can have up to (5) IPv4 CIDR blocks per VPC. You can have (1) IPv6 CIDR block per VPC. You must diligently manage the CIDR blocks present in the VPC to ensure that their IP addresses do not overlap.

The AWS customer controls the configuration of the VPC. Once you create the VPC, you can modify and change aspects of the VPC. However, ***once a VPC is created you cannot change its:***

- ***CIDR block of IP addresses***
- ***EC2 Instance Tenancy***

AWS offers 4 types of EC2 Instance Tenancy:

- ***Shared Tenancy;***
- ***Dedicated Instance;***
- ***Dedicated Host;***
- ***Placement Group.***

AWS VPC Prohibitions

The AWS VPC does not support:

IP Multicast – a way to transmit an IP datagram to multiple IP addresses.

Broadcast address – a network address to which all hosts connect to and by which all network connected hosts receive IP datagrams.

If the Business Process Model (BPM) requires either IP Multicast or Broadcast addressing, then an 'overlay network' (e.g., IPSec) must be created between the EC2 instances.

As part of the AWS shared responsibilities model, AWS is responsible for the physical network infrastructure. As such, AWS establishes two important VPC prohibitions:

Network Address Spoofing - by default, AWS also protects EC2 instances by treating the instance as a standalone network host. AWS automatically assigns to the EC2 instance its network MAC address. IP addresses are assigned to the EC2 instance either statically (by an administrator) using API request or are assigned dynamically by the AWS network infrastructure. The AWS network only allows EC2 instances to send traffic from IP and MAC addresses that AWS has specifically assigned to them, or the network traffic is dropped.

Packet Sniffing – an EC2 instance host interface configured in 'promiscuous mode' is attempting to receive or sniff network traffic that is intended for a different EC2 instance's host interface. If an EC2 instance host interface is place in promiscuous mode the hypervisor will ensure that traffic addressed to a different instance is not delivered to the promiscuous instance. Even if the two EC2 instance are located on the same physical host and owned by the same AWS account, neither can listen to the other's traffic. In addition, a cache poisoning ARP attack does not work within an EC2 instance or a VPC.

AWS VPC Subnet

The VPC and its subnets is present in the Network Layer of the OSI model, in the Internet Protocol (IP) layer. The AWS ***VPC contains 1 or more subnets, where each subnet is a subdivision (subrange) of IP addresses in a particular CIDR block.*** A subnet is a logical segment, is a contiguous range, of IP addresses. The typical use of subnet is to isolate a workload environment.

In this environment, all of your resources that require direct access to the internet (including public-facing load balancers, NAT instances, bastion hosts, etc.) would go into the public subnet, while all other instances would go into your private subnet. An exception would be resources that require absolutely no access to the Internet, either directly or indirectly. These resources would go into a separate private subnet.

Some environments try to use subnets to create layers of separation between "tiers" of resources, such as putting your backend application instances and your data resources into separate private subnets. This practice requires you to more accurately predict how many hosts you will need in each subnet, making it more likely that you will either run out of IP addresses more quickly, or leave too many IP addresses unused when they could be used elsewhere.

Subnets can provide a very basic element of segregation between resources by using a network access control list, or network ACL, rules. However, security groups can provide an even more fine-grained level of traffic control between your resources, without the risk of overcomplicating your infrastructure and wasting or running out of IP addresses.

With this approach, you just need to anticipate how many

public and how many private IP addresses your VPC needs and use other resources to create segregation between resources within a subnet.

Best practice - for a given VPC, subnets should be used to define internet accessibility, so there might not be a good reason to have more than one public and one private subnet per Availability Zone.

For each VPC, you can create 3 types of subnets:

1. Private or
2. Public, or a
3. Virtual Private Network (VPN).

You can create up to (200) subnets per VPC (if it's (5) CIDR blocks can support them all).

When you add an EC2 instance to a subnet, a private IP address of that subnet is automatically assigned to the instance.

Best practice - The majority of resources on AWS can be hosted in private subnets, using public subnets for controlled access to and from the internet as necessary.

Best practice - You'll always need more private IP addresses than public IP addresses because the more resources you expose to the internet, the more vulnerable you become.

Best practice - You can protect your IP resources by placing them in a private subnet.

Best practice - When you plan your architecture, it's important to try to anticipate how many hosts your VPC might need and how many of those hosts can be placed in private subnets.

VPC Network Topology

Nested within a VPC's CIDR block, you can create other subnets, of 3 different types (public; private; VPN), each of which is allocated a sub-range of the CIDR block's IP addresses.

A subnet nested inside a VPC's CIDR block subnet is as deep as it goes. The largest subnet that can be created in a VPC is accomplished by defining a subnet that includes the IP address range of the VPC in which the subnet is created. For example, if the VPC's CIDR block were 10.0.0.0/16, then its largest subnet is also 10.0.0.0/16.

What makes AWS somewhat complicated is that, you can have 1 VPC based on the 1 primary CIDR block that is an IPv4 block or is a IPv6 CIDR block and that same exact VPC can have up to 4 secondary IPv4 CIDR blocks as well. Of course, the 3 types of subnets can likewise be created from out of the secondary CIDR blocks as well.

A given AWS Account can create up to (5) VPCs per Region.

1 VPC Pattern

There are limited use cases where one Virtual Private Cloud could be appropriate.

High-performance computing environments might work best entirely within a single VPC, as a single VPC environment will have lower latency than one that's spread across multiple VPCs.

The use of Microsoft Active directory for identity management might best be limited to one VPC for the strongest security measures.

For small, single applications that are managed by one person or a very small team, it might be easiest to use one Virtual Private Cloud.

In most cases, there are two primary patterns for organizing your infrastructure: Multi-VPC or Multi-Account.

Multi-VPC & Multi-Account Patterns

The Multi-VPC pattern has one Region with four different VPCs—shared services, development, test and production each have their own VPC.

With the Multi-Account pattern, you can have multiple Amazon web services accounts with the same information—such as shared services, development, test and production—instead of having multiple VPCs.

The Multi-VPC Pattern

The Multi-VPC pattern with one account is easier to maintain for smaller organizations.

Multi-VPC patterns are best suited for a single team or for organizations, such as Managed Service Providers, or MSPs, that maintain full control over the provisioning and management of all resources in each application environment.

Limited teams make maintaining standards and managing access far easier.

For example, a single team developing a large e-commerce application might use this pattern when the developers have full access to the development and production environments.

Also, this pattern is very common with Managed Service Providers who manage all resources in test and production.

An exception would be governance and compliance standards that might require workload isolation, regardless of organizational complexity.

The Multi-Account Patterns

Multi-Account patterns are best suited for:

- larger organizations;
- organizations with multiple IT teams and
- medium-sized organizations that anticipate rapid growth.

It's easier with larger companies to manage with multiple accounts, versus having everything inside of one account with multiple VPCs.

AWS VPC Components

The AWS VPC consists of these (TCP/IP related) components:

- ***A Classless Inter-Domain Routes (CIDR) Block;***
- ***An Amazon DNS server and a Dynamic Host Configuration Protocol (DHCP) option set;***
- ***An implicit Router that is invisible to you, and Route tables;***
- ***A Main subnet and may have other subnets as well;***
- ***The Main subnet has a Default Route Table called the Main Route Table. The Default Route Table is a***

private route table, it does not allow any traffic with host interfaces located in the Internet;

- ***Security Group, which allows inbound traffic from instances assigned to the same Security Group and allow all IPv4 and IPv6 outbound traffic;***
- ***Network Access Control Lists (NACLs)), which allows all inbound and outbound traffic to a subnet and which can be modified;***

Optional VPC Components include:

- AWS Internet Gateways (IGWs);
- Elastic IP (EIP) addresses;
- Elastic Network Interface (ENI);
- VPC Endpoints;
- VPC Peering;
- AWS Network Address Translation (NATs) instances and NAT gateways;
- AWS Egress-only Internet Gateway;
- Virtual Private Networks (VPNs);
- AWS Direct Connect;
- Virtual Private Gateway (VPG);
- Customer Gateways (CGWs);
- VPN CloudHub;
- VPC Log Flows;

Default VPC

Each AWS Account has a default AWS VPS. The default AWS VPC contains 1 private subnet. However, ***you can create public and Virtual Private Network (VPN) types of subnets as well.***

Every AWS Account has a default Virtual Private Cloud (VPC).

When you create an AWS Account, within the Availability Zone (AZ) in the Region used to create that AWS Account, an AWS Virtual Private Cloud (VPC) – called the default VPC - is automatically created for the AWS Account.

Each Region in your AWS Account has a default VPC.

If you create a VPC-based resource (such as Amazon EC2, Amazon RDS, Elastic Load Balancing, etc.) but don't specify a custom VPC, it will be placed in your default VPC in that Region.

Default VPCs are configurable like other VPCs.

AWS accounts created before December 2013 do not have a default VPC.

The default VPC has:

- ***Default CIDR range is 172.31.0.0/16;***
- ***A Security Group (in which EC2 instances are launched by default);***
- ***Dynamic Private IP addresses (controlled by a Security Group);***
- ***Dynamic Public IP addresses (controlled by a Security Group);***
- ***AWS-provided DNS names;***
- ***Private DNS name;***
- ***Public DNS name;***
- ***Internet Gateway (IGW);***
- ***Default Main Route table (that connects the default subnet to the IGW);***
- ***Default Network ACL;***
- ***The default VPC has internet-routable traffic.***

Best practice - In general, this situation with the default VPC presents risk because many people know the default CIDR range and that those ranges are automatically connected to internet gateways by default unless they are disabled.

How to Use the Default VPC

Default VPCs are a quick start solution. They provide an easy way to test launching instances of your VPC-based resources without having to set up a new VPC.

When an EC2 instance is launched into a default VPC, AWS automatically provides the instance with both public and private DNS hostnames that correspond to the public IPv4 and private IPv4 addresses for the instance.

Best practice - use default VPCs and their subnets only for experimenting in your AWS account.

For real-world applications, create your own VPCs and subnets. You'll have greater control and knowledge of their configurations.

With the default VPC, you can:

- Create additional subnets and change Route Rules;
- Create additional network controls: Security Groups; NALs, Routing.
- Set hardware VPN options between the default VPC and an on-premise TCP/IP network

Do not delete the AWS Account's default VPC. You create many problems if you delete the AWS Account's default VPC. If the AWS Account's default VPC is deleted, you can re-create it by submitting a AWS Support Ticket.

Default Subnets in Default VPC

The default subnets in the default VPC:

- Are created within each Availability Zone for each default VPC.
- Have a public subnet with a CIDR block of /20 (with 4,096 IP addresses).
- Is a public subnet with a CIDR block range of /20 with over 4,000 IP addresses.
- Can be converted, like any public subnet, into a private subnet by removing its route to the internet gateway.

When a new AZ is added to a Region, your default VPC in that Region gets a subnet placed in the new AZ (unless you've made modifications to the default VPC).

Best practice - Using the default subnet and the default VPC is like leaving the router login and password set to admin. Many people might know how to use these default credentials and it's not very secure.

How to Create an AWS VPC

In AWS two types of virtual private cloud can be created:

1. EC2-Classic, and
2. VPC

AWS has deprecated the EC2-Classic type, so only the VPC type is covered in this manuscript.

Like all creative processes, creating an AWS VPC requires careful planning and the execution or a series of well executed tasks. ***The first two steps have inescapable consequences, for good or for ill: choosing a Region and choosing how many AZs to use.***

Step #1 - Select a Region

First, you need to determine where you want to host your data.

Before you can design and build a VPC, you have to choose the Region in which the VPC will exist.

Choosing a region involves 4 main considerations:

1. Data sovereignty and compliance
2. Proximity of users to the data
3. Service and feature availability
4. And cost effectiveness

Data Sovereignty & Compliance

Your first consideration is understanding where you can legally host your infrastructure.

What are the national and local data security laws?

Keep in mind that your data will be subject to the laws of the country and locality where it's stored.

Is customer data allowed outside of the country?

Some laws dictate that if you're operating your business in their jurisdiction, you can't store that data anywhere else.

Governance Requirements

Compliance standards, e.g., the Health Insurance Portability and Accountability Act (HIPA), have strict guidelines on how and where data can be stored.

AWS opened its first carbon-neutral Region in 2011 and AWS now offers 5 separate carbon-neutral Regions.

Proximity of Users to the Data

A second consideration to look for is proximity to your user base.

Proximity is a big factor in choosing your Region, especially when latency is critical.

In most cases, the latency difference between using the closest Region and the farthest Region is relatively small but even small differences in latency can impact a customer experience.

An AWS internal study in 2006 found that every 100-millisecond delay on Amazon.com corresponded to a 1 percent drop in sales.

Customers expect responsive environments and as time goes by and technology becomes more powerful, customers' expectations rise as well.

All AWS services are priced per Region, which means some Regions are more expensive than others.

Best practice - If you have two Regions that are equidistant from one another, compare the costs.

Service and Feature Availability

The next consideration should be understanding which services and features are available.

Some services are only available in limited Regions.

Some services can cross Regions but have increased latency.

Services are expanded to new Regions regularly.

Rather than waiting until a service is available everywhere before launching it, AWS releases a service when it's ready and expand its availability as soon as possible.

Cost Effectiveness

Finally, you want to consider cost effectiveness because service costs vary by Region.

However, in cases where the differences in latency, compliance, or service availability between Regions are minimal, you might be able to save money by using the lower-cost Region for your environment.

Some services, e.g., S3, have costs for transferring data out.

If you have Amazon EC2 instances, make sure that they're in the same Region because you start incurring costs when you transfer data outside of a Region.

Keep this in mind when you decide where to place your infrastructure and host your data.

Best practice - for an infrastructure is to use at least two Regions, so if one Region goes down because of a catastrophic event, your infrastructure can still serve your customers.

In circumstances where your customers are in different areas of the globe, you might consider optimizing the customer experience by replicating your entire environment to multiple Regions that are closer to your customers.

Because AWS is designed to allow you that kind of flexibility and because you only pay for what you use, you could easily scale your existing environment down as a way to mitigate the cost of adding another environment.

The downside to that approach is that you now have two environments to manage and not all of your components will scale down enough to mitigate all of the new component costs.

Additionally, you might have to maintain one single storage "source of truth" in one Region—such as a master Amazon Relational Database Service, or Amazon RDS, instance. Your secondary Region would have to communicate with the primary Region, which can increase latency and cost for those operations.

How Many AZs to use?

Best practice - start with 2 AZ per Region. If resources in one Availability Zone are unreachable, your application will be more fault tolerant.

Most applications can be designed to support two Availability Zones but may not benefit from more, because they use data sources that only support primary and secondary failures.

For heavy Amazon EC2 Spot instance usage or data sources that go beyond active or passive, such as Amazon DynamoDB, there might be a benefit to using more than two Availability Zones. However, using more than two Availability Zones isn't usually cost-effective.

For applications that heavily use Spot Instances, AWS recommends 2 AZ, or you can use more for additional price options. Because Spot instances are priced according to AZ, you could use two AZ to get the best price, even when prices change.

For applications that have relational database services, AWS recommends 2 AZs be used to support both active and passive.

For applications with Cassandra or MongoDB, AWS recommends 2:N AZs should be used for extremely high availability.

It is relatively easy to deploy a system across multiple AZs. However, as there can be governance issues specific to a Regions, governance issues can also be germane when selecting AZs to deploy into.

Creating a VPC

You can use the VPC Wizard to create a VPC but though the VPC Wizard is not covered in this lecture, the matters addressed do not differ fundamentally from what the VPC Wizard is able only in part to do.

After you select the Region in which the AWS VPC will exist, you assign a meaningful name to the new VPC.

To be restricted to 1 AZ in the Region (which makes the VPC a single point of failure):

You can specify which AZ in the Region the VPC will be created in.

To span all AZs in the Region (where there is 1 subnet of the

VPC in each AZ):

Do not specify which AZ in the Region the VPC will be created in.

A VPC is Region specific.

A Subnet is AZ specific.

After the VPC is created ***two things cannot be changed:***

1. ***The CIDR block***
2. ***EC2 Instance Tenancy***

VPC Immutable CIDR Blocks

The CIDR block (the IP address range) that you use when you create the VPC cannot be changed. You can modify the IP address range of the VPC by adding and removing secondary CIDR blocks.

The CIDR block(s) must not be the same or larger than the CIDR range of a route in any of the VPC route tables. When you associate a CIDR block with your VPC, a route is automatically added to your VPC route tables to enable routing within the VPC (the destination is the CIDR block and the target is 'Local').

AWS VPC Takes 5 IP Addresses from every CIDR Block

When you define the CIDR block of your subnet, AWS automatically consumes 5 of the IP addresses in every CIDR block:

- The 1st 4 IP addresses and
- The last IP address.

AWS uses these 5 IP addresses for internal networking purposes:

- 10.0.0.0: Network address;
- 10.0.0.1: reserved by AWS for the VPC Router;
- 10.0.0.2: reserved by AWS. The IP address of the DNS server is always the base of the VPC network range plus two. However, AWS also reserves the base of each subnet range plus two;
- 10.0.0.3: reserved by AWS for future use;

- 10.0.0.255: network broadcast address. ***AWS does not support broadcast in a VPC.***

In AWS the smallest IPV4 CIDR block you can define is a /28 which is a 16 IP address sized network. The maximum size of an IPv4 CIDR block is /16 which is 65,536 IP addresses.

If you choose IPv6, the size of the CIDR block is fixed to /56.

Remember to subtract the 5 IP address reserved by AWS, taken and held by the house. In AWS, therefore, the smallest subnet you can use has 11 IP addresses.

VPC's Amazon DNS Server

When a VPC is created in AWS, AWS automatically provisions within it an Amazon DNS server. The Amazon DNS server is used to resolve the DNS domain names.

In addition, for the VPC, ***AWS automatically creates and associates with the VPC a DHCP option set***. Each VPC must be associated with 1 and only 1 DHCP option set. The DHCP is used to pass information about a host interface in a TCP/IP network to other hosts in the network.

A host interface configuration parameter is called an option. By manipulating the values of DHCP options, ***you direct the host interface name assignments to the EC2 instances when they boot within the VPC.***

The set includes two options, to which AWS assigns default values:

- ***domain-name***=domain-name-for-your-region
- ***domain-name-servers=AmazonProvidedDNS***

The value AmazonProvidedDNS represent the Amazon DNS server that AWS automatically provisioned to the VPC. By default, ***the Amazon DNS server enables DNS for EC2 instances that need to communicate over the VPC's Internet Gateway (IGW)***.

The Amazon DNS uses an IP address at the base of the VPC's IPv4 CIDR block, plus two. The example that AWS gives is: for a DNS Server on a 10.0.0.0/16 network, its' reserved IP address is 10.0.0.2. For VPCs with multiple IPv4 CIDR blocks, the DNS server IP address is located in the primary CIDR block. If the allowed, AWS does allow queries of the Amazon DNS server at IP address 169.254.169.253 (not supported by Windows 2008) as well.

When an EC2 instance is launched in a VPC, AWS assigns private IP address and a private DNS hostname. If the EC2 instance also receives a public IP address, a public DNS hostname is assigned to the EC2 instance as well. AWS does not provide DNS hostnames for EC2 instances that use IPv6 addresses.

If the DCHP *domain-name-servers* option is set to *AmazonProvidedDNS*, that determines the format of both the private hostname and the public hostname, depending on the Region.

The private DNS hostname format for us-east-1 the format is ip-private-ipv4-address.ec2.internal. For all other Regions the format is ip-private-ipv4-address.region.compute.internal.

The AWS provided ***private (internal) DNS hostname resolves to the private IPv4 address*** assigned by AWS to the EC2 instance.

The public DNS hostname format for us-east-1 the format is ec2-public-ipv4-address.compute-1.amazonaws.com. For all other Regions the format is ec2-public-ipv4-address.region.compute.amazonaws.com.

Each EC2 instance is configured to limit the number of packets that it can send to the Amazon DNS server. The maximum is 1024 packets per second per network interface. That limit cannot be increased.

The number of queries that an Amazon DNS server can support per second is varies based on the type of query, the size of the response and the protocol used.

VPC DNS Attributes

Name resolution within the VPC must be supported, and that support is provided by a DNS service, or else name resolution will fail. AWS provides the Amazon Route 53 DNS server, and the AWS client can provide their own DNS server as well. To those ends, AWS provides VPC DNS attributes that the client can configured as needed.

If the ***VPC attribute enableDnsHostnames*** determines whether the EC2 instance launched in the VPC is assigned a public DNS hostname. If this attribute is set to true, the instances are assigned a public DNS hostname. If the VPC is created using the VPC wizard, by default AWS sets this attribute value to true. If the VPC is created using API, the AWS CLI, or AWS SDK, by default AWS sets this attribute value to false.

The ***VPC attribute enableDnsSupport*** determines whether the DNS resolution is supported for the VPC. If set to false, the resolution of public DNS hostnames to IP address is not enabled. If set to true, queries to the Amazon DNS server at the 169.254.169.253 IP address, or the reserved IP address at the base of the VPC IPv4 network range plus two will succeed. If set to false, then the Amazon DNS server is not able to provide DNS resolution for the EC2 instances launched in the VPC. If the VPC is created using the VPC wizard, by default AWS sets this attribute value to true. If the VPC is created using API, the AWS CLI, or AWS SDK, by default AWS sets this attribute value to true.

If either of these two VPC DNS attributes are set to false, then the DCHP domain-name-servers option must be set to a custom DNS server provided by the client. That custom DNS server must be configured to provide proper DNS resolution to the EC2 instance. The custom DNS server must assign the private DNS hostname to the EC2 instances, and also resolve them. If the custom DNS server assigns a public DNS hostname to the EC2 instance that public DNS hostname cannot be viewed in the Amazon Management Console, nor can it be manipulated by the AWS CLI or the AWS SDK.

VPC DHCP Option Set

DHCP options can be configured for your AWS VPC:

- ***domain-name-servers*** [the IP addresses of up to 4

domain name servers, separated by commas.]

- ***domain-name*** [the desired domain name, e.g., uc-denver.edu]
- ***ntp-servers*** [the IP addresses of up to 4 Network Time Protocol (NTP) servers, separated by commas.]
- ***netbios-name-servers*** [the IP addresses of up to 4 NetBIOS name servers (Microsoft WINS server address), separated by commas.]
- ***netbios-node-type*** [there are 4 netbios node types (1,2,4,8) but broadcast and multicast are not supported. When configured for an AWS VPC, set this option = 2]
- When you create an AWS VPC ***two DHCP options are automatically set by AWS***:
- ***domain-name-servers*** – the default value is set to AmazonProvidedDNS.

The AmazonProvidedDNS is an AWS DNS that provision DNS functions to EC2 instances that need to communicate over the VPC's IGW.

The DNS is a hierarchical and distributed system invented in 1985.

The function of the DNS is to it translate a domain name to its numerical IP address.

domain-name – the default is the domain name of the AWS Region in which you created the VPC.

To assign you own domain to you EC2 instances, you need to create a custom DHCP option set and assign it to your VPC.

Once you create a DHCP option set you cannot modify it. If you need to specify different DHCP option values, you need to create a new option set.

Launched EC2 instances pick up the new DHCP option set when they renew their DHCP lease. This allows all EC2 instances booted and launched in that VPC to point to the specified domain and DNS servers.

To use your own DNS server, you must create a new set of DHCP

options for your VPC.

Best practice – create a DHCP options set for your AWS Directory Service directory and assign the options set to the VPC in which your directory is located.

If a Windows DNS server is provisioned in the VPC:

1. The existing DCHP options set must be disassociated from the VPC.
2. A new DHCP option set must be created with the Windows DNS server IP address as the DNS server.
3. That new DHCP option set must then be associated with the VPC.

Auto-Assign Public IP Addresses

It is not possible to manually associate or disassociate a public IP address with an EC2 instance. At the ***subnet*** level of the VPC there is a ***configuration attribute called auto-assign*** that ***determines if a network interface*** created in the subnet is ***automatically assigned a public IP address***.

When the auto-assign is set as true, a public IP address from AWS's pool of public IP addresses (not from among those in your AWS account) ***is assigned to the EC2 instance's primary network interface*** (eth0). Through network address translation (NAT) the public IP address is mapped to the EC2 instance's primary private IP address. ***AWS decides when a public IP address is disassociated from the EC2 instance. A public IP address disassociated from an EC2 instance is returned to the AWS pool, and is no longer available for use by the EC2 instance.*** If there is a need to persist a public IP address of an EC2 instance, then use an Elastic IP Address.

If the subnet's auto-assign attribute setting if false, that setting can be overridden at instance launch, and a public IPv4 IP address can be assigned to the EC2 instance despite the subnet's auto-assign setting.

Types of VPC Subnets

Once you create the VPC, you can modify and change aspects of the VPC. For each VPC, you can create 3 types of subnets:

1. Private or
2. Public, or a
3. Virtual Private Network (VPN).

By default, all subnets can route between each other, whether they are private or public. You can create up to (200) subnets per VPC (if it's (5) CIDR blocks can support them all).

When you add an EC2 instance to a subnet, a private IP address of that subnet is automatically assigned to the instance.

If the cloud architecture consists of an Internet facing web service that communicates with back-end process, such as database services, AWS recommends that the VPC contain both a public subnet and a private subnet. In this scenario, the web service runs inside the public subnet, and the back-end process are deployed inside the private subnet (so that they are not accessible from routes over the Internet). Route tables and Security Groups are configured to allow authorized network traffic between the web service and the back-end processes.

How to Create a Public Subnet in an AWS VPC

Required changes to the VPC:

- Attach an IGW to the VPC;
- Create a subnet route table rule to send all non-local traffic (0.0.0.0/0) to the IGW;
- Or you can scope the non-local traffic to a narrow range of IP addresses, even to just known IP Addresses, of interfaces in the Internet, or even EIP Addresses.
- Carefully configure your Network ACLs and Security Group rules to allow only authorized traffic to flow between EC2 instances in the VPC.

Required change to an EC2 instance in the now Public subnet:

- Assign a Public IP Address to the instance, or

- Assign an Elastic IP (EIP) Address to the instance.

VPC Router

The Router takes packages off of the Ethernet layer, examines the package's destination IP address and compares it with information about directly connected subnets and remote networks, kept in its Route Table (which it accesses in RAM).

A directly connected subnet is one associated with an interface on the Router itself.

Remote networks are added to the routing table using either a dynamic routing protocol or by configuring static routes.

The Router uses the route table to determine which is the best way to direct that package through the neighborhood Network Layer topology.

Directing Traffic Between VPC Resources

As we have discussed, your Amazon VPC is your own logically isolated part of the AWS Cloud. Every VPC has a default route table.

A route table is a map that tells you how to enter and leave your network. It contains a set of rules, called routes, which are used to determine where network traffic is directed. You can have main route tables, which is the default that's displayed and custom route tables. For example, you can use custom route tables if you need infrastructure within your VPC that can connect back to your on-premises environment.

All route tables include a local route entry. When you create a VPC, it automatically has a main route table. Initially, the main route table—and every route table in a VPC —contains only a single route: a local route that enables communication within the VPC. ***You can't delete the local route in a route table.*** When you launch an instance in the VPC, the local route automatically covers that instance. You don't need to add the new instance to a route table. You can create additional custom route tables for your VPC.

Each subnet in your VPC must be associated with a route table, which controls the routing for the subnet. If you don't explicitly associate a subnet with a particular route table, the subnet is implicitly associated with—and uses—the main route table. A subnet can be associated with only one route table at a time, but you can associate multiple subnets with the same route table.

A best practice is to use custom route tables for each subnet, which enables granular routing for destinations.

Route Table

The Router service and Route tables are present in the Network Layer of the OSI model, in the Internet Protocol (IP) layer. Every subnet has 1 route table. A Route Table can be associated with 2-N subnets. A Route table contains a set of allow rules/routes. These rules are applied to network traffic in a subnet and are used to determine where network traffic is directed. You can have up to (50) rules/routes per Route table.

A Route table (typically in RAM) contains information about the network topology in its immediate surroundings. For each destination interface, the network address and subnet mask of the interface, the metric (a path through which the package is to be sent), along with the interface type and number, are entered into the routing table.

VPC's CIDR's Main Subnet's Main Route Table

A VPC's CIDR block has a Main subnet. The VPC's CIDR block's Main subnet has a Main Route Table. ***The Main Route Table is the VPC's CIDR block's default route table.***

The default, or main, route table cannot be deleted. You can modify the Main Route Table. But, it is best not to. You can replace the Main Route Table. But, it is best not to.

Best practice – don't fix what ain't broken. Work above the system.

Custom Route Table

All subnets within a VPC's CIDR block that are not explicitly associated with a Custom Route Table use (are by inheritance automatically associated with) the VPC's Main subnet's Main Route Table.

Best Practice – leave the Main Route Table of the Main subnet of the VPC in its original state, even with only the local route. Assign a Custom Route Table to subnets 2-N that you create from the VPC's CIDR block. In the CIDR block's 2-N subnets, replace the Default Route Table with a Custom Route Table. Provision AWS resources and services in the 2-N subnets.

When you create a Custom Route Table it is a private route table, until you explicitly add to it those rules that allow traffic with interfaces in the Internet.

Immutable Local Route

If your VPC has more than one IPv4 CIDR block, your route tables contain a local route for each IPv4 CIDR block.

If you've associated an IPv6 CIDR block with your VPC, your route tables contain a local route for the IPv6 CIDR block.

The local route is a rule that:

- Enables the exchange of messages within the VPC.
- Cannot be modified, cannot be deleted.

Given a route rule, the target of 'Local' means only traffic can flow within the subnet and no other traffic is allowed – the rule refers to a private subnet.

Non-Routable VPC IP Addresses

The IP Addresses of the AWS VPC subnet are always Private IP Addresses, that is, ***are non-routable on the Internet***. An EC2 instance is only aware of its Private IP Address.

The EC2 instances in different subnets within a given VPC use the rules/routes in the Route tables to exchange messages. To ensure that an EC2 instance in one subnet (of a VPC) cannot communicate with an EC2 instance in another subnet (of the same VPC), you must ensure that there are no routes in (the route table of each subnet) which allow traffic from one subnet to the other.

Route Table per Subnet Type

A subnet's route table dictate's the subnet type:

1. Public subnet has a route table that directs the subnet's traffic to the Amazon VPC's Internet Gateway (IGW).
2. VPN-only subnet has a route table that directs the subnet's traffic to a VPC's Virtual Private Gateway (VPG).
3. Private subnet has a route table that does not direct the subnet's traffic to an IGW. However, EC2 instances in a private subnet can use a NAT Gateway or a NAT Instance to communicate with host interfaces in the Internet.

AWS Route Table Facts

Keep the following facts in mind about AWS route tables:

- The VPC's default route table routes traffic between subnets in a VPC.
- You can have up to (250) route tables per VPC.
- A Route Table can be associated with 1-N subnets.
- You can create additional Custom Route Tables for your VPC and its subnets.
- You can replace the VPC's Main subnet's main route table with your custom route table.
- Any new VPC that you create will automatically use your custom route table by default.
- After adding an IGW to the VPC remember to add the 1.0.0.0/0 route to the subnet's Route table, otherwise instance launched within the subnet cannot be reached through routes from the Internet.

AWS VPC Security Groups

AWS supports two types of permissions:

1. User-based, and

2. Resource-based

A Security Group is a virtual stateful firewall present in your VPC. A ***Security Group controls inbound and outbound network traffic to EC2 instances and AWS resources in the VPC***. When you ***change a Security Group, the effect is immediate.***

All EC2 instances must be launched into a Security Group. The VPC ***Security Group operates at the EC2 instance level and is your 1st line of defense.***

VPC's Default Security Group

A VPC has a default Security Group. ***The default Security Group allows inbound traffic from EC2 instances assigned to the same Security Group. The default Security Group allows all outbound IPv4 and IPv6 traffic.***

You can change the rules of the VPC's Default Security Group, but you cannot delete it. When an EC2 instance is launched, if a Security Group is not specified, then the EC2 instance is launched into the VPC's Default Security Group.

Best practice – refrain from using the VPC's default Security Group, and instead create your own Security Groups which AWS ensures by default does not allow inbound network traffic to EC2 instances and which ensures that EC2 instances launched within that security group are not able to exchange messages unless the required allow rules exists.

Security Groups Secure Traffic to EC2 Instances

Even if 2 EC2 instances are launched in the same (not the default) ***Security Group they cannot exchange messages until the required allow rules are created.***

By design, in your Security Group ***inbound network traffic not explicitly allowed by a rule is prohibited to/between EC2 instances*** and all other AWS resources in you VPC. By default, ***network traffic outbound from EC2 instances is allowed*** in your VPC.

By default, a security group will deny all incoming traffic. You can use rules to control that traffic that filter based network protocols such as Transmission Control Protocol, or TCP, User Datagram Protocol, or UDP and Internet Control Message Protocol, or ICMP.

Because ***a security group is stateful, if your inbound request is allowed, the outbound response is allowed automatically.*** For example, if you initiate an HTTP request to your instance from your home computer and your inbound security group rules allow HTTP traffic, information about the connection including the source IP address and port number) is tracked. The HTTP response from your instance to your home computer is recognized as part of an established connection and allowed through the security group, even if the security group rules restrict outbound HTTP Traffic.

Security Groups Secure Application Tiers

You can use an entire CIDR block or another security group to create layers of security to define who or what has access to your cloud resources.

Multiple tiers is a common application architecture, one in which there is an Internet-facing auto-scaling load balancer in front of an auto-scaling website behind which there is an internal auto-scaling load balancer in front of an auto-scaling application service behind which there is an auto-scaling information storage service.

Each application tier scales horizontally based on a schedule or on demand adding/removing resources. When doing so, each tier uses its own dedicated Security Group. The EC2 instances that make up the load balancer tier in front of the website tier exist in their own Security Group that is different and distinct from the Security Group in which the EC2 instances exist that make up the load balancer tier in front of the application.

It is best practice to create a Security Group per tier that defines inbound rules that allow specific traffic per protocol. Because a security group is stateful, given an allowed inbound request, the outbound response is allowed automatically (and therefore does not need to be defined - as an outbound rule in a security group).

Continuing with the common multi-tier application architecture as our example, the Internet facing load balancer security group has an inbound rule that allows TCP on port 443 where the source is 0.0.0.0/0 (Any). The website security group has an inbound rule that allows TCP on port 80 where the source is the website's load balancer tier. The security group of the internal load balancer has an inbound rule that allows TCP on port 8080 where the source is the website tier. The application service's security group has an inbound rule that allows TCP on port 8080 where the source is the application load balancer tier. The information storage security group has an inbound rule that allows TCP on port 3306 where the source is the application tier.

Custom Application Ports

Applications can be built to use custom ports (a valid port number that is not already claimed and in use (on the host interface)) and of course that application's custom port has to be reachable by network traffic. When such an application that uses a custom port is hosted by an EC2 instance, that port has to be opened. To open a custom port, the Security Group needs to be changed. The Security Group Inbound Rules need to be changed to allow network traffic to reach the custom port.

It is important to take note that ***un-authorized port scans*** of an EC2 instance by customers is a violation of the AWS Acceptable Use Policy.

AWS VPC Security Group Facts

1. By default, Security Groups do not allow any inbound ICMP traffic.
2. A Security Group can span multiple AZs in the same Region.
3. You can create up to 500 Security Groups per VPC.

4. You can create up to 2,500 Security Groups per Region.
5. For each host interface, you can associate 1-5 Security Groups.
6. For each Security Group, you can add 1-60 inbound and 1-60 outbound traffic rules.
7. That's a maximum of 600 rules per host interface.
8. AWS evaluates all 'allow rules' in the Security Group before deciding whether to allow traffic.
9. Because the Security Group is stateful, responses to allowed inbound traffic are allowed to flow outbound regardless of outbound rules and vice versa. The preceding fact is an important distinct difference between Security Groups and Network ACLs.

AWS VPC Network ACL (NACL)

When each VPC is created, it has associated with it a ***default Network ACL***, which you can modify, that ***allows all inbound and outbound traffic. A subnet NACL is optional,*** you can choose to configure one or not.

The VPC's ***Network ACL is your 2nd layer of defense and is applied to all EC2 instances present in the subnet.***

Best practice – though a NACL is optional, every subnet, VPC, must have a NACL.

Due to the subnet's default Network ACL, EC2 instances on the same subnet are not able to exchange messages with each other, until you add the allow rules to the subnet's Network ACL. When you can create a custom network ACL, its initial configuration denies all inbound and outbound traffic, until you create rules that allow the traffic.

The Network ACL does not filter traffic between instances residing in the same subnet.

A Network ACL is a numbered list of 'allow rules' and 'deny rules' that AWS evaluates in sequential order, starting from the lowest numbered rule, whether deciding if traffic is allowed in to or out of any subnet associated with the Network ACL. ***As***

soon as a rule matches traffic, it's applied regardless of any higher-numbered rule in the NACL. You can have up to (20) rules per Network ACL.

Best practice – to be able to easily add rules, use rule numbers that are multiples of 100.

When you ***change a NACL, the effect is immediate.***

A Network Access Control List (ACL) is an optional layer of security that ***acts as a stateless firewall*** on a subnet level and traversing the subnet boundary. Return traffic must be explicitly allowed.

A NACL is stateless: ***responses allowed inbound traffic are subject to the rule for outbound traffic.***

A NACL rule is a combination of IP address, port #, protocol and allow/deny for a subnet. A NACL can have up to 32,766 rules.

There exists a 1-to-N relationship between a Network ACL and subnets. You can have up to (200) Network ACL per VPC.

A NACL can be used to deny the traffic from a set of IP addresses.

Best practice – ***to quickly and temporarily deny access from specified IP addresses*** (e.g., multiple port scans are originating over the Internet from these addresses), modify the Network ACLs associated with all public subnets in the VPC to deny access from the block of IP addresses.

Two Tier Application

In a single AZ, it is common for an EC2 instance in a public subnet to that hosts a web application to need to communicate with a database service in a private subnet, where both subnets are in the same VPC. Given this use case, the Security Groups must be set to allow the application host to communicate with the database host on a specific port, using a specific protocol. In addition, the VPC's Network ACL must have rules that allow communication between the two subnets.

AWS VPC and IPv6

At present, in 15 of its Regions ***AWS supports IPv6 IP addresses with Elastic Load Balancing (ELB), AWS IoT, S3 (and Transfer Acceleration), CloudFront, WAF, Route 53, VPC and EC2 instances.*** Support for both versions of IP addresses (IPv4 and IPv6) ensures compatibility and flexibility to access resources and applications.

To support IPv6, ***AWS makes use of a dual-stack model*** that assigns each instance/endpoint an IPv4 address and an IPv6 address, along with their corresponding DNS entries.

The AWS customer can assign IPv6 IP addresses to their VPC. However, the support that AWS provides for IPv6 IP addresses is not equivalent to how AWS supports IPv4. The range of IPv6 addresses is automatically allocated from Amazon's pool of IPv6 addresses (you cannot select the range yourself). The size of the IPv6 CIDR block is fixed (/64). You can have (1) IPv6 CIDR block per VPC. Each VPC is given a unique /56 address prefix from within Amazon's GUA (Global Unicast Address).

Within a VPC Security Groups, Route Tables, Network ACLs, as well as VPC Peering, Internet Gateway, Direct Connect, VPC Flow Logs, and DNS resolution all operate in the same way for IPv6 as for IPv4, performance is equivalent as well.

To support IPv6, the VPC Security Group, to allow inbound HTTP access from all IPv6 addresses, the source IP is ::/0. Before trying to access a bucket using IPv6, you must ensure that any IAM user or S3 bucket polices that are used for IP address filtering include IPv6 address ranges.

Other VPC Considerations

- The majority of AWS services do not actually sit within a VPC.
- Although Amazon EC2 instances are configured with public IP addresses, network traffic between

AWS Regions traverse the AWS global network backbone by default, which typically provides more consistent, lower-latency network connectivity than equivalent internet-based connections.

- On occasion, some traffic between Regions uses the public internet.
- Best practice - if you use the public internet for to connect to AWS services, you should use a VPC endpoint.
- You can use a VPC endpoint to privately connect your VPC to supported AWS services and to VPC endpoint services that are powered by PrivateLink without using an internet gateway; network address translation, or NAT, device; VPN connection, or AWS Direct Connect connection.
- Instances in your VPC do not require public IP addresses to communicate with resources in the service.
- Traffic between your VPC and the other service does not leave the Amazon network.

VPC Best Practices

Some best practices include:

- Choosing CIDR block or IP address ranges wisely by selecting a range large enough for future growth (or run multiple VPCs). Start with /16.
- Using subnets to divide resources based on access, which is their primary purpose.
- Using Multi-Availability Zone deployments in a VPC for high availability (you will learn more on that in the next module).
- Using security groups to control traffic between Amazon EC2 instances and elastic load balancers. You can specify a granular security policy for Amazon EC2 instances by using a security group.
- Using VPC Flow Logs to track and monitor VPC

traffic. Store traffic logs for a particular VPC, VPC subnet, or Elastic Network Interface to CloudWatch Logs, where they can be accessed by third-party tools for storage and analysis.
- Checking the health of the VPN link via API calls or in the AWS Management Console.

I CAME, I SAW, I LEFT

There are many different mechanisms (or ways) you can use to enter, traverse, and exit an AWS VPC. Rules/ routes can be added to a Route table which direct traffic to exit the subnet by using the:

- AWS Internet Gateways (IGW);
- AWS NAT Gateway or NAT instance;
- Amazon Virtual Private Gateway (VPG);
- AWS Egress-only Internet Gateway;
- VPC Peering;
- Virtual Private Network (VPN);
- AWS VPC Endpoint, and
- Bastion Host.

When you add an Internet gateway, an egress-only Internet gateway, a virtual private gateway, a NAT device, a peering connection, or a VPC endpoint in your VPC, etc., you must update the route table for any subnet that uses these gateways or connections.

AWS Internet Gateway (IGW)

The IGW is an AWS VPC component that you use to permit the exchange of messages between the Internet and EC2 instances in your subnet. The IGW is compatible with both IPv4 and IPv6 IP addresses.

The IGW is a:

- horizontally scaled,

- redundant and
- highly available,

The IGW functions as a target in your VPC/subnet route table for Internet-routable traffic. The IGW also ***performs network address translation for EC2 instances that have been assigned a public IP address.***

You add the IGW to the VPC. You are limited to 1 IGW per VPC. Any subnet inside the VPC can add the IGW to its route table and gain access to the Internet. If you encounter an error while attempting to add an IGW to a VPC, check to see if there is already an IGW attached to the VPC.

You are limited to (5) IGW per Region.

The IPv4 Route table entry for the IGW is 0.0.0.0 and ::/0 for IPv6. The IGW name has the 'igw-' prefix.

An IGW can only support packet MTU size of 1500 bytes. If the packet is a jumbo, then the packet is either fragmented into 1500 chunks, but if the IP header's Don't Fragment flag is set on the message, the message is dropped by the IGW.

IGW Network Address Translation

The IGW maintains a map of each EC2 instance's Public IP Address and Private IP Address.

When a message is received from a node/interface in the Internet, the IGW translates the message's target address – the EC2 instance's Public IP Address – to the EC2 instance's Private IP Address and forwards the message to the EC2 instance in the VPC.

When a message is sent from an EC2 instance in the VPC to a node/interface in the Internet, the IGW translates the EC2 instance's reply IP address to the EC2 instance's Public IP Address, or its Elastic IP (EIP) Address if the instance uses one.

AWS Network Address Translation (NAT) Instances & NAT Gateways

Host interfaces in the Internet cannot initiate a connection to the EC2 instance in the private subnet.

After you have secured the network traffic inbound and outbound to your EC2 instance located in your private subnet and have ensured that no communications are possible between your EC2 instance and host interfaces in the Internet, there comes a time when the EC2 instance requires software (e.g., security patches; application upgrades; etc.) that can only be downloaded from a host interface located in the Internet.

AWS provides you with NAT Instances and NAT Gateways that enable your EC2 instance in your private subnet to communicate with host interfaces in the Internet.

The NAT Instances and NAT Gateway can be used only with IPv4 IP addresses.

NAT Instances

An AWS NAT Instance is an AWS Linux Amazon Machine Image (AMI) that has been modified and enhanced to:

Accept network traffic from EC2 instances within a private subnet.

Translate the EC2 instance's private IP address to the public IP address of the NAT Instance.

Forward network traffic to an IGW within the VPC.

Maintain the state of the forwarded network traffic to return response traffic from the interface in the Internet to the correct EC2 instance in the private subnet.

Within the AWS Management Console, the AWS NAT Instance has this string in their name: amzn-ami-vpc-nat.

The IPv4 Route table entry for the NAT is 0.0.0.0 and ::/0 for IPv6.

In the NAT name has the 'nat-' prefix.

How to Create an AWS NAT Instance

To create a NAT Instance in your VPC, a public subnet that contains an IGW must exist in the VPC.

The goal is 2-fold:

- Prevent EC2 instances in a private subnet from re-

ceiving inbound traffic initiated from a host interface in the Internet and
- Allow EC2 instances in a private subnet to send outbound Internet communications.

Complete these tasks:

- Create a Security Group in which you will launch the NAT Instance. This Security Group has outbound rules that specify host interfaces in the Internet by network protocol, IP address and port #.
- Within that Security Group, launch an Amazon Linux NAT AMI as an EC2 instance in a public subnet in the VPC.
- Disable the Source/Destination Check attribute of the NAT Instance.
- In the private subnet (that contains the EC2 instances that need to communicate with the host interfaces in the Internet), configure the Route table to direct Internet bound traffic to the NAT Instance.
- Reserve an EIP and associate that public IP address with the NAT Instance.

What else do you need to do to handle the scenario where the NAT Instance fails and goes off-line?

AWS NAT Gateways

When a single NAT Instance is no longer able to support the all of your EC2 instances the next step up is the NAT Gateway.

You use the NAT Gateway to allow EC2 instances in your private subnet to access host interfaces in the Internet. The AWS NAT Gateway is a managed service that is highly available within an Availability Zone (AZ), however is does not support auto scaling.

The NAT Gateway is deployed in a public subnet of a specific AZ, and is implemented with redundancy in that AZ. You are limited to (5) NAT Gateway per Availability Zone (AZ).

The NAT Gateway functions like a NAT Instance:

Prevents EC2 instances in a private subnet from receiving inbound traffic initiated from a host interface in the Internet and

Allows EC2 instances in a private subnet to send outbound Internet communications.

For common use cases, AWS recommends that you use a NAT Gateway rather than a NAT Instance.

The NAT Gateway has built-in redundancy:

- Automatically scales horizontally;
- Provides better availability;
- Provides higher bandwidth (10Gbps based on demand) and
- Requires less administration effort.

How to Use an AWS NAT Gateway

Deploy an AWS NAT Gateway in the public subnet of the VPC. An IGW must be deployed to that public subnet.

In a VPC that already has an IGW, it is easy to use an AWS NAT Gateway:

- In the private subnet, configure its Route table to route Internet-bound traffic to 0.0.0.0/0 with the NAT Gateway as the destination.
- Add egress rules to VPC Security Groups applied to the private EC2 instances, to allow network traffic to the Internet destinations.
- Reserve an EIP and associate that public IP address with the NAT Gateway.

Best practice – to create a solution that is less dependent on a particular AZ, create a NAT Gateway in each AZ and configure the Route tables (of the private subnets in the VPCs in the AZ) to ensure that EC2 instances use the NAT Gateway in the AZ in which they are launched.

Best practice – though resources in multiple AZ can share one NAT Gateway, this is not advisable. If the NAT Gateway is down, then all resources in all AZ lose Internet access.

The IPv4 Route table entry for the NAT is 0.0.0.0 and ::/0 for IPv6. And, the NAT name has the 'nat-' prefix.

Given resources in multiple AZ which share a single NAT Gateway, in the event that that NAT Gateway's AZ fails, the resources in the other AZs will not have Internet access. To make the NAT Gateway more highly available, create a second NAT Gateway in another AZ.

AWS Egress-only Internet Gateway

You can add an Egress-only Internet Gateway to a VPC. ***The Egress-only Internet Gateway can be used only with IPv6 IP Addresses***. All IPv6 subnets in the VPC can access the Internet by placing its entry in the subnet's route tables. Since it is egress-only, ***the gateway allows outbound traffic only and it prevents host interfaces in the Internet initiating a IPv6 connection to an EC2 instance in a private subnet.***

You are limited to (5) Egress-only Internet Gateways per Region.

VPC Peering

By design, EC2 instances in one VPC cannot communicate with EC2 instances in other VPCs.

An AWS VPC Peering connection is a 1-to-1 network connection between 2 different VPCs in the same Region, that ***enables EC2 instances in either VPC to communicate with each other*** (as if they were on the same network). ***The VPCs to be connected can be owned by different AWS accounts. You cannot peer VPCs across Regions.***

A VPC can have up to (50) Peering connections. The 5 VPCs you can create per Region can support only (10) peering connections between them.

VPC Peering relies on special hardware. AWS uses the internal infrastructure to peer VPCs:

- There is no single point of failure;
- There is no throttling of bandwidth when the traffic flows across VPCs.

How to Create a Peering Connection

To initiate a new peering connection, these 3 facts must be known first:

- Peering target AWS Account ID;
- Local VPC ID, and
- Target VPC ID.

The owner of VPC #1 sends a request to create a peer connection to the owner of VPC #2. In the case where VPC #1 and #2 are owned by the same AWS account, that request contains VPC #1's ID. In the case where VPC #1 and VPC #2 are owned by different AWS accounts, that request contains VPC #1's ID and the AWS Account ID that owns VPC #1.

After receiving a request to create the peer connection, the AWS Account that owns VPC #2 has 1 week to accept or reject the request to peer with VPC #1, before the request expires.

Prohibitions on Creating a Peering Connection

There are a few prohibitions on creating a VPC peering connection:

- You cannot create a Peering connection between VPCs that have either matching or over-lapping CIDR blocks.
- You cannot create a Peering connection between VPCs that exist in different Regions.
- A Peering connection does not support transitive routing.
- Given a peering connection between node-A and node-B and another peering connection between node-A and node-C, a message from node-B cannot reach node-C by transiting through node-A.
- 2 VPCs cannot have >1 Peering connections between them.

Virtual Private Networks (VPNs)

The use case is the one where you have an on-premise network of host interfaces and you need them in part or in whole to communicate with host interfaces present in your AWS VPC. Or, vice versa.

You have 4 options, both of which require using a Virtual Private Network (VPN) over TCP/IP. You can use a:

1. Hardware-based VPN;
2. Software-based VPN
3. AWS Direct Connect;
4. VPN CloudHub;

Hardware-based VPN

The Virtual Private Gateway (VPG) is a network traffic concentrator, is a software device, that exists inside the AWS VPC. The VPG provides 2 VPN Internet Protocol Security (IPSec) protocol Tunnels, terminated in 2 different AZs for automatic failover. IPSec authenticates and encrypts each IP packet of a communication session.

You are limited to (5) VPG per Region.

Software-based VPN

You can create a Software VPN to your on-premise network by running a software VPN application on an EC2 instance in the VPC.

AWS does not provide or maintain you applications.

AWS Direct Connect

AWS Direct Connect is the easiest way to establish a dedicated network connection from on-premise into AWS. Due to its' increased bandwidth, Direct Connect, compared to using an Internet-based connection, provides a superior experience when on-premise users access AWS resources and services.

Direct Connect provides a dedicated private connection/pipes from you on-premise network to you AWS VPC. Direct Connect ***requires the BGP protocol***. Direct Connects ports support 1 Gbps and 10 Gbps connection speeds.

Each AWS Region has 1:N Direct Connect locations available in various co-location facilities, e.g. Equinix, Coresite, etc.. There are no set-up charges and you can cancel anytime. Pricing is based on port-hour and data transferred. Port-hour consumed is per port type, with partial hours being billed as full hours. Data transfer is bill in the same month that it occurred.

If you do not already have a footprint in one of the co-location facilities, you can work with AWS telco partners to establish the last-mile connection.

A Direct Connect connection ***can be configured with 1:N virtual interfaces.*** A virtual interface is configured for access to EC2, to S3 using a public IP address, or to EC2 instances in a VPC by using their private IP address.

You can ***combine the Direct Connect with an AWS hardware-based VPN to create an IPSec encrypted connection.***

Best practice - to get redundancy, use 2 Direct Connect connections over independent circuits.

AWS VPN CloudHub

In the scenario where you have multiple on-premise sites (e.g., branch offices), to enable communications between these networks, you can create multiple AWS hardware-based VPN connections to your VPC.

In the above scenario, when you use AWS VPN CloudHub configuration, multiple networks can assess you VPC and securely access each other, using a simple hub-and-spoke model.

Each CGW is configured to advertise a site-specific prefix to its VPG.

The VPG routes traffic to the appropriate site and advertises the reachability of one on-premise site to all other on-premise sites.

How to Configure the VPN

AWS automatically propagates routes, to allow your EC2 instances to route traffic to the on-premise TCP/IP network through the VPG and across the VPN Tunnel.

Security groups and route tables must be modified to allow and route traffic over the VPN. The security groups in which

EC2 instances are launched must allow traffic from the on-premise host interfaces to the EC2 instances running inside the VPC subnets. In addition, ***ensure route propagation from the VGW is enabled for the route tables for the VPC subnets*** in which the EC2 instances are launched.

AWS VPN Facts

An AWS VPC can contain 0-N VPN-only subnets. An AWS VPN-only subnet has a route table that directs the subnet's traffic to the Amazon VPC's Virtual Private Gateway (VPG).

Your VPC can contain 0-N VPGs. Each VPG connects to 1-and-only-1 CGW. For your VPC to be able to support 2-N VPGs, the IP Address of each CGW must be unique within the AWS Region.

To support high availability of the VPC to your on-premise network, each VPN within your VPC consists of 2 Internet Protocol Security (IPSec) Tunnels.

AWS VPC Gateways

AWS provides 2 gateways you can use to securely connect an on-premise TCP/IP network to a VPC:

Virtual Private Gateways (VPGs) and

Customer Gateway (CGW).

Virtual Private Gateway (VPG)

A Virtual Private Gateway (VPG) is the VPN gateway (aka, concentrator) ***on the AWS VPC side of the site-to-site VPN connection.*** A VPG is created and attached to a VPC that you want to be connected with an on-premise TCP/IP network.

When a VPG is created, its private Autonomous System Number (ASN) can be specified. If not specified than the default ASN (64512) is used. Once the VPG is created, its ASN cannot be changed.

Customer Gateway (CGW)

As its name implies, ***the Customer Gateway (CGW)*** is the gateway that ***exists within the on-premise TCP/IP network***. The

CGW ***can be a hardware device or a software device.***

The network ***traffic that leaves the AWS VPC and traverses the Internet onto the on-premise CGW.*** Therefore, ***the CGW needs to be assigned a static Internet-routable IP address.***

After you provision (a VPG or) a CGW, you next initialize the VPN Tunnel. To initialize the VPN Tunnel, outbound traffic must be generated from the on-premise CGW.

You are limited to (50) CGW per Region.

When the connection is initiated from the CGW, you specify the type of routing to be used with the VPN connection.

If the CGW supports ***Border Gateway Protocol (BGP),*** then the VPN can be configured for dynamic routing. Otherwise, configure the VPN connections for static routing. BGP is the protocol used to exchange routing information on the Internet. IP routes, called prefixes, are advertised dynamically over BGP and maintained automatically. BGP has a maximum limit of (100) prefixes. You can have up to (50) BGP routes per Route table.

If the CGW supports ***static routing***, you must enter the routes that your EC2 instances will use to communicate with the VPG.

AWS VPC Endpoints

Often, a BPM requires that Internet connectivity to/from EC2 instances not be permitted. Yet, the BPM still requires access to S3 from within the VPC. In that access to S3, by default, occurs over the Internet, these requirements are in conflict, and a viable remedy is needed, that supports both requirements.

An AWS VPC Endpoint is a virtual device you use to create a private connection between your VPC and an AWS service (at present, only S3 and DynamoDB are supported), without requiring access:

- Over the Internet, or
- Through a NAT instance, or
- Through a VPN connection, or

- Through an AWS Direct Connect.
- The Endpoint:
- Scales horizontally and is redundant;
- Provides high availability.

In your VPC, you can:

- Have up to (20) Endpoints per region
- Create multiple Endpoints for a single AWS service and
- Use different Route tables to enforce access policies from subnets to a given AWS service.

An EC2 instance in the VPC uses their private IP address to communicate with the resource accessed through the VPC Endpoint.

How to Create a VPC Endpoint

It is relatively easy to create a VPC Endpoint:

1. Select a VPC.
2. Select an AWS service (at present either S3 or DynamoDB). An AWS service is identified by the form com.amazonaws.<region>.<service>
3. Specify the access policy. An access policy can be changed at any time.
4. Specify the route tables and the rules. Add to each specific route table, a rule that states the AWS service as the destination and the Endpoint as the target.

When the EC2 instance in a private subnet is connected to S3 via the Endpoints, ***the traffic never leaves the Amazon network so there are no data transfer charges*** (as occurs when S3 is accessed via the Internet).

You can tag an AMI image, you can tag an EBS volume, you can tag a VPC, but ***you cannot tag a VPC Endpoint.***

Bastion Host

As more EC2 instances are added to the VPC, each has a network interface that can be used as an access point, for use by authorized systems administrators as well as by hackers. ***A bastion host is a dedicated EC2 instance with a special purpose in life: to be a proxy.***

The ***bastion host is deployed into a public subnet that can be reached from the Internet and accessed using SSH or Remote Desktop Protocol (RDP).*** The bastion host serves as the primary access point from the Internet and acts as a proxy to the other EC2 instances, ***acts as a jump server to the resources within the other subnets.***

Once the network connection is established with the bastion host, from it SSH or RDP can be used to log into other EC2 instances deployed deeper within the VPC, i.e., inside a private subnet. Before that is allowed however, precautions are taken (i.e., all unnecessary applications and libraries are removed) to ensure that the bastion host is unable to support any other function or purpose than the jumps to other EC2 instances. To support these jumps, the ***Security Groups and the Network ACLs (NACLs) must be configured as required.***

AWS IDENTITY

AWS provides the following Identity and Access Management tools and services:

- AWS IAM
- AWS Certificate Manager
- AWS Security Token Service (STS)
- AWS Single Sign-On
- AWS Cognito
- MFA Token
- AWS Organizations
- AWS Directory Service
- Simple AD
- AD Connector

AWS IAM Service

The AWS Identity and Access Management (IAM) service secures interactions with AWS resources and an AWS Account.

IAM controls how each principle is authenticated. IAM policies are written to specify the access privileges of principles. IAM policies are associated with principles.

IAM can secure your infrastructure through:

- Multi-factor Authentication (MFA) and
- Key Rotation.

IAM Roles can be used to delegate permissions and to federate users (see IAM Roles).

IAM resolves multiple, possibly conflicting, IAM permissions.

The IAM is controlled through the:

- AWS Management Console;
- AWS CLI and
- AWS SDK.

IAM Identity Concepts

IAM uses traditional identity concepts:

1. IAM Users
2. IAM Groups
3. Access control policies

To control:

1. Who can use your AWS account,
2. What AWS services and resources the account can use and;
3. How the account can use the AWS service.

The control is enough to limit 1 user to the ability to perform 1 action on a specific resource from a specific IP address during a specific window of time.

IAM can be used to allow an application to be granted access to AWS resources, whether they are running on-premises or in the AWS cloud.

What IAM is not

IAM is not an identity store/authorization system for your applications. The permissions you assign using IAM are permissions to manipulate AWS resources and services.

IAM Principles

An IAM principle is an entity that is allowed to interact with AWS resources.

A principle can be persistent or temporary.

A principle can represent a human being or an application.

IAM defines 3 types of principles:

1. ***Root User*** (cannot be limited; permanent);
2. ***IAM User*** (access controlled by policy; durable; can be removed by IAM administrator) and

3. ***IAM Role and Temporary Security Token*** (access controlled by policy; temporary; expires after specific time interval).

IAM Root User

An IAM Root User is automatically created by AWS when you create an AWS Account. The ***AWS Account is a single-sign-on principle*** that ***has complete access to all AWS services and resources*** associated with that account, ***on a fee basis***.

The IAM Root User:

- is that single-sign-on principle.
- has full privileges (like UNIX root; Windows Administrator), including closing the AWS Account.

Best practice – do not use the IAM Root User for everyday tasks, including administrative tasks.

Best practice – use the IAM Root User only to create your 1st IAM user and then securely lock away the IAM Root User credentials.

To access AWS services and resources, the IAM Root User can use the:

- Amazon Management Console;
- AWS CLI;
- AWS SDK;

Oddly, even though the CLI and SDK can be used, the CLI and SDK are not part of the AWS Cloud Architect Associate training or certification.

IAM Root User Access Key

Use an access key (an access key ID and secret access key) to make programmatic requests to AWS.

Do not use your AWS account Root User access key.

The access key for your AWS account Root User gives full access to all your resources for all AWS services, including your billing information.

You cannot reduce the permissions associated with your AWS account Root User access key.

Therefore, protect your Root User access key like you would your credit card numbers or any other sensitive secret.

Tasks That Require IAM Root User

The following list contains most of the tasks known to require use of the IAM Root User account:

- Modify Root User details. This includes changing the Root User's password.
- Change your AWS support plan.
- Change or delete your payment options. An IAM user can also perform this after you enable billing access for all IAM users.
- View your account's billing information. An IAM user can also perform this after you enable billing access for all IAM users.
- View Billing tax invoices.
- Open Billing support cases.
- Close an AWS account.
- Sign up for GovCloud.
- Submit a Reverse DNS for Amazon EC2 request.
- Create a CloudFront key pair.
- Change the Amazon EC2 setting for longer resource IDs.
- Configuring an Amazon S3 bucket to enable MFA (multi-factor authentication) Delete.
- Editing or deleting an Amazon S3 bucket policy that includes an invalid VPC ID or VPC endpoint ID.
- Submit a request to perform penetration testing on your AWS infrastructure using the web form.
- Request removal of the port 25 email throttle on your EC2 instance.
- Find your AWS account canonical user ID in the console. You can view your canonical user ID from the AWS Management Console only while signed in as the AWS account Root User.
- Restoring IAM user permissions. You cannot use

policies within your account to explicitly deny access to the Root User.

Securing the IAM Root User Account

AWS strongly advises securing the IAM Root User account and recommends the completing the following steps:

1. Decide to stop using the IAM Root User account;
2. For the IAM Root User account, create an IAM user.
3. Create an IAM Group, grant it full administrative permissions, and add the above IAM user to that IAM Group.
4. If there exists IAM Root User account access keys, establish that those access keys are not being used anywhere in the solution. Where in use, stop using those access keys.
5. Store the IAM Root User account credentials in a very secure place.
6. Require multi-factor authentication (MFA) for the IAM Root User account and use MFA to control access to AWS service APIs.
7. Enable CloudTrail so that all API request to resources/services are recorded in logs. Apply the trail to all Regions and identify the S3 bucket to be used to store those logs and restrict access to that bucket to only those authorized.
8. Enable the AWS Cost and Usage Report, to provide information about IAM Root user account usage of AWS resources and estimated costs.
9. If there exists IAM Root User account access keys, disable and remove those access keys from the root account.
10. Stop using the IAM Root User account.
11. Sign into the AWS cloud using the IAM user credentials.

IAM User

An IAM User is a persistent entity that represents either 1 human being or 1 application. ***The IAM User provides authentication.***

The IAM User is a way to enforce the principle of least privilege. When the IAM User is created, it has neither a 2-part access key or a password. The IAM administrator can set up either or both. ***After creating a new IAM user, before they can make API calls a set of Access Keys have to be created for the IAM user.***

An IAM principle with AdministratorAccess can create an IAM user by using the Management Console, CLI or SDK.

A persistent IAM principle has no expiration date. An IAM principle is persistent until an IAM principle with AdministratorAccess deletes them.

To control the granular permissions of an IAM user, they are associated with an IAM Policy.

IAM Groups

An IAM Group is used to manage permissions for groups of IAM users.

IAM Authentication

There are 3 ways that IAM authenticates a principle:

1. ***UserName/Password*** *- Used when principle represents a human being; in IAM you can create a password policy that enforces password complexity and expiration.*
2. ***Access Key*** *- A combination of an access key ID (20 characters) and an access secret key (40 characters); A program using the AWS infrastructure via a service API will use these values to sign the REST calls to the services.*
3. ***Access Key/Session Token*** *- A process/application operates under an assumed IAM role, the temporary security token provides a 2-part access key for authenti-*

cation. In addition, the token includes a session token. To authenticate, calls to AWS must include both the 2-part access key and the session token.

Multi-Factor Authentication (MFA) Token

Multi-Factor Authentication (MFA) requires you to verify your identity with both something you know and something that you have.

MFA adds another layer of security beyond password or access key.

MFA requires a One-Time Password (OTP) from a small device.

The MFA device can be either a hardware or software device (e.g., Amazon MFA app for smart phones).

MFA can be assigned to an IAM User, whether the principle is a human being or a process/application.

When human being using an IAM user configured with MFA attempts to access the Management Console, after providing their password will be prompted to enter the current code displayed in their MFA device before gaining access.

A process/application using an IAM user configured with MFA must query the application user to provide the current code, which the application then passes to the API.

Best practice – add MFA to the IAM Root User.

IAM Policy

An ***IAM Policy is a JSON document*** that contains 1:N permissions, with each permission defining:

- ***Effect*** – a single word (Allow or Deny);
- ***Service*** – the identity of the AWS service;
- ***Resource*** – the Amazon Resource Name (ARN) value that AWS assigns to the resource;
- ***Action*** – the action value specifies the subset of actions within an AWS service that the permission allows or denies;
- ***Condition*** – defines 1:N additional restraints that

limit the actions allowed by the permission (e.g., restricted to time period, IP address, etc.).

IAM Authorization

Authorization is handled in IAM by defining specific privileges in Policies and associating those policies with principles. An ***IAM Policy provides authorization.***

Associating Policies with Principles

A policy is associate with a ***principle*** in 1 of 2 ways:

1. ***User Policy*** – the policy exists only in the context of the IAM user to which it is attached (using the IAM User page in the Management Console).
2. ***Managed Policies*** – these policies exist independently of any individual IAM user. In this way the same policy can be associated with 0:N IAM Users or IAM Group (using the Management Console, the CLI and SDK).

After a policy is assigned to the group, all users in that group assume those allow/deny permissions. There are 2 ways to associate a policy with an IAM group:

1. ***Group Policy*** – these policies exist only in the context of the IAM Group to which they are attached (using the IAM Group page in the Management Console).
2. ***Managed Policies*** – the managed policies can be associated with an IAM Group just as with an IAM User.

Best practice – to ensure that people who are responsible in one environment (say development) do not have access to EC2 instances in another environment (say production), add tags to differentiate EC2 instances by the environment they are launched within. Next, use the (environment) tag in combination with an IAM policy to control access to them.

IAM Role - Temporary Security Credentials

An IAM Role is used to grant specific privileges to specific 'actors' for a specific period of time. These actors can be authenticated by AWS or some trusted external system. ***The actor uses AWS Security Token Service (STS) to access the AWS cloud.***

An IAM Role is global service that is available across all Regions. For example, the same IAM role can be assigned to EC2 instances launched in different Regions.

When the actor assumes the IAM Role, ***AWS provides the actor with a temporary Security Token*** from the STS. Requesting a Security Token requires specifying the period of time in which the token needs to exist before it expires. ***The range of time in which a security token can exist is 15 minutes to 36 hours.***

IAM Role use cases:

1. ***EC2 Instance*** – grant permissions to applications running on the instance;
2. ***Cross-Account Access*** – grant permission to IAM users from other AWS accounts, whether you control those accounts or not.
3. ***Federation*** – grant permissions to IAM users authenticated by a trusted external system
4. ***Service-linked*** - *a unique type of IAM role that is linked directly to an AWS service.*

IAM Role – EC2 Instance

An IAM role can be attached to an existing EC2 instance. The IAM role enables the EC2 instance to use temporary security credentials that AWS creates, distributes, and rotates automatically.

Using IAM Roles for EC2 instances removes the need to store AWS account credentials on the instance, secure credentials, rotate keys, etc.

The IAM Role is used to grant permissions to applications running on the instance that use the AWS SDK to access an API of an AWS services.

When the EC2 instance is launched the IAM Role is assigned to the instance.

When an application running on that EC2 instance accesses an AWS service's API, the application (using the SDK) assumes the IAM Role assigned to the instance and obtains a temporary security token from AWS STS, which it sends to the API and allowing the application to make a call to access the AWS service (without worry about authentication).

Best practice – refrain from hard coding IAM credentials using AWS SDK, and switch to using IAM EC2 instance roles.

IAM Role - Cross-Account Access

It is a common need to grant permission to IAM users from other AWS accounts, whether you control those accounts or not, whether they are controls by a counter-party.

Best practice – do not distribute access keys outside your organization.

Set up an IAM role with the needed permissions.

Then have the IAM users in the other accounts use that IAM role when they access the resources.

IAM Role – Identity Provider (IdP) Federation

AWS is able to interoperate with Identity Providers (IdPs) that support ***OpenID Connect (OIDC)*** (e.g., Facebook; Google; login to Amazon) and federate these outside identities with IAM. ***An IAM Role can be used to assign privileges those users authenticated trusted external system outside of IAM.***

AWS is able to interoperate with IdPs that support ***Security Assert Markup Language 2.0 (SAML),*** e.g., Active Directory or LDAP, or SAML-compliant e.g., Active Directory Federation Services (ADFS) and federate these outside identities with IAM. An IAM Role can be used to assign privileges those users authenticated trusted external system outside of IAM.

Federation works by returning a temporary security token associated with an IAM role to the IdP for the authenticated iden-

tity used for calls to the AWS API.

Best practice – to enable IT administrators of an environment in which resources are hosted on-premise as well as the AWS cloud to use their on-premise credentials that are stored in Microsoft Active Directory, use SAML Federation.

IAM Role – Service Link

A service linked role is an IAM role linked directly to an AWS service, such as GuardDuty. The role is predefined by the particular service and includes all of the permissions required to use the service on your behalf.

IAM Rotating Keys

Security risk of any credential increases with the age of the credential.

Best practice - rotate the access key associated with an IAM user, on a regular basis.

The IAM user access key can be changed using the Management Console, the CLI and the SDK:

1. Create a new access key for the user;
2. Reconfigure all applications to use the new access key;
3. Disable the original access key (disable instead of deleting this allows rollback if there are issues with the rotation process);
4. Verify the operation of all applications using the new access key;
5. Delete the original access key;

IAM Resolves Multiple Permissions

IAM resolves permission conflicts in this way:

- Initially the request is denied by default;
- All the appropriate policies are evaluated; if there is an explicit deny found in any policy, the request is denied and evaluation stops;
- If no explicit deny is found and an explicit allow is found in any policy the request is allowed;

- If there are no explicit allow or deny permissions found, then the default deny is maintained and the request is denied.

AWS Organizations

AWS Organizations is an account management service you can use to centrally apply policy-based controls across multiple accounts in the AWS Cloud. You can consolidate all of your AWS accounts into an organization and arrange all AWS accounts into distinct organizational units.

Organizations includes consolidated billing and account management capabilities that enable you to better meet the budgetary, security and compliance needs of your business.

AWS Organization Features

As an administrator of the master account of an organization, there is a hierarchical grouping of your accounts, so you can restrict which AWS services the users and roles in each member account can access.

This restriction even overrides the administrators of member accounts in the organization.

When Organizations blocks access to a service or action for a member account, a user or role in that account can't access any prohibited service or action, even if an administrator of a member account explicitly grants such permissions in an IAM policy.

Organization permissions overrule account permissions.

IAM provides granular control over users and roles in individual accounts.

Organizations expands that control to the account level by giving you control over what users and roles in an account or a group of accounts can do.

The resulting permissions are the logical intersection of what is allowed by Organizations at the account level and what permissions are explicitly granted by IAM at the user or role level within that account.

In other words, the user can access only what is allowed by both Organizations policies and IAM policies. If either blocks an operation, the user can't access that operation.

Organizations integrate with other Amazon web services.

You can enable select AWS services to access accounts in your organization and perform actions on the resources in the accounts.

When you configure an AWS service and authorize it to integrate with your organization, Organizations creates an IAM service-linked role in each member account.

The service-linked role has predefined IAM permissions that allow the other service to perform specific tasks in your organization's accounts.

For this service to work, all accounts in an organization have a service-linked role that enables AWS Organizations to create other service-linked roles.

These other roles are required by the AWS services that you configure to perform organizational-level tasks.

These additional service-linked roles come with policies that enable the specified service to perform only those tasks that are required by your configuration choices.

AWS Organizations uses a distributed computing model called eventual consistency.

Any change that you make in Organizations takes time to become visible from all possible endpoints.

Some of the delay results from the time it takes to send the data from server to server, or from replication zone to replication zone.

Best practice - design your global applications to account for these potential delays and ensure that they work as expected, even when a change made in one location is not instantly visible at another.

The Organization

An organization is an entity that you create to consolidate your AWS accounts.

You can use the AWS Organizations console to centrally view and manage all of your accounts within your organization.

An organization has 1 master account along with 0:N member accounts.

You can organize the accounts in a hierarchical, tree-like structure with a root at the top and organizational units nested under the root.

Each account can be located directly in the root or placed in one of the organization units (OUs) in the hierarchy.

An organization has the functionality that is determined by the feature set that you enable.

Organization Root & Organization Units (OUs)

The root is the parent container for all the accounts for your organization.

If you apply a policy to the root, it applies to all the organizational unit and accounts in the organization.

An OU is a container for accounts within a root.

An OU also can contain other OUs, which enables you to create a hierarchy that resembles an upside-down tree.

This hierarchy has a root at the top and the branches of OUs reach down, which end in accounts that are like the leaves of the tree.

When you attach a policy to one of the nodes in the hierarchy, it flows down and affects all OUs and accounts that are beneath it.

An OU can have exactly one parent and currently each account can be a member of exactly one OU.

Organization Master Account

An account is a standard AWS account that contains your AWS resources.

You can attach a policy to an account and apply controls to only that one account.

An organization has one account that is designed as the

master account.

This is the account that creates the organization.

The rest of the accounts that belong to an organization are called member accounts.

From the organization's master account, you can:

1. create accounts in the organization,
2. invite other existing accounts to the organization,
3. remove accounts from the organization,
4. manage invitations and
5. apply policies to entities within the organization, such as roots, OUs, or accounts.

An account can be a member of only one organization at a time.

The master account has the responsibilities of a payer account and it's responsible for paying all charges that are accrued by the member accounts.

Organization Invitation

An invitation is the process of asking another account to join your organization.

An invitation can be issued only by the organization's master account and it's extended to either the account ID or email address that is associated with the invited account.

After the invited account accepts an invitation, it becomes a member account in the organization.

Invitations also can be sent to all current member accounts when the organization needs all members to approve the change from supporting only consolidated billing features to supporting all features in the organization.

Organization Invitation Handshake

Invitations work by accounts exchanging handshakes.

Although you might not see handshakes when you work in the AWS Organizations console, you must work directly with handshakes if you use the AWS Command Line Interface, or AWS CLI, or AWS Organizations API.

A handshake is a multi-step process of exchanging information between two parties.

One of its primaries uses in AWS Organizations is to serve as the underlying implementation for invitations.

Handshake messages are passed between and responded to by the handshake initiator and the recipient so that it ensures that both parties always know the current status.

Handshakes are also used when you change the organization from supporting only consolidated billing features to supporting all features that Organizations offer.

Organization Service Control Policy

A service control policy, or SCP, is a policy that specifies the services and actions that users and roles can use in the accounts that the SCP affects.

SCPs are similar to IAM permission policies except that they don't grant any permissions.

Instead, SCPs are filters that allow only the specified services and actions to be used in affected accounts.

Even if a user is granted full administrator permissions with an IAM permission policy, any access that is not explicitly allowed or that is explicitly denied by the SCPs that affect that account is blocked.

You can attach an SCP to the following entities:

- A root, which affects all accounts in the organization;
- An OU, which affects all accounts in that OU and all accounts in any OUs in that OU subtree;
- Or an individual account.

Organization & Consolidated Billing

If you previously had a Consolidated Billing family of accounts, your accounts were migrated to a new organization in AWS Organizations and the payer account in your Consolidated Billing family has become the master account in your organization.

All linked accounts in the Consolidated Billing family become member accounts in the organization and continue to be linked to the master account.

Your bills continue to reflect the relationship between the payer account and the linked accounts.

AWS and the Microsoft Active Directory

AWS extends its identity management capabilities by providing 3 services that allow you to integrate Microsoft Active Directory with your AWS cloud solutions:

1. AWS Directory Service;
2. Simple AD and
3. AD Connector.

AWS Directory Service

AWS Directory Service is a managed service for Microsoft Active Directory [Enterprise Edition], used when there are >5,000 users and ***a trust relationship between the AWS hosted-directory and an on-premise directory is required***. In addition, ***a VPN from the AWS cloud VPC to the on-premise facility is required*** for AWS Directory Service to work.

AWS Directory Service is powered by Windows Server 2012 Revision 2 and is created as a highly available pair of domain controllers that are connected to your VPC. Each directory is deployed across multiple AZs and AWS monitoring automatically the domain controllers, detects if one fails and replaces it if needed. As a managed service, AWS handles data replication and daily snapshots per your configuration and handles all software patches and upgrades.

As you'd expect, AWS Directory Service functions like any other Microsoft Active Directory but is also able to integrate with AWS resources and services, such as IAM, both in the cloud and on-premise (i.e., Amazon WorkSpaces and Amazon WorkDocs). IAM roles can be used to allow Active Directory identity credentials to be used to access AWS resources and services.

Simple AD

The Simple AD is a Microsoft Active Directory-compatible directory service, that provides launch-managed, ***stand-alone directories*** powered by Samba 4 Active Directory Compatible Server. Simple AD is used when there are < 5,000 users and there is no need of the more advanced features of Microsoft Active Directory, such as:

- A trust relationship with other Active Directory domains;
- Communication over Lightweight Directory Access Protocol (LDAP);
- Multi-factor Authentication;
- PowerShell AD command-lets, etc..
- By using Simple AD, you can manage:
- Users accounts (can access AWS WorkSpaces, WorkDocs and WorkMail; can use IAM roles to access the AWS Management Console and manage AWS resources and services);
- Group memberships;
- Domain-joining;
- EC2 instances running Linux and Microsoft Windows,
- Kerberos-based Single Sign-On (SSO);
- Group policies;
- Daily snapshots;
- Point-in-time recovery.

Simple AD provides audit trail and event logs that enable you to track how the directory is used, including which users logged in, when they logged in and reports on any accounts that have been locked because of failed login attempts. The Microsoft Windows event log tools can be used to view and analyze the audit trail and event logs.

AD Connector

The AD Connector is a proxy service that is used to connect an on-premise Microsoft Active Directory to the AWS cloud, but without requiring complex Active Directory synchronizations or the complexity of hosting an Active Directory federation. The connection requires a VPC VPN, or an AWS Direct Connect, be used. Once setup, you can continue to use the on-premise Microsoft Active Directory as usual, but now extend your security policies into your AWS cloud.

AD Connector works by forwarding sign-in requests to you AD domain controllers for authentication and provides applications with the ability to query the directory for information. Users are able to use their existing AD credentials to log on to AWS applications (AWS WorkSpaces, WorkDocs and WorkMail) and the AWS Management Console from where they can manage AWS resources.

If required, AD Connector can be enabled to enforce MFA, by integrating with an existing on-premise Remote Authentication Dial-Up Service (RADIUS) based MFA infrastructure.

AWS Certificate Manager (ACM)

It's desirable to establish the identity of a website in the Internet and to encrypt communications over the Internet. The industry standard Secure Sockets Layer/Transport Layer Security (SSL/TLS) protocol is used to encrypt messages exchanged between a web browser/application and a website. In addition, the industry standard SSL/TLS certificates are used to establish the identity of a website.

The AWS Certificate Manager (ACM) is a highly-available service that provisions and manages SSL/TLS certificates to an AWS hosted website/application, and which can be used to easily configure that same website/application to use the SSL/TLS protocol. ACM is integrated for free with AWS resources/services, such as Elastic Load Balancers (ELBs), CloudFront distributions, EC2 instances, IoT devices, and APIs on API Gateway.

For a monthly fee based on the certificates that they create, the ACM's built-in Private Certificate Authority (CA) service enables the AWS client to centrally manage public and private certificates for their websites/applications. ACM is automated and eliminates the manual process of purchasing, uploading and renewing SSL/TLS certificates.

IdP Single-Sign-On (SSO)

A user (i.e., a host interface) can be authenticated in your organization's network (both those on-premise or in the clouds), and then provide that user with credentials that provide them with access to computing resources and systems, without creating a new identity for the user and requiring the user to log-in with a separate identity (i.e., user-name and password). This technique is called Single-Sign-On (SSO).

Identity Providers (IdPs) e.g., Facebook; Google; login to Amazon, provide the Internet marketplace with the ability to federate these outside identities with cloud utilities, such as AWS, Azure, etc.

To use outside identities AWS can integrate with 2 types of IdPs:

1. OpenID Connect (OIDC) – the major web-based IdPs (Facebook; Google; login to Amazon).
2. Security Assert Markup Language 2.0 (SAML) - IdPs such as Active Directory or LDAP, or SAML-compliant such as Active Directory Federation Services (ADFS).

As such, clients of AWS can also integrate with the Microsoft Active Directory (AD). To leverage Microsoft AD identities, AWS provides these services:

- AWS Directory Service;
- Simple AD, and
- AD Connector.

AWS and Identity Federation

Identity federation makes it easier to manage user identities by maintaining their identities in a single place, thereby enabling federated Single-Sign-On (SSO). At present, AWS supports both OIDC and SAML IdPs and so both types of IdPs can be used to manage access to AWS resources and services, the AWS Management Console, or to make AWS API and AWS SDK calls.

All of the integration authentication and authorization events are transparent to the user. In the end, the user obtains from AWS STS temporary credentials, which can be used, by default, for one (1) hour.

AWS Security Token Service

The ***AWS Security Token Service (STS)*** is a lightweight web service that ***enables you to request temporary, limited-privilege credentials for IAM users or for users that you authenticate*** by using either cross-account access or federated users (see below for descriptions of these two techniques).

A trusted entity that is allowed to assume a role, calls the STS AssumeRole API and obtains a temporary security credentials made of an ***access key ID, a secret access key and a security token***. The temporary security credentials are then used to gain access temporary access to an AWS resource or service.

AWS STS can be integrated with the AWS CloudTrail service, so that AWS calls from AWS accounts are logged (i.e., who made what call when) and those logs delivered to an S3 bucket.

AWS Single Sign-On

Given an AWS Organization, ***the AWS Single Sign-On (SSO) is a highly-available service that lets the AWS client easily manage SSO and identity privileges of all of the accounts in the AWS Organization***, and ***provides users with one place to access their business resources/services***.

There is no additional infrastructure that the AWS client needs to maintain or deploy to use AWS SSO. It takes a few clicks in the Management Console to integrate an AWS Organization with the AWS SSO.

In addition to native support of AWS Identity Access Management (IAM), AWS SSO also contains a built-in component used to integrate with Security Access Markup Language (SAML) 2.0 compatible services/applications, e.g., Office 365, Salesforces, etc..

Through the AWS Directory Service, AWS SSO can be integrated with the Microsoft Active Directory (AD). With AD integration, the end user (as a SAML-enabled application, an individual user or as a member of a group) can sign into the AWS SSO portal using their corporate AD credentials (that are managed within their corporate directory).

AWS SSO provides a central point to manage SSO, as well as a place to view the history of each application/user lifecycle and the privileges granted-to/removed-from the application/user. In addition, AWS SSO provides a centralized view of application/user attempts to access resources/services including the requestor's IP address. By default, to meet audit and compliance requirements, all AWS SSO administrator activities are traced using AWS CloudTrail.

Amazon Cognito

Amazon Cognito is a highly-available and highly scalable Single Sign-On (SSO) service that supports OpenID IdPs and SAML 2.0 identity providers and lets the AWS client quickly and easily add users and provide/control SSO access to web and mobile applications. There is no additional infrastructure that the AWS client needs to maintain or deploy to use Amazon Cognito.

Lastly, Amazon Cognito supports multi-factor authentication (MFA), as well as encryption of data in motion as well as at rest.

AWS COMPUTE

Virtual computing resources (e.g., EC2 instances), like virtual private networks and cloud storage, are ubiquitous to the AWS cloud, as well as to most AWS customers' systems running in the cloud. Like networking and storage, EC2 instances must be understood by the AWS consumer. When paying the fees for partially managed services, the AWS consumer has to determine the EC2 instance(s) that best fit their use case. Even when consuming fully managed AWS serverless services, underlying these are EC2 instances as well which you can scale vertically. In the cloud, there's no escaping the virtual machines: they are everywhere, hosting computations of every imaginable flavor. So, to obtain the best results, understanding EC2 instances is a must.

AWS Compute Resources and Services

AWS Compute includes:

1. Amazon Elastic Cloud Compute (EC2)
2. Amazon Elastic Block Storage (EBS) and
3. Amazon Lightsail

Amazon Elastic Cloud Compute (EC2)

An Amazon EC2 instance is a virtual machine you obtain on a pay-per-use basis. The type of virtualization depends on the type of Amazon Machine Image (AMI) used to launch the EC2 instance.

You launch an EC2 instance and manage EC2 instances, over the Internet. The instance type determines the hardware of the host computer used for your virtual EC2 instance. You configure the virtual CPU, RAM and block-storage resources used to host web applications and other types of software systems.

There are current-generation and the 1-2 previous-generation EC2 instances available in AWS

There is a limit on the number of instances you can start in a particular Region. The limit ***depends on the instance type***.

Resources in one Region are not automatically replicated to other Regions. When data is stored in one Region it is not replicated outside that Region. AWS never moves customer resources or data out of the Region the customer placed them in. It is the responsibility of the AWS customer to replicate data across Regions, based on the customers' business requirements.

EC2 Benefits

Benefits of EC2 instances include:

- ***Time to market*** – deploy a new EC2 instance in minutes;
- ***Scalability*** – at any moment, you can scale up and down CPU, RAM, block-storage resources;
- ***Control*** – at any moment, start and or stop an EC2 instance, interact with the it (via SSH; the AWS Management Console; the AWS CLI; the AWS SDK). You can control how the it boots (via bootstrapping);
- ***Reliable*** – available 99.95% of the time, for each Region;
- ***Secure*** – the VPC provides network traffic security of the EC2 instances;
- ***Multiple instance types*** – select from a variety of AWS EC2 instance types and sizes. You can also choose a pre-packaged EC2 instance in the Amazon

Marketplace form 3rd party vendors.
- ***Integration*** – most AWS services (VPC; S3; Lambda; Redshift; RDS; EMR, etc.) can be easily integrated with an EC2 instance;
- ***Cost Effective*** – pay for use of EC2 instance on an hourly basis or per second.

EC2 Operating Systems

EC2 instances are available with various operating systems:

- Amazon Linux;
- Windows 2003R2, 2008/2008R2, 2012/2012R2, 2016;
- Debian;
- SUSE;
- CentOS;
- Red Hat Enterprise Linux;
- Ubuntu.

EC2 Instance's Root Device

Underlying the virtual EC2 instance is a host computer. In that machine is a local block storage device. Each virtual EC2 instance running on a machine is allocated a portion of that local block storage device that is ***called the instance root device.*** The size of the temporary block storage depends on the instance type. The size can range from 0 to (24) 2 TB instance stores.

An instance root device contains the AMI image that is used to boot the EC2 instance.

The EC2 instance type also determines the type of local block storage hardware:

Hard Disk Drive (HDD,) or

Solid-State Drives (SDDs).

EC2's Instance Store

The instance root device has temporary block-level storage, called the instance store. The ***ephemeral storage is located on***

disks that are physically attached to the underlying host machine. You have to buy durable information storage, e.g., Amazon S3, EBS.

Suited for temporary information, which changes frequently, such as buffers, caches, scratch data

Amazon Machine Images (AMIs)

An instance is customizable by you, in various ways. However, each instance is available with a pre-built Amazon Machine Image (AMI) so that the instance can be launched and operated immediately and successfully.

The AMI contains:

- The operating system, either Linux or Microsoft Windows, and its default/custom configuration
- The initial state of installed patches
- Application or system software.

For example, when an AMI is to be used to instantiate an EC2 instance that is an ELB, best practice is to configure the operating system by enabling the keep-alive option in the kernel of the operating system. When enabled, keep-alive allows the ELB to reuse connections to the back-end EC2 instances, thereby reducing CPU utilization on the ELB EC2 instance.

A single AMI can be used to launch different types of EC2 instances.

AMI Maximum Transmission Unit (MTU)

Certain AMI support the configuration of network packet size, the ***Maximum Transmission Unit*** (MTU). The AMI configured for jumbo frames supports packets that are 9001 bytes in size, while the standard frame size is 1500 bytes.

If there are different MTU between EC2 instances in a VPC subnet, then this creates issues that must be handled. If an EC2 instance sends a packet that is larger than then receiving EC2 instance MTU, the receiving EC2 instance returns this ICMP message that instructs the sender to adjust the size of the MTU packet that it sends to the receiving instance. By default,

Security Groups do not allow any inbound ICMP traffic. To ensure that the sending instance does not drop the ICMP message, a custom ICMP rule with the Destination Unreachable protocol must be added to the Security Group.

In addition, inbound and outbound network ACL rules are required to ensure that the ***Path MTU Discovery*** can function correctly. The Path MTU Discovery functions to prevent packet loss. Path MTU Discovery is used to determine the path MTU between two EC2 instances or network devices.

AMI Root Volume

The AMI contains a root volume. The AMI root volume is a blueprint that contains information about:

- ***Template for the root volume*** of the EC2 instance (the operating systems; the applications running on the OS (e.g., the LAMP stack);
- ***EBS mappings to the instance*** launched from the AMI;
- AWS account ***AMI launch permissions*** that control which accounts can launch instance from the AMI.

AMI Launch Permission Categories

AMI launch permissions are categorized as:

1. Public – the owner grants launch permission to all AWS Accounts;
2. Explicit – the owner grants launch permissions to specific AWS Accounts;
3. Implicit – the owner has implicit launch permissions for the AMI.

S3-Backed (aka Instance Store-Backed) EC2 Instance Root Device

An Instance Store-Backed EC2 instance root device image is <u>backed up by S3</u>. The AMI is sourced from S3 and at launch the AMI used to boot the instance is copied to the instance root device. An instance store-backed EC2 instances ***cannot enter the***

Stop state.

When an Instance store-backed AMI instance is used, all data in the instance store is lost whenever:

- ***The host computer's disk drive fails;***
- ***The EC2 instance enters the Hibernate or Terminate state (it cannot enter the Stop state).***

EBS-Backed EC2 Instance Root Device

An EBS-backed EC2 instance root device image is backed up by an EBS volume and at launch the AMI used to boot the instance is copied to the instance root device. For example, the t2.medium EC2 instance requires an EBS-backed HVM AMI.

When an EBS-backed AMI instance is used the data in its instance store persists whenever:

- ***Can enter the Stop state and then re-Started (reboots),***
- ***The EC2 instance enters the Stop, Hibernate, or Terminate state, or fails.***

You can ***detach an EBS-backed instance store from one EC2 instance and attach it to another*** EC2 instance.

Golden Images

An EC2 instance can be customized. The configuration of a customized EC2 instance can be saved by creating an AMI. Each time an ***AMI configuration is changed*** there is the need to create a new ***golden image of the AMI.*** Up to the AWS account limit, as many EC2 instances made from the golden image AMI can be launched as needed (and all of which will embody the customized configuration).

These golden image AMIs are assets and must be managed appropriately.

Best practice – use a version control system to manage the golden image of AMIs.

Best practice – to ensure that the EC2 instances in an Auto Scaling Group are installed with the required configuration, base them on a golden image AMI.

Moving AMIs Across Regions

AWS never moves your data or your resources out of the Region that you placed them in. It is the clients' responsibility to move data and resources across Regions as required by their BPM. However, an EC2 instance cannot be moved across Regions, neither can a custom configured EC2 instance. ***To move a custom configure EC2 instance across Regions, create a golden image,*** an AMI image, of the instance.

In support of disaster recovery, the AMI image is copied to the destination Region using the AWS Management Console, or the AWS CLI or the AWS SDK (both of which support the CopyImage action). Both EBS-backed AMI images and Instance Stored-backed AMI images can be copied in this way. As can AMIs created from encrypted snapshots as well as from encrypted AMIs. ***Each copy of the AMI is identical and is assigned a unique identifier.***

Linux AMIs

An EC2 instance created from a Linux AMI does not have a password.

Linux AMIs use one of two types of virtualization:

1 - Hardware Virtual Machine (HVM)

The ***operating system runs directly on top of the virtual machine***, without modification, similar to the way the OS runs directly on top of the underlying hardware

The HVM ***can take advantage of hardware extensions*** (e.g., enhanced networking; GPU processing, etc.).

All current generation instance types support the HVM AMIs.

Only an HVM AMI is able to support enhanced networking;

2 - Paravirtual (PV)

The PV AMI is boot loaded using PV-GRUB.

The PV runs on host hardware that does not explicitly support virtualization.

The PV cannot take advantage of hardware extensions.

Sources of AMIs

There are a variety of different sources AMIs, such as:

AWS - For a given operating system, multiple releases are supported. The OS is a standard image, so you will have to ensure that all patches required to support your workload are installed on the instance.

AWS Marketplace - AWS partners sell AMIs with their proprietary software or services installed and configured on the instance. The Buyers of AWS partner instances incur the usual AWS charges plus the additional charges by the AWS partner.

Generated from existing instances - The buyer configures an AMI to meet their specific workload needs, security requirements, company standards, government regulations, etc. The buyer then uses that company AMI to launch customized instances. You can choose between instance store-backed or EBS-backed images.

Uploaded Virtual Servers - The buyer has an in-house virtualized image (Open Virtualization Format; Hyper-V; OVA). You use the AWS VM Import/Export service to import your private virtual machine images to instances and vice versa. You can choose between instance store-backed or EBS-backed images.

Shared AMI - Shared by the developer community.

VM Import/Export

To import and export your VM images for use with EC2 instance, AWS provides at no additional charge the VM Import/Export tool.

To upload a VM into AWS, you must provide an S3 bucket and an IAM role named vmiport. The VM image must be stored in an S3 bucket located in the Region in which you want to import the VM. The vmiport IAM role needs the appropriate bucket policy for the bucket in which the VM image will be stored.

If you want to export a VM image, the EC2 instance must

first be stopped. When in a stopped state, an AMI of the EC2 instance can be created.

EC2 Instance Type Categories

AWS offers 5 EC2 instance type categories.

General purpose

Provides a balance of CPU, RAM and network resources that is good for general use. The T2 type provides burstable performance.

The T2 instance provides a base-line performance with the ability to burst above the base-line. When the CPU is idle it accrues credits and when it is active it consumes those credits.

Instance types M5, M4 and M# do not provide burstable performance.

Compute optimized

Has high-performance processors. For CPU-intense workloads, like media transcoding, applications supporting large numbers of concurrent users, long-running batch jobs, gaming servers, etc.

Memory optimized

For processing large data sets in RAM, such as SAP HANA, Oracle dbs, MongoDB, Cassandra, Presto, Spark, high-performance computing (HPC) and Electronic Design Automation (EDA), Genome computations, etc.

Storage optimized

For workloads that require high-performance sequential read/write access to very large data sets on local storage. Optimized for low-latency, random I/O operations per second (IOPS), such as I/O bound applications, NoSQL databases, data warehouses, MapReduce, etc.

Advanced computing

Provide hardware accelerators, such as graphic processing units (GPUs), field programmable gate arrays (FPGAs), which enable parallelism. Used for machine learning algorithms, genome computations, fluid dynamics.

EC2 Instance Intel Processor

The EC2 instance uses an Intel processor, with:

Intel AES Instructions (AES-NI) – this encryption uses the Advanced Encryption Standard (AES) algorithm.

Intel Advanced Vector Extensions (AVX) – improves performance for image and audio/video processing. Available on HVM AMI based instances.

Intel Turbo Boost Technology – provides more performance when needed.

The EC2's Block Storage Features

The primary and permanent volume of block storage you attach to an EC2 instance that is called Elastic Block Storage (EBS).

Though a virtual device that has an existence independent from the EC2 instance, the EBS is used by the EC2 instance as if it were its physical hard drive.

When you terminate the EC2 to which the EBS is attached, the EC2 disappears but the EBS persists (and therefore, you continue to pay for its use after the EC2 is terminated).

There are 3 types of block storage:

General purpose – uses Solid-State Drives (SSDs); this is the default EBS of most EC2 instance types;

Provisioned IOPS (PIOPS) – you get > IOPS than general purpose SSDs; provisioned IOPS maximizes I/O throughput; typically needed by database CRUD.

Magnetic – provides the lowest cost per GB for all volume time; for non-mission-critical workloads; for batch workloads; for development workloads.

Provisioned IOPS

PIOPS SSD volumes are designed for I/O intensive workloads, that are sensitive to storage performance and consistency in random access I/O throughput.

They are the most expensive EBS per GB, but they provide the highest performance in a predictable manner.

The size of the PIOPS SSD volume ranges from 4GB to 16TB

When you provision PIOPS SSD you specify both the volume size and the desired number of IOPS.

IOPS can be up to the lower of the maximum of 30 times the number of GB of the volume, or 20,000 IOPS.

You can stripe multiple PIOPS SSD volumes to create a RAID 0 configuration. The resulting size of the RAID 0 array is the sum of the storage capacity of the volumes within it, and the expected IOPS is the sum of the available bandwidth of the volumes within it.

EC2's Block Storage Comparison

Some EC2 instances are EBS-optimized. What that means is the EC2 instance has be modified to support dedicated throughput between the EBS volume and the EC2 instance.

To gain the best EBS I/O performance, dedicated throughput minimizes contention between the EBS I/O network traffic and other traffic outbound from the EC2 instance.

With this optimization, depending on the EC2 instance type, throughputs between 500 Mbps and 14,000 Mbps can be purchased.

Ways to Address an EC2 instance

To address an EC2 instance you don't say, 'hello EC,' or 'e2?'. None of those salutations will do the trick.

If you launch ***the EC2 instance*** in a VPC's public subnet, it ***is assigned***:

1. ***a public IP address and public DNS name, as well as***
2. ***a private IP address and private DNS name.***

When you create the instance, you define how it will be addressed over the Internet. There are 3 ways ***to address the instance from a route over the Internet***:

1. ***Public Domain Name System (DNS) Name***;
2. ***Public IP***, and
3. ***Elastic IP***.

Public Domain Name System (DNS) Name Address

When you launch an instance, AWS automatically generates a DNS name and assigns it to that instance. The buyer cannot specify the instance's DNS Name.

The DNS Name is accessible via the AWS Management Console web service, or from its API by using the AWS Command Line Interface (CLI) library.

EC2 Private IP Address

An EC2 instance is only aware of its private IP Address. The private IP addresses are used to communicate between instances in the same network (EC2-Classic of VPC).

When an EC2 instance is launched in a VPC, the private IP address (from its CIDR block range) associated with the network interface remains associated with the network interface when the instance enters the stopped and the restarted states. The private IP address is only release when the instance is terminated.

When an EC2 instance is launched in the EC2-Classic, the private IP address is released when the instance is stopped or terminated. If the instance is restarted, it is assigned a new private IP address.

How Internet Hosts Access EC2 Instances

The key requirements to providing host interfaces in the Internet with access to EC2 instances are:

1 Attach an Internet Gateway (IGW) to the VPC that contains the subnet in which the EC2 instance is launched.

2 Attach a public IP address (or Elastic IP) to the EC2 instance;

3 Add a route entry for the IGW in the Route table.

As will be revealed, there are other important matters that may need to be addressed as well.

EC2 Public IP address

A launched instance may also have a public IP address assigned to it, from among the IP addresses reserved by AWS. The Public IP address cannot be transferred to another instance. The buyer cannot specify the public IP address. The IP address is unique on the internet but only lasts as long as the instance is running.

By default, the public IP address of the EC2 instance is released after the instance is stopped and started.

Best practice – when an EC2 instance's has a public IP address, refrain from programmatically accessing the instance by using to the instance's domain name.

EC2 Elastic IP Address

An Elastic IP is a static public IP address, unique to the Internet, that the buyer reserves independently and assigns to the EC2 instance. It is a public IP address that can be shared externally without coupling end users to a particular instance.

This EIP is tied to the AWS account. The EIP is not tied to the lifetime of the instance, or its run state but persists. This EIP address can be transferred to another instance. This makes if possible to use the EIP to mask the failure of an EC2 instance or of an application service (by rapidly disassociating (and unmapping) the EIP for the unhealthy Instance and associating (and mapping) the EIP to another instance (in your AWS account).

Source/Destination Check Attribute

Each EC2 instance has a source/destination check attribute that controls whether the source/destination of network traffic is enabled on the instance. By default source/destination check is enabled, therefore the instance does not handle network traffic that isn't specifically destined for that EC2 instance. Configure VPC route tables to send outbound traffic through the EC2 instance.

When an EC2 instance is used to support network address translation, routing, or functions as a firewall, this attribute must be disabled. In addition, when a VPN IPSec tunnel is provisioned to support traffic from on-premise hosts to EC2 instances launched in the AWS VPC, this attribute must be disabled otherwise the EC2 instances will not be accessible to the on-premise hosts.

In addition, configure to VPC route tables to send outbound traffic through the EC2 instance as needed.

EC2 Scheduled Events

Periodically, AWS maintenance conducts EC2 Scheduled Events. These events result in down time. When that scheduled down time conflicts with the client's BPM, those interruptions must be managed effectively by the client.

Best practice – after receiving a notice of an EC2 Scheduled Event which will result in EC2 instance down time, during your regularly scheduled down time, stop and start the instance. Doing so will force the migration to the new EC2 instance configuration.

The EC2 Instance Key-Pair

Amazon EC2 uses a public-key cryptography to encrypt and decrypt login information

See URL https://en.wikipedia.org/wiki/Public-key_cryptography

A key-pair is made of:

1. A private key that is used to encrypt the information and
2. A public key that is used to decrypt the information

The keys that AWS uses are 2,048-bit SSH-2 RSA keys.

Amazon stores the public key and the private key is kept by the buyer.

A buyer can upload a key-pair and can also use the AWS Management Console, the CLI, or the API, to create a key-pair through AWS.

You can have up to 5,000 key-pairs per Region.

Where does Amazon keep the public key? That depends on the OS.

Linux instance:

- ***Has no password;***
- The public key is stored in the ~/.ssh/authorized keys file
- An ***initial user, ec2_user,*** is created
- To access the Linux instance, you ***use the ec2_user login, your private key and the Secure Shell (SSH) tool.***
- After the initial login you can configure SSO and log in via LDAP.

Windows instance:

- ***AWS generates a random password for the local administrator account and encrypts that password using the public key***
- Initial access to the instance occurs by decrypting the local administrator password, by using your private key
- Initial access can happen via the AWS Management console or its API
- That decrypted password can be used to log into the instance, as the local admin account, using the Microsoft Remote Desktop Protocol (RDP)

Best practice – change the instance's random password as needed.

Logging into the EC2 Instance

Now that you've launched the instance, how can you access that virtual machine? ***For a Linux instance you will login using the Secure Shell (SSH) tool.*** You will ***use SSH along with the private key of the instance's Key-Pair to log into the EC2 instance*** and manipulate the instance.

SSH is a very important tool in cloud environments

SSH is a cryptographic network protocol for use over unsecured networks, e.g., the world-wide web

SSH provides a secure channel between the SSH client and the SSH server.

SSH is used to:

- log into a remote machine, i.e., your instance and
- execute commands on an instance and
- transfer files to and from the instance

An SSH client or server is typically on a Linux machine and are available for Windows machines.

Best practice - root credentials are not allowed to login over Secure Shell, or SSH, to an EC2 launched instance.

The standard/default port for SSH is 22. Therefore, ***the Security Group in which the EC2 instance is launched must have an inbound rule to allow TCP*** (on the default) ***port 22*** - without that rule, no host interface located in the Internet will be able to SSH into the instance. In addition, ***the target EC2 instance must have a public IP address and the VPC's IGW and route table entries must be in place as well.*** To SSH into a Linux EC2 instance *it is not required that the instance have a private IP address.*

For SSH access to an EC2 instance, the protocol referenced by the Security Group rule must be TCP. The default SSH port is 22. To limit which IP addresses can SSH into the EC2 instance, ***it is possible in the security group rule to specify the range of IP addresses, or of a single IP address, of permitted host interfaces***.

For an EC2 instance to allow SSH inbound and outbound traffic, there must exist an inbound Network ACL allow rule as well as an outbound Network ACL allow rule (Network ACLs are stateless therefore they require an allow rule for each direction of the network traffic).

Lastly, if you are able to SSH to an EC2 instance that is hosting a web application but cannot connect to that web service when using a web browser, check to be sure that an HTTP rule exists in the instance's Security Group.

AWS does not permit SSH connections with all EC2 instances, and ***specifically SSH connections with those instances used by a managed AWS service.***

In addition, ***it is not possible to establish an SSH connection with a Windows EC2 instance***. For a Windows instance you will

login using the Remote Desktop Protocol (RDP).

You can use Amazon Run Command from the Amazon EC2 Console to configure the instances without having to login to the instance, i.e., no need for SSH of RDP.

EC2 Instance Security Groups

How do you secure (control the network traffic inbound to and outbound from) an EC2 instance in a subnet of your VPC? You do this by creating ***a Security Group***, which ***functions as a stateful firewall***.

There are 2 types of security groups:

EC2-Classic - you can only control out-going traffic from the instance

VPC - you can control both incoming and out-going traffic to the instance.

A Security Group controls traffic at the EC2 instance level.

The hacker has to breach the Security Group repeatedly for each EC2 instance.

A ***Security Group Rules is defined by 3 attributes: port #, protocol and source/destination identity***.

In turn, ***a source/destination identity is defined*** in 1 of 2 ways:

CIDR block - which defines a specific range of IP addresses

Security group – includes any instance in a group. Helps prevent coupling rules with a specific IP address

The default rule is to deny (to not allow any) traffic that is not explicitly allowed by a rule.

Security Groups and Ping

To be able to Ping from an EC2 instance in one subnet to an EC2 instance in another subnet, where both subnets are in the same VPC, ***the Security Group needs to be configured to allow ICMP network traffic***. The Ping tool uses the ICMP echo request and echo reply messages (the Internet Control Message Protocol (ICMP) protocol runs within the Network Layer of the OSI Model) to test if a host interface can communicate with another host interface.

Changing a Security Group

An instance is associated with a Security Group the moment that it is launched.

Every instance must belong to 1 security group but can join more than 1. When an instance belongs to N security groups, the security rules are aggregated and all traffic allowed by each group is allowed.

While an instance is running within an Amazon VPC, you can change which security group the instance is associated with.

While an instance is running outside of an Amazon VPC, you cannot change which security group the instance is associated with.

EC2 Instance Life-Cycle

An instance life-cycle has 5 stages:

Launch

- When you launch an instance, the AMI boots, health checks are performed to make sure there are no hardware issues. ***Once 'up and running'*** the instance is ready to work and can be connected to. ***At this moment, the hourly billing for the instance starts and you are liable to pay that bill.***

Start and Stop

- ***Starting and stopping an EC2 instance causes the instance to be provisioned on different AWS hardware.*** If the health check fails, the instance does not start. You can attempt to fix the problem or start up another instance. ***You can stop an instance only if it is backed-up by an Elastic Block Storage (EBS). Amazon does not charge a buyer while an instance is stopped but you are charged for the EBS service. When stopped, an instance type can be changed and the re-started. If started with a different instance type the public IPv4 address of the instance will***

change, but the private IP address will stay the same.

Reboot

- ***You can reboot an instance only if it is backed up by instance store or backed up by EBS. All data persists after the reboot event, even the contents of the instance store. The IP address remains the same after the reboot.*** You can reboot an instance using the AWS Management console or the CLI.

Termination

- You can shut down or terminate an instance. ***When the instance is terminated, the billing stops.*** If an EBS is backing up the instance, ***you must end the EBS service after terminating the instance, or you will be billed for the EBS use.***

Retirement

- An instance is retired when an unrepairable hardware issue is detected. As soon as the instance reaches this state, it is stopped and terminated by AWS.

If an EC2 instance is launched within an Auto Scaling Group, Running, Terminated, and Stopped are no longer valid instance states.

EC2 Instance Bootstrapping at Launch

Once an instance is launched, the buyer can programmatically configure the instance. This is called bootstrapping. In Linux, this is done with a bash shell script. In Windows, this is done (usually) with a PowerShell script.

When the EC2 instance is launched, AWS executes that script in the form of a string, ***called UserData***

During bootstrapping two types of UserData can be passed to the EC2 Instance:

1. ***Run a shell script that:***

- Applying patches;
- Installing software (such as the Perl language);
- Configuring a daemon to start, a root directory of a

web service, ...;
- Enrolling in the Active Directory Service;
- Installing an application runtime.

2. ***Cloud-init directives (common automated configuration tasks).***

Modifying a Launched EC2 Instance

The top 3 modifications to a launched instance include:

3. Changing the instance type or size,
4. Changing a security group, the instance belongs to, or
5. Terminating an instance.

Changing the Instance Type or Size

You can change the instance type using the AWS Management Console, its API, or the CLI. ***To change the type of or to resize an instance, the state of that EC2 instance must be transitioned to Stopped.***

After the instance is stopped, the instance type and or size can be changed. Once the change task concludes, the instance is restarted (the usual way) and the change process is complete (for the time being).

Diagnose EC2 Instance Termination Events

EC2 instances can terminate for reasons that are unanticipated and are at first unknown. To gather data about the instance termination event use the AWS CLI. The AWS CLI provides the 'aws ec2 describe-instances' command which takes the instance ID as input. Within the JSON document that this command returns is data that will help you understand the reasons for the unanticipated termination event.

In that neither the CF or the CA certification exams cover either the AWS CLI or the AWS SDK, this information is being shared for its practical use value. Put it inside your virtual toolbox, and don't depart for the clouds without it.

Amazon EC2 Pricing Options

AWS offers multiple EC2 pricing options, based on:

1. The duration of the instance;
2. Hourly price of the instance;
3. Performance of the instance, and
4. Security.

The 3 pricing options offered by AWS are:

1. ***On-demand*** instance;
2. ***Reserved*** instance and
3. ***Spot*** instance.

On-Demand Instance Pricing Option

This is the most popular pricing option. You pay just for the usage on a flat hourly rate or per-second billing. There is no up-front or hidden charges. There is no commitment to a minimum term and so you can scale up or down at any point in time.

You can vary provisioning based on un-predictable loads.

Reserved Instance Pricing Option

With Reserved Instances:

- ***Ensures capacity reservations*** for predictable workloads (how many resources for how long);
- Can be up to a 75% discount over On-Demand Instances;
- The contract terms apply to EC2 instances in a Region, or in a specific AZ.

There are ***2 factors that determine the pricing***:

The ***term commitment***, which is the length of time, of ***either 1 year or 3 years***, during which the instances are reserved by the buyer and

The ***Payment option***, of which there are 3

1. ***Upfront*** – pay in-full for the entire term of the reservation
2. ***Partial Upfront*** – a portion of the reservation cost is paid and the remainder is paid in monthly in-

stallments for the duration of the term

3. ***No Upfront*** – the entire reservation cost is paid in monthly installments for the duration of the term.

You can modify the:

- AZ;
- Scope;
- Network platform, or
- Instance size within the same instance family.

Of your Reserved Instance.

Sub-Categories of Reserved Instance

Standard

- The Standard Reserved Instance pricing options are the 3 explained above.
- A standard reserved instance can be applied to instances launched by Auto Scaling.
- The buyer can modify a reservation in 3 ways, at no fee:
- Can be migrated across Availability Zones, within the same Region;
- Change between the old EC2-Classic and the current EC2-VPC;
- Change the Linux instance Type, within the same Instance Family.

Convertible

- ***You can exchange an EC2 instance of one class of family to another class, another instance type, platform, scope, or tenancy;***
- ***There is no limit to the number of times an exchange can be performed***, just as long as the exchange is of equal or greater value;
- ***There is no exchange fee***, other than the up-cost to acquire a greater value through the exchange;
- An exchange can be made to exploit price reductions of EC2 instances over time;
- Provides some flexibility if the computing needs

change during the 3-year term of the contract.

Scheduled

- Regularly scheduled batch computations are common to most BPM;
- Scheduled Reserved Instances are available for clients to ***reserve, for predefined blocks of time that recur over a 1-year term;***
- ***Can be run on a daily, weekly, or monthly basis***, at a 5-10% discount of On-Demand Instance rates;
- For a Linux instance the fee is per second, for other operating systems the fee is per hour;
- Are ***only available to be launched within the predefined blocks of time***;

Reserved Instance Marketplace

For AWS accounts with a US-only bank account that want to stop paying for a Standard Reserved instance, they must:

Terminate the Standard Reserved instance as soon as possible (which helps to preserve the remaining term), and

Sell the Standard Reserved Instance along with its remaining term on the AWS Reserved Instance Marketplace.

The Reserved Instance Marketplace is a platform that ***supports the sale of*** 3rd-party and AWS customers' ***unused Standard Reserved Instances***. As to be expected, across collection of offers, the length of the term varies as do the pricing options.

There are a variety of reason why an AWS client wants to see the unused portion of their Standard Reserved Instances: moving instance across Regions; changing to a new instance type; a business need ends before the length of the term expires; etc.

Spot Instance Pricing Option

AWS has excess unused compute capacity which it offers for sale. ***Spot Instances are intended for workloads that are not time critical and are tolerant of interruption***. This option offers discounts that can be up to 90%. Spot instances can be a good fit for workloads that are for data analysis, batch jobs, background processing, or optional (none critical) computations.

For each instance type, there is a Spot Price. The buyer offers the Bid Price that they are willing to pay for a type of instance. If the Bid Price > Spot Price, the buyer can receive the requested Spot instance type. You gain or lose the Spot instance at very short notice. The buyer pays the Spot Price for the hours that the Spot instance runs.

The Spot instance runs until 1 of these events occurs:

- The buyer terminates the instance;
- The Spot Price goes above the buyer's Bid Price;
- There is not enough unused capacity to meet the demand for Spot instances;
- Tenancy based pricing models.

AWS Tenancy Options

The tenancy option chosen at the time when the VPC is created cannot be changed. The AWS architecture is based on tenancy, on how the buyer wants to occupy, or inhabit, the AWS cloud. ***Each tenancy option has a different pricing model, with a different cost-efficiency.***

The AWS pricing models are based on which tenancy option a buyer chooses. ***AWS offers 4 types of tenancy:***

1. ***Shared Tenancy;***
2. ***Dedicated Instance;***
3. ***Dedicated Host;***
4. ***Placement Group.***

Shared Tenancy

Shared tenancy is where:

- ***A single host machine houses 1-N instances*** from different AWS accounts, that is ***from different buyers;***
- AWS securely isolates each instance on a host machine;

- ***This is the default pricing model for all instances.***
- ***Multiple EC2 instances*** on the same host computer ***are isolated from each other via the Xen Hypervisor***.

The hypervisor ensures that network packet sniffing is ineffective.

Clients have ***no direct access to the raw disk devices*** on the host computer.

Dedicated Host Tenancy

A Dedicated host is:

- ***A physical machine with a single instance dedicated to a single buyer.***
- ***You can use your existing software licensing*** by consuming dedicated hosts.

If you want, ***you can create virtual machines on the dedicated host***.

A dedicated host ***can be purchase on-demand or on a reservation***.

For added security, clients ***can encrypt the raw disk device.***

Dedicated Instances Tenancy

Dedicated instances are:

- A dedicated instance is the EC2 instance that you launch within your Virtual Private Cloud (VPC).
- You dedicated instance is physically isolated at the host hardware level from the EC2 instances that belong to other AWS Accounts.

Specific instances of a single buyer, of a single AWS account, marked as being 'dedicated,' run on a host machine.

Dedicated Instance Auto Recovery

The Dedicated Instance has an Auto Recovery feature (now available in all AWS Regions) that increases individual EC2 instance availability. ***The Auto Recovery feature uses CloudWatch to detect when an instance is impaired and automatically recover the Dedicated Instance.***

The instance is recovered on a different physical server and decreases the efforts required by the client to manually intervene in the recovery process. Thought there is no fee to enabling the Auto Recovery feature, the *related CloudWatch charges do apply*.

The Placement Group (Cluster Networking)

A Placement Group is a logical cluster of EC2 instances that maximizes the bandwidth and network performance. EC2 instance types R4, X1, M5, M4, C5, C4, C3, I2, P3, P2, G3 and D2, support cluster networking.

When you launch any of these EC2 instance types into a Placement Group, they can use up to 10 Gbps for a single-flow and up to 25 Gbps for multi-flow, network traffic in each direction (inbound and outbound).

Here are a few important facts about placement groups:

- ***A Placement Group cannot span AZs.***
- A running Placement Group cannot be moved.
- The name of the Placement Group must be unique within your AWS Account.
- A single Placement Group can contain multiple types of instances.
- An existing EC2 instance cannot be added to a placement group.
- The maximum throughput between EC2 instances in the placement group is limited by the slowest of the two instances.

Best practice – use the same EC2 instance type in a given Placement Group.

There is no charge for creating a Placement Group. You are billed for the EC2 instances used within the Placement Group.

Placement Group with Enhanced Networking

EC2 instance types that support cluster networking, might also support enhanced networking.

An EC2 instance with ***enhanced networking uses a Single Root Virtualization (SR-IOV) that provides higher I/O perform-***

ance and lower CPU utilization. Only a Hardware Virtual Machine AMI supports enhanced networking.

SR-IOV increases the quantity of packets per second (PPS), lowering latency and smoothing out the peaks and valleys

Their network enhancements provide:

- Higher bandwidth;
- Higher packet per second (PPS) performance;
- Lower inter-instance latencies.

There is no additional cost for enhanced networking beyond that of its instance type fee.

Steps for Using an AWS EC2 Instance

After you have done the main lifting of configuring and securing you network (have chosen the Regions, created the VPCs and CIDR blocks, chosen the AZs and created the subnets, Security Groups, routes, NACLs, etc.):

1. Either select from among the existing AMIs, or create your custom AMI, you will use as an EC2 instance;
2. Choose the EC2 pricing option;
3. Choose EC2 instance type;
4. Choose the subnet, attach the EBS and optionally choose a static EIP, or EIN, for use with the EC2 instance.
5. Launch the instance in its Security Group and complete its configuration.

Amazon Resource Name (ARN)

A unique identifier called an ARN is automatically assigned by AWS to a resource, e.g., EC2 instance, that is created in AWS.

EC2 Instance Tag

An AWS tag is a useful way to categorize AWS resources, such as by purpose, environment, account owner, etc. In addition to being used to segregate resources, ***tags are also used for cost reporting and billing purposes.*** Access to a tagged EC2 instance can be by associating an IAM policy which sets conditions for access to the instance.

Best practice – associate a meaningful tag with each EC2 instance.

EC2 Instance Metadata

Each EC2 instance is uniquely identified by its instance metadata. The instance metadata is a set of properties that you use to configure and manage the instance. You obtain the values of properties of the instance from within its OS, without making a call to the AWS API.

Instance metadata properties and their values include, these and others:

- Associated security group or groups
- The ID of the instance
- The instance type.
- The AMI used to create the instance.

To ***retrieve the public IP address*** assigned to a running EC2 instance, log into the instance and use a GET request to this local URL http://169.254.169.254/latest/meta-data/public-ipv4

To ***retrieve the private IP address*** assigned to a running EC2 instance, log into the instance and use a GET request to this local URL http://169.254.169.254/latest/meta-data/local-ipv4

To ***retrieve both the private IP address and the public IP address*** of the EC2 instance, log into the instance and use a GET request to this local URL http://169.254.169.254/latest/meta-data/

Instance Identity Document

When an EC2 instance is launched, its instance identity document is generated, and exposed through instance metadata. The document is used to validate the attributes of the instances, such as instance size, instance type, operating system, AMI, etc.

To retrieve the instance identity document, log

into the instance and use a GET request to this local URL http://169.254.169.254/latest/dynamic/instance-identity/document

Managing & Monitoring EC2 Instances

To manage the EC2 instances, there are also tags associated with your instance. A tag is a key/value pair that is used by AWS services to manage the instance. An instance can have a maximum of 10 tags associated with it.

AWS offers Amazon ***CloudWatch, a service that provides monitoring and alerting for EC2 instances*** and also other AWS infrastructure. A ***CloudWatch Alarm can monitor an EC2 instance and automatically recover the instance*** if it fails due to hardware problems or incurs problems that require AWS involvement to repair. The recovered instance is identical to the original instance, including instance ID, private IP address, instance metadata, etc.

Terminating an EC2 Instance

At the end of its life-cycle, the state of an instance is set to Terminated. ***A terminated instance cannot be recovered.***

When an instance is terminated, its OS is shut-down and that instance is removed from the AWS infrastructure.

The ***termination protection setting*** can be enabled for an instance. While termination protection is enabled, calls from the AWS Management Console, API or CLI will fail. This setting offers no protection from:

- the OS shutdown command, or from
- shutdown by AWS Auto Scaling, or from
- termination by a Spot Price change.

EC2 Penetration Testing

Per the AWS Acceptable Use Policy, penetration testing of EC2 instances may be performed on their own EC2 instances with prior authorization from AWS.

AWS Elastic IP Addresses (EIPs)

An EIP is a static, public IP address, reachable from the Internet, ***that you associate with an EC2 instance. In each Region, AWS maintains an inventory of public IP addresses.*** You can release an EIP that you associate with your EC2 instance.

In multitier solutions, each application maps to an IP address. When you launch an EC2 instance, it is given a new private IP address. Changes to an instance's IP address breaks the multitier solution, until it is remapped.

AWS makes static public IP addresses – in the form of an EIP – available to you so that you can associate a static public IP address with your EC2 instance in your VPC. Applications connect using the same static EIP. Your EIPs remains fixed in place in you VPC even while the EC2 instance associated with them may change over time.

You are limited to (5) EIP per Region. You are able to acquire, preserve and grow, your own inventory of EIPs.

Keep the following facts about EIPs in mind:

- EIP supports only IPv4, not IPv6, IP addresses.
- ***EIPs are specific to the AWS Region they are created in and cannot be assigned to an EC2 instance launched in an alternative Region.***

There exists a 1-to-1 relationship between a host interface and an EIP.

Your first step is to ***allocate an EIP for use within your VPC*** and the 2nd step is to ***assign the EIP to an EC2 instance in the VPC.***

You can move an EIP from one EC2 instance to another EC2 instance, either when the EC2 instances are in the same VPC or in different VPCs (in the same Region).

You are charged a fee for each EIP allocated to your AWS account, whether that EIP is or is not associated with an EC2 instance. ***But, you are not charged that fee when an EIP is associated with a launched EC2 instance.***

You are charged a fee if the EIP is attached to a stopped EC2

instance.

An EIP remains associated with your AWS account until you explicitly release the EIP.

AWS Elastic Network Interfaces (ENIs)

There exists network appliances and security appliances, as well as computations, that require EC2 instances that have 2-N host interfaces.

You cannot change the default, or primary, interface of any EC2 instance (known as eth0).

The ENI is a virtual network interface that you create independently of any host, of any EC2 instance.

The ENI does not impact/increase the network bandwidth to the EC2 instance.

The ENI is permanently associated with the VPC in which it is created.

The ENI persists (for a fee) whether or not it is associated with an EC2 instance.

You can 'attach' an ENI to an EC2 instance that exists in the ENI's home VPC when the instance is:

- Running (***hot attach***);
- Stopped (***warm attached***), and
- Being launched (***cold attached***)

The maximum number of ENI you can attach to an EC2 instance depends on the type of instance, as does the maximum counts of public IP and private IP addresses per ENI.

You can have up to (350) ENIs per Region.

ENI Attributes

An ENI has the following attributes:

- A MAC Address;
- 1 public IP address is used to communicate with interfaces in the Internet (which can be auto assigned to the ENI for eth0 when the instance is being launched);
- 1 private IP address taken from the range of a VPC's

CIDR block;

- 1:N secondary private IPv4 IP addresses;
- 1 Elastic IP IPv4 IP address per private IPv4 IP address;
- 1:N IPv6 IP Addresses;
- 1:N Security Group;
- A source/destination check flag and description.

How EC2 Instances in a VPC Communicate With Each Other

The predominant characteristic of AWS infrastructure is tenant isolation. Every part of every virtual private cloud (VPC) is a logical model that AWS maps to the underlying AWS physical resources. The ***AWS mapping service captures and manages that logical model, all virtual resources contained in it, as well as their IP addresses.*** AWS maps these logical components to the IP address of the physical servers on which the virtual resources are deployed.

In a VPC, the EC2 instance initiates communication with another instance by broadcasting an Address Resolution Protocol (ARP) packet, intended to obtain the Media Access Control (MAC) address of the target EC2 instance.

The local hypervisor intercepts the EC2 instance's ARP packet and queries the AWS mapping service to verify the existence of the target EC2 instance and to obtain its MAC address. If the target exists in the VPC, the hypervisor returns its MAC address to the initiating EC2 instance.

Next, the EC2 instance sends an IP packet (containing its MAC address and the target's MAC address) to the target instance, which the hypervisor intercepts. The hypervisor queries the AWS mapping service for the IPv4 IP address of the physical server on which the target instances is running.

When the AWS mapping service returns that IPv4 IP address to the hypervisor, the packet from the initiating EC2 instance is encapsulated in a VPC identifier (that identifies the source VPC). That packet is next encapsulated in an IP packet containing both the source instance's IP address and the target instance's IP address. Then, the hypervisor drops that packet on the AWS network media.

The target physical server picks the packet off the AWS network media, and hands that packet to its local hypervisor, which queries the AWS mapping service to validate the existence of the source EC2 instance on that specific physical server in that specific source VPC. Once validated, the hypervisor on the target removes the outer envelopes and delivers the packet to the target EC2 instance that it is hosting.

Elastic Block Storage (Amazon EBS)

The persistence of data flowing into and out of the workload is dictated by the life-cycle of an EC2 instance. ***Certain states that an EC2 instance enters literally obliterate data.*** The data of a typical workload on ***an EC2 instance requires protection to ensure that its data persists.*** Because ***the EBS volumes persist data when an EC2 instance fails, it is possible to recover that data.***

Amazon ***EBS is disk-storage - persistent block-level storage volumes*** - that is ***attached to an Amazon EC2 instance.*** However, ***the EBS volume is automatically replicated across multiple servers within its AZ***, that protects your data from instance failure, that ***offers high availability and durability***.

An EBS volume available in one AZ is not available in any other AZ. ***Data stored in an EBS volume is not equally accessible from all AWS Regions. An EBS volume is only accessible from 1 AZ. EBS does not tolerate an AZ failure.***

There are 3 types of EBS volumes available, at different prices, depending on the instance type chosen:

1. ***Magnetic volumes***
2. ***General-purpose SSD***
3. ***Provisioned IOPS SSD***

Multiple EBS volumes can be attached to 1 EC2 instance.

The size of the EBS volume can be changed, and a change in size can also happen with the EBS volume is attached to an EC2

instance.

EBS Use Cases

The EBS is used when data input and output to a workload is best kept proximate to the instance on which the computation is running.

Moreover, ***this data has value and needs to persist beyond the time when the instance is stopped or terminated or may be rebooted.***

The EBS is useful when:

- The disk drive underlying the EC2 instance fails;
- The instance is stopped (and data in the instance store needs to persist);
- The instance terminates (and data needs to persist).

Magnetic Volumes

The magnetic volumes have the lowest performance characteristics and have the lowest price per GB.

- The size of the magnetic volume can range from 1GB to 1TB.
- The average IOPS is 100 but burst speeds can reach into the 100s of IOPS.
- The magnetic volume EBS is suited for:
- Workloads where data is accessed infrequently;
- The workload involves sequential reads of data records;
- The situation requires the lowest-cost storage.

You are charged for the size of the volume chosen, not for the quantity of data physically present on the volume.

Magnetic Types

AWS has two new types of magnetic EBS volumes, which are intended to replace the older style volume

Through-put Optimized

- A low-cost HDD volume designed for frequent data access in support of analysis. This is for use with workloads typical of big data, data warehousing and log processing

- The volume size can be up to 16TB
- With a maximum IOPS of 500 and a maximum throughput of 500 MB/sec
- This type of volume is significantly cheaper than General-purpose SSD volumes.
- Uses a 'burst bucket model.'

Cold HDD

- These volumes are designed for workloads where the data is access infrequently, perhaps once in 24 hours
- Volume size can be up to 16 TB
- With a maximum IOPS of 250 and a maximum throughput to 250 MB/sec.
- Uses a 'burst bucket model.'

General-Purpose SSD

The General-purpose SSD (aka, gp2) offers cost-effective storage which is suitable for a variety of workloads. They deliver single-digit millisecond latencies. The size of the SSD ranges from 1GB to 16TB.

The baseline performance is 3 IOPS per GB, capping at 10,000 IOPS. The most important factor that determines baseline performance is the size of the volume.

The general-purpose SSD uses a 'burst bucket model.' The burst speech can be up to 3,000 IOPS, for extended periods of time. I/O credits represent the available bandwidth that the general-purpose SSD volume can burst large amounts of I/O. The more I/O credits the volume has the more time it can burst beyond its baseline level. A general-purpose SSD earns I/I credits at the rate of 3 IOPS per GB of volume size.

You are ***billed based on the quantity of storage provisioned***. These volumes are suited for workloads with:

- Small to medium-sized databases
- Development and test environments

- System boot volumes.

Provisioned IOPS SSD

Provisioned IOPS SSD support I/O intensive workloads that are vulnerable to physical storage CRUD performance and random I/O access. The ***size of the volume ranges from 4GB to 16TB.***

You specify not just the size of the volume but the desired IOPS. ***The lower maximum is 30 times the number of GB of the volume, or 20,000 IOPS. The highest maximum is 50 times the GB count of the volume.*** The volume delivers within 10% of the IOPS performance 99.9% of the time.

You can stripe multiple volumes together to create RAID 0. The resulting size of the RAID 0 array is the sum of the storage capacity of the volumes within it, and the expected IOPS is the sum of the available bandwidth of the volumes within it.

Provisioned IOPS SSD volumes are suited where the workload:

- Requires sustain high-volume I/O;
- Processes large database volumes.

EBS-Optimized EC2 Instance

When I/O is critical to the workload, you are advised to select ***an EC2 instance type that has been optimized for I/O.*** An I/O optimized instance ***uses a different OS stack, with additional and dedicated capacity for I/O. These optimizations ensure the best I/O performance and minimizes I/O contention*** issues. You will pay an additional hourly charge for an I/O optimized EC2 instance.

EBS Volume Encryption

Without need of your own key management infrastructure, ***you can enable EBS volume encryption, but only when the EBS volume is created.*** Once encrypted, ***encryption cannot be removed*** from the EBS volume.

When an AWS account is created, AWS automatically creates for that account a unique AWS Key Management Service

(KMS) managed customer master key (CMK). Unless the client specifies a customer-managed CMK, that KMS CMK is used when the AWS account creates an encrypted EBS volume. The CMK associated with an encrypted volume (or snapshot) cannot be changed.

With the CMK, the EBS encrypts the volume using a data key (based on the AES-256 algorithm). That encrypted data key is stored on the disk along with the encrypted data. All snapshots made for the volume share that same data key, as do any volumes subsequently created from those snapshots.

Encryption is supported by all types of EBS volumes. However, ***not all EC2 instance types support encrypted EBS volumes***, but these do:

- General purpose: A1, M3, M4, M5, M5a, M5ad, M5d, T2, and T3
- Compute optimized: C3, C4, C5, C5d, and C5n
- Memory optimized: cr1.8xlarge, R3, R4, R5, R5a, R5ad, R5d, X1, X1e, and z1d
- Storage optimized: D2, h1.2xlarge, h1.4xlarge, I2, and I3
- Accelerated computing: F1, G2, G3, P2, and P3
- Bare metal: i3.metal, m5.metal, m5d.metal, r5.metal, r5d.metal, u-6tb1.metal, u-9tb1.metal, u-12tb1.metal, and z1d.metal

Encryption operations run on the physical servers that host the EC2 instance to which the encrypted EBS volume is attached. ***Encrypted EBS volumes are accessed in the same way as unencrypted volumes.*** Encryption is handled transparently for the client and no additional actions are needed by the client or by their application. You can expect the data transfer rates on an encrypted EBS volume to be the same/slight-latency as a similar unencrypted volume.

When an encrypted EBS volume is attached to an EC2 instance the following types of data are encrypted:

- Data at rest inside the EBS volume;
- All data moving between the EBS volume and the

EC2 instance;

- All snapshots created from the EBS volume (encryption cannot be removed from an encrypted snapshot);
- All EBS volumes created from those encrypted snapshots (you can assign a new CMK to the created volume).

You can move encrypted data to an unencrypted EBS volume, and the decryption is handled transparently by the EC2 instance.

An EBS volume attached to a Linux EC2 instance can use operating system tools to encrypt the file system on the EBS volume. If after the EBS volume is created, ***an encrypted file system can be overlaid on the EBS volume.***

Durable EBS Snapshot

For every type of EBS volume storage you use, ***you are able to make an incremental point-in-time snapshot. Only the blocks which have changed (since the last snapshot event) are recorded in the snapshot image.*** A snapshot can be created using the AWS Management console, its API and the CLI.

Best practice – to routinely protect data, on a scheduled basis, on the EC2 instance to which the EBS volume is attached, create a cronjob that uses the AWS CLI to take a snapshot of the volume.

AWS stores EBS snapshot images within AWS-controlled S3 storage and not within the buyer's S3 storage. ***A snapshot can be used to create new volumes but only in the same Region in which the snapshot was created***. You cannot manipulate a snapshot image as you do an object in an S3 bucket.

When you create a snapshot, asynchronously the point-in-time image is created immediately but the data changes are loaded into it lazily. If you access a snapshot before it is fully loaded, it will become fully loaded upon request.

The first snapshot you create is the baseline image for new volumes or for data backup. After that initial snapshot, ***peri-***

odic snapshots are incremental, and ***only capture the blocks that changed since the prior snapshot event***. The snapshot feature has a delete sub-process which ensures that ***you only need the most recent snapshot to restore the entire volume.***

You can take a snapshot of a volume while it is in use. The in-progress snapshot is unaffected by ongoing reads and writes to the volume. The snapshot only captures changes written to the blocks. Data that has been cached by an application or by the operating system might be excluded if the EBS volume is in use when the snapshot is taken.

Best practice – fully initialize a volume created from a snapshot by accessing all of the blocks in that volume image.

EBS Snapshot and RAID 0

RAID arrays introduce data interdependencies and a level of complexity not present in single EBS volume configurations, interdependencies and complexities that the snapshot process is unable to handle. Therefore, it is critically important to ensure that no data I/O is happening with a RAID configuration when a snapshot is in-progress. All writes to the RAID array must stop, and all RAID caches flushed to disk. Writes can be stopped by unmounting the RAID array, by freezing the file system, by shutting down the EC2 instance on which the application runs. Wait until all I/O has fully stopped before taking the snapshot of the RAID 0 array.

EBS Snapshot Encryption

The typical workload requires that the data it inputs and outputs, are encrypted. AWS offers encrypted EBS volumes. When the encrypted EBS volume is launched, AWS uses the Key Management Service (KMS) to handle keys.

Unless the buyer uses a key which they have created separately, AWS KMS creates a new key. That key, as well as your data, are encrypted using the industry standard AES-256 algorithm. ***The encryption is native; encryption occurs on the physical computer that the EC2 instance runs on.***

The data is encrypted on the storage media as well as between the host computer and the volume.

Encrypted data has the same IOPS rates as un-encrypted data. ***Snapshots taken from encrypted volumes are automatically encrypted. A new volume restored from an encrypted snapshot is automatically encrypted.***

If an AWS KMS encrypted EBS snapshot needs to be shared across AWS accounts a customer managed CMK has to be used, and the other accounts need access to that CMK used to encrypt the snapshot. Use a custom CMK, not the AWS account's default CMK, to encrypt the EBS volume. Grant access to the custom CMK to the other accounts. Next take the snapshot, and then give the other accounts access to the snapshot.

Moving EBS Volume Across AZs

Resources in one Region are not automatically replicated to other Regions. When data is stored in one Region it is not replicated outside that Region. AWS never moves customer resources or data out of the Region the customer placed them in. It is the responsibility of the AWS customer to replicate data across Regions, based on the customers' business requirements.

An EBS volume available in one AZ is not available in any other AZ. ***To make an EBS volume available in another AZ it has to be moved into that other AZ.*** To move an EBS volume to another AZ, first create a snapshot from that EBS volume. Next, use that snapshot to create a new EBS volume and when doing so specify the new desired AZ.

EBS Volume Check

Basic monitoring of the EBS volume happens automatically every 5 minutes, at no charge.

AWS automatically performs checks on the status of each EBS volume. The volume status checks help us understand, track and manage potential inconsistencies in the blocks of data written onto the volume. The status will reveal if the volume is impaired/corrupted and helps us to respond to a potentially inconsistent volume.

If all checks have passed the status is 'OK.' If the status is 'insufficient-data' then the check is still in-progress. Any other status value indicates the volume is impaired.

EBS Snapshot Best Practices

When storage blocks are restored from snapshots, the volumes must be initialized (read from S3 and written to the volume) before the data can be accessed. This write takes time and is the cause of a significant increase in the latency of I/O operations the first time each block is accessed.

Best practice – to ensure that the snapshot initialized EBS delivers expected levels of IOPS performance, read all of the blocks in the volume before using it in production.

When you need to increase the size of the EBS volume:

1. Take a snapshot of the existing volume
2. Create a new EBS volume of the needed size
3. Replace the current EBS volume with the new volume
4. Restore the snapshot onto the new volume.

When an instance fails and there is data on the boot drive, it is easy to detach an EBS volume from it and then to attach that volume to a new instance which will access the volume.

Unless, the DeleteOnTermination flag on the instance has been set to false, all EBS volumes are to be detached before the instance is terminated.

Best practice – for high durability, keep EBS volume snapshots in a S3 bucket.

AWS STORAGE

It is difficult to imagine a cloud solution that does not involve information storage, of some type or fashion. From the simplest hybrid design pattern that archives stale data in Glacier, to an Auto Scaling Group using Elastic File Service (EFS), or an upload of massive volumes of information into the AWS infrastructure, information storage is fundamental to, is a foundation of, cloud solutions.

Given its REST API, Information storage in the cloud can be radically different from information storage on-premise. Information storage on-premise typically uses JDBC and ODBC interfaces to some flavor of relational database engine, or as often data processing involves the API of a distributed/local file system. In these traditional information storage systems we have defined hierarchical and relational data structures, to which most (stateful) applications hard-wire themselves.

So, when thinking in terms of cloud storage, if you are familiar with on-premise information storage systems using SQL, set that understanding aside, and think of information management as a web service that supports GETs and PUTs of a stream of bytes into a bucket. Try to keep a vision of cloud storage processing that is simple, where it is understood how to secure that storage as well as the objects placed therein. That vision is the focus of this chapter.

Of critical importance to appreciate, because the cloud storage has a REST API, a storage bucket is (also) a web site.

And, in AWS a web site is an origin of content for CloudFront (the AWS Content Delivery Network (CDN) service). AWS storage appears simple but there is immense potential in that simplicity.

AWS Storage Services

AWS Storage consists of the following services:

- AWS Storage Gateway
- Elastic File System (EFS)
- Amazon Simple Storage Service (S3),
- Amazon Glacier
- AWS Snowball
- AWS Snowball Edge
- AWS Snowmobile
- AWS Import/Export Disk

AWS Storage Gateway

AWS Storage Gateway is a data storage software appliance used to connect an on-premise software appliance with AWS cloud storage. Provides low latency to the entire data sets, and the ***caching of frequently accessed data on-premise,*** while ***encrypting and asynchronous storing all data in Amazon S3 or Amazon Glacier.***

The Storage Gateway software appliance is a virtual machine (VM) that you download, install and operate on an on-premise host computer. The storage is exposed as an iSCSI device that can be mounted by the on-premise software application.

The Storage Gateway VM is registered with your AWS Account (using the Management Console). Can be integrated with CloudWatch, CloudTrail and IAM.

Types of Storage Gateway Interfaces

The Storage Gateway supports industry standard storage protocols and 3 types of industry standard storage interfaces:

1. ***File gateway***
2. ***Volume gateway, of which there are 2 sub-types (stored and cached)***

3. ***Virtual Tape Library gateway***

File Gateway

The File gateway presents an on-premise application with a ***Network Files System (NFS) mount point***. The File gateway ***supports storing and retrieving objects in S3, using the NFS industry standard file protocols***. Provides low-latency access to data through ***transparent local caching***.

Data files are stored ***as objects in S3 buckets and accessed through a Network Files System (NFS) mount point.*** The user metadata of the object (ownership, permissions and timestamps) are stored in S3.

The data files, as objects, can be managed as such and bucket policies (versioning, lifecycle management and cross-region replication) apply directly to objects stored in a bucket.

Volume Gateways

The Volume gateway presents you on-premise application with disk volumes using the iSCSI block protocol. For each volume, you create its EBS volume. You take point-in-time snapshots of the volume.

When the snapshot, it is incremental (only the new/changed data is captured and stored). You can initiate a snapshot on a scheduled basis. The data is backed up in the form of an Amazon EBS snapshot.

The volume and the snapshot are transferred to S3 over encrypted SSL connections. The data is encrypted at rest in S3 using SSE.

This data cannot be accessed using the S3 Console or the S3 API, is accessed through the AWS Storage Gateway service.

A Volume gateway can be operated in 2 modes:

1. ***Cached***
2. ***Stored***

Cached Volume Gateway

With Cached Volume gateways, you store data kept in an on-premise cache called a volume, which is asynchronously backed

up to Amazon S3. Provides low-latency access to cached data.

Each volume is limited in size to 32TB and attach the volume as iSCSI devices to the on-premise application servers. 1 Cached Volume gateway can support up to 32 volumes, for a total of 1 PB storage.

Stored Volume Gateway

With Stored Volume gateways, you ***store data kept in an on-premise storage*** called a volume, which is ***asynchronously backed up to Amazon S3. Provides low-latency access to the entire data set.*** Provides off-site backups, thereby taking advantage of S3 durability.

Each volume is limited in size to 16TB. 1 Gateway Stored Volume can support up to 32 volumes, for a total of 512TB storage.

Virtual Tape Libraries (VTL) Gateway

A Virtual Tape Libraries (VTL) gateway presents you on-premise back-up application with an industry-standard iSCSI-based virtual tape library (VTL), containing a virtual media changer and virtual tape drives. ***You store data on virtual tape cartridges, which is stored in the AWS cloud.***

Each virtual tape is stored in S3. A blank tape is created using the Management Console or the CLI. A VTL can contain up to 1,500 tapes (1 PB) of total tape data. A VTL appears to your on-premise tape service as if it were a physical tape library.

A Gateway VTL is archived on a Virtual Tape Shelf (VTS) and stored in Amazon Glacier.

There is 1 VTS per Region and multiple Gateway VTLs in the Region share the VTS.

Amazon Elastic File System (EFS)

EFS works with NFS protocol, is provisioned to a VPC and is attached to an EC2 instance. The ***EFS can store data and metadata across multiple AZs in a region***, can drive high levels of throughput, ***can grow to petabyte scale, and allow massively***

parallel access to data from EC2 instances. To an EC2 instance, the EFS appears like any other file system to the EC2 instance's operating system (OS).

You pay for the storage space used. There is no minimum fee or minimum commitment.

The EFS is a shared file system, so it can be mounted across multiple EC2 instances and ***can support 1,000s of concurrent NFS connections.***

Attributes of the EFS:

- ***Fully managed*** – you do not manage any hardware or software.
- ***Elastic and scalable*** – elastically scales up to PBs and shrinks down, automatically.
- ***Highly available and durable*** – EFS is automatically replicated across AZs within a Region.
- ***File system interface*** – compatible with standard OS APIs.
- ***File system access semantics*** – a hierarchical directory structure, locking, read-after-write consistency, etc. Shared storage – all EC2 instances have concurrent access to the same data set. Performance – consistent high IOPS.

Making EFS Available in a VPC

The primary resource in EFS is the file system, where you create directories and store files. You can create up to 10 file systems per AWS Account.

To access an EFS file system, you create an NFS v4 endpoint, which functions as a mount target, in the VPC where the EC2 instances are launched. An EFS file system mount target has an IP address and a DNS name. For each EFS file system, create a mount point in each AZ used by the VPC.

EFS integrates with Amazon CloudWatch. I/O metrics can be collected and analyzed for best performance. Using a Direct Connect and VPC, the EFS can be mounted on an on-premise server via the NFS 4.1 protocol.

Administering EFS

EFS can be administered using the:

1. Management Console;
2. AWS CLI;
3. AWS SDK;
4. EFS API.

Amazon Simple Storage Service (Amazon S3)

Amazon S3 is highly scalable and durable object storage, that has a native REST API. S3 was ***designed for high availability and fault tolerance.***

The S3 service is Region specific. The AWS ***client chooses the Region in which they use S3.*** Which Region chosen can depend on the location of the end users of S3, can depend on the location of the EC2 instances and AWS services that read/write data to S3. Often, the cost of transferring data between S3 and EC2 instances or with other AWS services is reduce when all component are located in the same Region.

The Amazon ***S3 data model is a flat structure, devoid of a physical hierarchy: you create a bucket and store digital objects in the bucket.***

S3 does not have a file system. All objects are stored in a flat namespace, organized by buckets. In S3 there are no subfolders or sub-buckets. You cannot place a bucket inside another bucket. The useful illusion of a logical hierarchy is created using key name prefixes and delimiters.

You can store nearly any type of digital object:

- Source code files
- JSON files
- HTML files
- Image files
- Encrypted files, etc.

S3 provides access to that data over the Internet. All and all, integrating S3 storage with a web-based solution is a straightforward matter.

There is no physical limit to the amount of data you can store in S3, because there is no size limit at the bucket level.

S3 automatically performs backups in at least 3 different AWS Data Centers of the Region chosen, and so S3 has extremely high durability. Durability of S3 has been measured at over 99.99% (out to 11 digits). If you store 10,000 objects in S3, then over a 10-million-year period, the average loss is 1 object.

S3 features:

Simple – easy to use web page UI, with which you can upload, download and manage objects;

Scalable – Petabytes of objects can be stored and accessed quickly;

Durable – 1 object in 10,000,000 destroyed over 10,000 years;

Secured – object encryption and AWS Identity and Access Management (IAM) are supported. Information is transferred over SSL;

High Performance – supports multipart object uploads; you can choose which Region to locate your objects to minimize access latency;

Available – annually, 99.99% of the objects are available;

Low Cost – you only pay for what you need, with a volume discount;

Easy to manage – uses a task-based approach to object management;

Easy integration – easily integrates with other AWS services.

S3 Use Cases

S3 is optimized for READS. If the use case need optimized reads, then be certain to determine if S3 is or is not a good fit for the BPM.

To be in the cloud, is to operate instances of virtual machines and storage deployed in a virtual network. As such, the ***use of Amazon S3 storage for a fee*** underlies nearly all cloud workloads, nearly all cloud use cases:

- Backup – used for storing backup images. Three copies of the backup image file are distributed across multiple Availability Zones within a Region. Versioning is also supported;
- Tape replacement;
- Static web site hosting;
- Mobile and Internet-based application hosting;
- Disaster Recovery – using Cross-Region replication;
- Content Distribution over the Internet;
- Data Lake – a central place to store massive amounts of information for processing and analysis;
- Private software repository.

Block and File Storage vs S3 Object Storage

Block storage:

- Operates at the level of the raw storage device;
- Manages data files as a set of numbered and fixed-size blocks;
- Storage Area Network (SAN) is block storage accessed over the network, using protocols such as iSCSI or Fibre Channel.

File storage:

- Operates at the operating system level, above the block storage level;
- Manages files as a named hierarchy of folders/directories;

Network Attached Storage (NAS)is file storage accessed over the network, using protocols such as Common Internet File System (CIFS) or Network File System (NFS).

S3 Buckets

Buckets form the top-level namespace for S3. Each bucket is created in a specific AWS Region, that you choose. ***There is no***

size limit enforced by AWS at the bucket level.

By default, ***you can have up to 100 buckets per AWS account. Each bucket can hold an unlimited number of objects.***

By default, all S3 buckets are private and AWS credentials are required to access the bucket. In this context, private means that only the bucket owner can access their bucket. Access to an S3 bucket is controlled by the AWS account that owns that bucket.

And, ***S3 content is automatically replicated*** on multiple storage devices, ***in multiple facilities within a Region.*** Consequently, ***S3 can sustain concurrent loss of data in 2 AWS data centers.***

AWS automatically ***partitions buckets*** to support very high request rates and concurrent access. ***There is no difference in performance whether you stored all object in 1 bucket, or if you organize the object across multiple buckets.*** The bucket namespaces have to convey the meaning of the whole as well as all of its parts (so, do not create fewer, or more, buckets than needed to achieve that gestalt for the use case).

Bucket Name

Bucket names can contain at least 3 and no more than 63 lowercase letters, numbers, hyphens. The name must start with either a lowercase letter or number.

Best practice – a bucket name must not be formatted like an IP address.

Bucket names are global. Bucket names ***must be unique across all AWS accounts***, not just within your AWS account.

A bucket name is a series of 1:N labels, where each adjacent label is separated by a single period (.).

Best practice – use names that contain your domain name and which conform to the rules for DNS names.

When using virtual-style buckets with SSL, the SSL wild card certificate will only match bucket names that do not contain periods. To work around this problem, use HTTP or write your own certificate verification logic.

Best practice – refrain from using periods in the bucket name.

Bucket Operations

What types of bucket activities does S3 support? You can:

- Create and delete a bucket.
- List the names of the objects (the keys) contained in a bucket.
- Secure access to a bucket and its objects.

By default, when you create a bucket, only your AWS account has access to it and all of the files in it are private. By default, only the AWS account that created the bucket has permission to read or write the files in it.

S3 Bucket ACLs

By default, when you create a bucket, only your AWS account has access to it and all of the files in it are private. By default, only the AWS account that created the bucket has permission to read or write the files in it.

You grant controlled bucket access to others, by:

1. ***Bucket Access Control List (ACL)***
2. ***Course-grained permissions at the bucket or object level;***
3. READ, WRITE, or FULL-CONTROL;

ACLs are legacy.

The only way to grant write permission is to an S3 Log Delivery Group.

S3 Bucket Policies

A bucket policy is associated with a bucket;

Supports finer-grained permissions very similar to IAM policies;

You can specify who can access the bucket, from where (by CIDR block or IP address) and during what time of day;

Allows you to assign cross-account access to S3 buckets and objects by other AWS accounts;

Can explicitly reference an IAM principal policy;

Is ***the recommended access control mechanism***.

S3 Bucket IAM Policy

IAM policies:

1. *Are associated with an AIM principal;*
2. ***Grants access to an S3 bucket***;
3. Grant access to a bucket by other AWS services and resources.

S3 Server Access Logging

By default, S3 bucket logging is turned off. ***To track all requests to a given S3 bucket***, you ***enable server access logs*** on that bucket. ***Server access logs are very useful in security and access audits of S3 buckets.*** However, ***the owner of the bucket can at any time delete the server access log files.***

S3 server access logs include such data as:

1. Requestor AWS account and IP address;
2. Bucket name;
3. Request time;
4. Request action (GET, PUT, LIST, etc.);
5. Response status or error code.

The AWS account can choose to store the server access logs of a bucket in their bucket or in another bucket that they own (in the same Region as the source S3 bucket). If you want ***Amazon S3 to automatically deliver server access logs to a bucket***, then ***write permission*** on the target ***bucket must be granted to*** the ***Log Delivery Group by using a Bucket ACL.***

Best practice – ***when the server access logs are stored in their source bucket, there are logs about those logs which result in increased bucket volumes and consequently in increased bucket charges.*** Therefore, minimize bucket costs by storing the server access logs in a bucket other than their source bucket.

To learn about the end user access patterns and discover precisely where you are spending your S3 dollars, you need to examine the server access logs. ***AWS does not charge a fee when server access logging is enabled on an S3 bucket***. AWS does not charge a fee to generate and deliver the log files. No data transfer charges are accrued for log file delivery. However:

- ***the server access log files delivered to the bucket owner do accrue the usual S3 storage fees, and***
- ***access to the delivered log files accrues the usual data transfer charges.***

S3 Objects

An object is a digital entity stored within an S3 bucket. S3 treats an object as ***a simple stream of bytes***. An ***object size can range from 0 bytes to 5 TB***.

Objects are redundantly stored on multiple devices across multiple AZs in a single S3 Region (in which its home S3 bucket is located).

An object can store data in a large variety of formats. ***The total number of objects (and volume of data) you can store in an S3 bucket is unlimited.***

By default, all objects are private and AWS credentials are required to access the object. In this context, private means that only the object owner can access their object. ***Access to an object stored in a bucket is controlled by the AWS account that owns that object.***

Each object is identified by a unique user-specified file name, which is also known as the object key. The object key must be unique within the bucket it is stored within. An object key can contain up to 1024 bytes of Unicode UTF-8 characters. A key can contain characters like slashes and backslashes to help logically organize objects.

The combination of bucket name, object key, and optional object version ID provides a globally uniquely identify for each S3 object.

Object Metadata

Object metadata is a set of key/value pairs that describe the object.

There are 2 types of object metadata:

1. ***System metadata*** – is created by AWS and used by S3. Includes facts like object size, MD5 digest, HTTP Content-type, etc.
2. ***User metadata*** – these are custom tags you associate with your data.

Object Operations

By default, only the AWS account that created the bucket has permission to read or write the files in it.

Unlike a file, ***you operate on the object*** (in the bucket) ***as a whole.***

You GET an object from a bucket.

You PUT an object into a bucket.

You can DELETE an object from a bucket.

When an object is successfully stored in the bucket, the operation returns the HTTP 200 result code and the MD5 checksum.

Amazon recommends using HTTPS to ensure that your S3 requests and replies are secure.

You use standard HTTP verbs to create and delete buckets, to list object keys, as well as read and write objects:

- Create in HTTP is PUT.
- Read in HTTP is GET.
- Delete in HTTP is DELETE.
- Update in HTTP is POST (or in some cases PUT).

It is unlikely that you will have a need to use the native REST API directly. Most often the REST API will be manipulated indirectly, by using the AWS Management Console, the AWS CLI or AWS SDK.

The better ensure data durability, the ***PUT requests synchronously store the object across multiple AZs before returning SUCCESS.***

Multi-Part Upload

Break a file larger than 100 Mbytes into smaller chunks and use the Multipart Upload API. The maximum object size allowed for multi-part upload is 5 TB.

The chunks are transferred in parallel, the upload can be paused and resumed if need be. When all of the chunks are completed being uploaded, S3 re-assembles them into a single object.

Multi-part upload can also be used to make a copy of an existing S3 object.

Multi-Object Delete

The multi-object delete is used to delete a large number of objects from S3 in a single process.

Object ACLs

By default, the object is private and AWS credentials are required to access the object. The digital identity (which is usually an AWS account) that writes an object into a bucket is the owner of that object. The owner of the object retains control over individual object access privileges granted to other digital identities.

Multiple Object Owners Sharing One Bucket

As determined by the bucket policy, more than one digital identity (which is usually an AWS account) can be granted permission writes an object into a bucket. Therefore, when access privileges to objects in a bucket need to be managed, it is the object owner that must manage those access privileges.

Consequently, the owner of the bucket can be in a position where the owner of the bucket does not control access privileges to all of the objects located in the bucket that they own. For example, if the owner of the bucket wants to limit read access privileges to objects in a bucket that they own the bucket owner is only able to limit read access to just those individual objects that the bucket owner also owns. All objects the bucket owner does not own are not affected by the bucket owner's object security settings.

Versioning Objects

S3 allows you to keep multiple versions of a given object. ***Versioning is turned on at the bucket level. Versioning of an object allows you to preserve, retrieve and restore every version of an object.***

Once enabled, versioning cannot be turned off, it can only be suspended. When versioning is enabled on a bucket, the DELETE command no longer permanently deletes an object. All versions of the object remain within the versioned bucket, and S3 assigns a logical DELETE marker to the object version. That marker functions as the object's version ID. A GET request (for an object in a versioned bucket) that does not include the object's version ID returns a '404 Not Found' error: S3 acts-as-if the object were deleted even though it has not in fact been deleted. You restore a version of an object by referencing the version ID of the object, the bucket name and the object key/filename.

Object Keys and S3 Bucket Partitions

The name of the S3 bucket is a namespace. To keep track of the objects ***S3 maintains a key map of each object key in a given bucket***, i.e., in a given namespace. Using the namespace as a prefix, a key value pair containing 'bucket name/object key' is created transparently to the AWS client.

In addition, each namespace, i.e., ***each bucket, contains multiple partitions***. Reads and writes of objects can and does occur in parallel when the bucket has multiple partitions. ***An object is stored within a partition*** of an S3 bucket.

The object key is used to partition the bucket. Therefore, ***the object key defines the S3 bucket partition that that individual object is stored within.*** The object key dictates which partition it is stored within and subsequently retrieved from. Therefore, while AWS maintains a map of buckets and their objects, it is ***the AWS client who defines that key map.***

So as not to impair performance, AWS recommends the following best practices:

- Recognize the critical impact of both bucket name and object name on performance;
- To spread the transaction load across multiple buckets, use a hex hash code as the prefix of the bucket name;
- Reference the bucket using this convention: <bucketname>.s3.amazonaws.com
- Avoid object key names that result in a bucket that has only 1 partition.
- Refrain from using globally unique identifiers (GUID), timestamps, and running counters since they are not good candidates for object key names (because they use repeating prefixes). Alternately, the object key prefix can use a reversed timestamp, a reversed epoch time, or a reversed counter. Reversing their order is a simple way of pseudo-randomizing their values;

Take advantage of the fact that the ***object key prefix,*** i.e., ***the first 3-4 characters of the object key***, are most significant. In fact, ***the S3 bucket is partitioned by the object key prefix.*** Therefore, ***to maximize performance randomize the object key prefix*** (by using a hex hash as the prefix) so that transactions are spread across the bucket partitions;

There are no limits to the number of object key prefixes in a given bucket. This makes exponential growth in read and write performance possible. Typically, a well object key prefix can support 3,500 PUT, POST, or DELETE requests and 5,500 GET requests per second, per prefix. Conceivably, by introducing 10 object key prefixes the reads will occur in parallel and read performance could then scale to 55,000 requests per second.

Even though S3 is optimized for READs, it is still possible, given a large number of objects in a bucket that is not partitioned, for a poor quality object key name to result in GET requests that degrade S3 read limits and raise exceptions (which must be handled programmatically as errors).

Lastly, when a hex hash code is used as the object key prefix, these values can be stored in a DynamoDB secondary index functions as a legend which specifies the location to all objects.

S3 Secure Socket Layer (SSL) API Endpoints

An S3 bucket can be accessed over HTTP or HTTPS. To secure data in motion, S3 supports the HTTPS protocol. To create an S3 SSL endpoint, create a S3 bucket policies that requires requests to use Secure Socket Layer (SSL).

S3 as REST API Endpoint

In S3, data is managed as objects that contain both data and metadata. ***By default, both S3 object storage as well as the objects stored within it are manipulated through a REST API*** using standard HTTP verbs, invoked from the AWS CLI or an AWS SDK. Consequently, given its REST API, an S3 bucket can also be configured as a website endpoint and therefore become optimized for a web browser.

As stated by AWS, here are the key features of an S3 bucket that has been configured as a REST API Endpoint:

- Access control – ***supports both public and private content***;
- Error message handling – returns an XML-formatted error response;
- Redirection support – not applicable;
- Requests supported – ***supports all bucket and object operations***;
- Responses to GET and HEAD requests at the root of a bucket – returns a list of the object keys in the bucket;
- Secure Sockets Layer (SSL) support – ***supports SSL connections***.

By default, all S3 buckets are private, and all objects are private as well. Access to the S3 bucket through its REST API is controlled by the owner of that bucket. Access to the REST API of an object stored in a bucker is controlled by the owner of that object.

S3 Pre-Signed URLs

By default, all S3 buckets are private, and all objects are private as well. However, ***temporary access to a bucket, or to an object in a bucket, can be granted by their owner to other AWS accounts as well as by authorized federated identities, for a specified window in time***.

The pre-signed URL supports the use case where:

An S3 bucket owner needs to grant temporary permission to another identity (that may or may not have an AWS account) to upload a specific object into that bucket.

An S3 bucket owner needs to grant temporary permissions to download an object (that they own) to another identity (that may or may not have an AWS account).

S3 as Website Endpoints

Given the S3's REST API, an S3 bucket can be configured as a public website endpoint. Since the S3 service is Region specific, the website endpoint is therefore Region specific. Unlike the REST API, the S3 Website Endpoints are optimized for use by web browsers.

When configured as a website endpoint, S3 is frequently used to store static URL content, e.g., HTML files, Cascading Style Sheets (CSS), image files, and multimedia content.

As stated by AWS, here are the key features of an S3 bucket that has been configured as a Website Endpoint:

- Access control – ***supports only publicly readable content;***
- Error message handling – returns an HTML document;
- Redirection support – supports both object-level and bucket-level redirects;
- Requests supported – supports only GET and HEAD

requests on objects;
- Responses to GET and HEAD requests at the root of a bucket – returns the index document that is specified in the website configuration;
- Secure Sockets Layer (SSL) support – ***does not support SSL connections***. Does not support HTTPS.

By default, all S3 buckets are private, and all objects are private as well. Access to the S3 bucket through its website endpoint is controlled by the owner of that bucket. Access through the website endpoint to an object stored in a bucker is controlled by the owner of that object. Access to the bucket is provided by a bucket policy, and access to an object is provided any an object ACL.

Best practice – do not return a 403 or 404 error message to a host interface. It is best not to disclose such material facts to a host interface. Instead, best practice is to keep the host interface in the dark regarding such material facts, and instead remit meaningless ambiguous information to the host interface. Hackers can use those error codes to break into the website.

Best practice - when an S3 bucket supports a web site endpoint, use Route 53 as its DNS server. Be certain to add an alias record to your (Route 53) DNS server that points to the S3 endpoint.

S3 Object URLs

An object stored in an S3 bucket can be addressed by a unique Uniform Resource Locator (URL). Objects stored within an S3 bucket are equally accessible from all AWS Regions.

The object URL is formed using the:

1. Web service endpoint, which for S3 is s3.amazonaws.com
2. The bucket name and
3. The object key (or filename).

For example: https://mybucketname.s3.amazonaws.com/

myfilename

Multi-Factor Authentication (MFA) Delete

In addition to versioning, MFA Delete requires additional authentication in order to permanently delete an object version, or to change the versioning state of the bucket.

MFA Delete requires a temporary, on-time, password authentication code, which is generated by a hardware, or virtual, Multi-Factor Authentication (MFA) device.

MFA can only be enabled by the AWS root account.

Transfer Acceleration

Transfer Acceleration is the ability, provided by AWS, to enable fast, easy and secure transfer of files over long distances between the AWS client and their S3 bucket. Transfer Acceleration is useful when gigabytes to terabytes of data need to be transferred over the Internet into an S3 bucket. When using Transfer Acceleration additional data transfer fees may apply.

Bucket Event Notification

Event notifications can be sent in response to actions taken on objects. They allow you to run workflows, send alerts, or perform actions in response to changes of objects. ***In S3, you set up triggers to perform these actions.***

Event notification is set up at the bucket level. They are set up using the AWS Management Console, or its REST API and the AWS SDK.

Notifications can be set up for when:

- A new object is created (by POST, PUT, COPY, or multi-part upload);
- When an object is removed (by DELETE);
- When S3 detects that a Reduced Redundancy Storage (RRS) object is lost.
- Notifications ***can be based on the object key*** as well.

Notification are sent using the Amazon Simple Notification Service (SNS) or delivered directly to AWS Lambda to invoke Lambda functions.

S3 Data Consistency Model

Objects in buckets are replicated across multiple servers and locations, within a Region. Therefore, changes to objects take time to propagate to all locations.

If a new object is PUT, then S3 provides read-after-write consistency.

If an existing object is PUT, or if an object DELETEs, then S3 provides eventual consistency. For eventual consistency reads, you will get the old object or the new object but never an inconsistent mix.

Updates on a single key are atomic.

Cross-Region Replication

S3 allows you to choose to ***asynchronously replicate all new objects in a given source bucket, in 1 Region, to a target bucket in another Region***. Existing objects will not be replicated and must be copied using separate commands. The object metadata and ACLs associated with it, are replicated as well.

Cross-replication must be enabled on both the source and target buckets and each bucket must have versioning enabled on it. Object from 1 bucket can be replicated to only 1 different bucket. And, you must create an IAM policy to grant S3 permission to replicate objects.

Cross-replication is often used to:

1. Reduce READ latency by moving the objects closer to their end users and
2. Store backups at a safe distance from the originals.

If both the source and the destination buckets are not owned by the same AWS account, the source bucket owner must be granted permissions to replicate objects to the destination bucket.

Bucket and Object Encryption

Amazon ***S3 does not support bucket level encryption***. However, ***S3 does support both object level, as well as data in motion, encryption. For any object you can enable S3 server-side encryp-***

tion.

Best practice – encrypt all data at rest and while in motion.

There are several options for encrypting objects at rest in S3:

1. ***Server-Side Encryption*** (SSE) – encrypts and decrypts individual objects, by S3 and
2. ***AWS Key Management Service*** (KMS), using 256-bit Advanced Encryption Standard (AES).

You can also encrypt your objects before writing them into S3, using Client-Side encryption.

To encrypt data while in motion, you can use Amazon S3 Secure Socket Layer (SSL) API endpoints.

Client-Side Object Encryption

You retain end-to-end control of the encryption process, including management of the encryption keys.

You have 2 options for using encryption keys:

- Use an AWS KMS-managed customer master key, or
- Use a client-side master key.

3 Ways AWS Encrypts/Decrypts Objects at Rest

There are 3 ways by which AWS encrypts/decrypts object:

SSE-S3 (AWS Managed Keys)

- Every object is encrypted with a unique key and then the actual object is then further encrypted using a separate master key;
- A new master key is issued at least monthly, with AWS rotating these keys;
- Encrypted data, encryption keys and master keys are all stored separately on secure hosts.

SSE-KMS (AWS KMS Keys)

- AWS handles your key management and protection for S3 but where you manage the keys;
- There are separate permissions for using the master key, which provides protection against unauthorized access of objects;

- Provides auditing, where you can see who used the key to access the object and when;
- You can view all failed access attempts by un-authorized parties.

SSE-C (Customer-Provided Keys)

- You maintain your own encryption keys but don't manage or implement Client-Side encryption
- AWS does the encryption/decryption of the objects, while you maintain full control of the keys used to encrypt/decrypt the objects.

Best practice – for simplicity and ease –of-use, it is advisable to use Server-Side Encryption with AWS SSE-S3 or SSE-KMS.

Best practice – ***to comply with HIPPA laws***, encrypt the data locally using your own encryption keys, enable SSE on the S3 bucket to make use of AES-256 encryption, and then copy the data to S3 over HTTPS endpoints.

S3 and IPv6

The same S3 operations are available over IPv6, and they work the same way as with IPv4. When using the S3 REST API the dual-stack endpoint is directly accessed. The dual-stack endpoint can also be accessed directly by using the AWS CLI and the AWS SDK.

However, not all S3 features are supported over IPv6:

- Static website hosting from an S3 bucket;
- BitTorrent;

Lastly, when IAM users or S3 bucket policies are used for IP address filtering, these must reflect the IPv6 address range.

Storage Classes & Object Life-Cycle Management

Objects have a life-cycle and this provides you with the opportunity to significantly reduce the cost of owning and managing objects. Objects transition through 4 stages and for each life stage there is a corresponding storage service.

The object life-cycle configuration is a set of 1:N rules that define an action that is S3 applies to a group of objects. There are two types of life-cycle actions:

Transition actions – defines when an object transitions to another storage class;

Expiration actions – defines when the objects expire.

There are four storage classes:

S3 Standard – store objects here, initially. For general purposes. Delivers low 1st-byte latency and high throughput. For frequently accessed objects.

S3 Standard-Infrequent Access (IA) – after 30-days, objects are transitioned here. Delivers low latency and high throughput. For less-frequently accessed objects.

S3 Reduced Redundancy Storage (RRS) – lower durability (99.99%) and lower availability (99.99%). For use with objects which can easily be reproduced, e.g., a thumbnail image. The need to design automation around replacing lost objects may exist in the BPM.

Amazon Glacier – after 90-days, objects are transitioned here.

The S3 Standard, Standard – IA, and Glacier storage, services support lifecycle management for automatic migration of objects and are equally durable (99.999999999%) as well.

The 4th stage addresses objects which are 3-years or older. The value, if any, of a 4th stage object is directly dependent upon the BPM policies, rules and regulations.

Best practice – determine the policies, rules, regulations and laws, which govern object retention and enforce them consistently.

Data Transfer Charges

There is no charge to transfer data from an EC2 instance into S3 if they are both in the same Region.

Amazon S3 Glacier

Amazon Glacier is a low-cost, secure, durable storage service, which is suitable for infrequently accessed content It is usable where retrieval time is measured in several hours.

S3 Glacier is used mainly for:

- data archiving and long-term backup;
- Magnetic tape replacement;
- Healthcare/life-sciences/scientific data storage – to meet patient record compliance requirements; to run analytics over long-duration data sets;
- Media assets archiving/digital preservation;
- Compliance archiving/long-term backup – storage for x-years.

Glacier functions as a write-once archive. You are not able to modify a file in Glacier; it is immutable data.

There is no limit to the number of files you can archive in Glacier.

Jargon – a single file is called an archive.

Each archive is assigned a unique ID, created by Glacier, at the time it is created in Glacier. All archives are ***automatically encrypted and decrypted*** by Glacier.

A single archive can range in size from 1 byte to 40TB. You can archive individual files, but you pay per file/archive you store.

Best practice – aggregate individual files, using TAR or ZIP, and thereby create 1 Glacier archive.

Glacier is designed for 99.99% (11 digits out) durability of objects over a given year.

Glacier Vaults

Jargon - a vault is a container that gives you the ability to logically organize your files. You can create up to 1,000 vaults per account, per Region.

You can set different access policies for each vault. You can use IAM and create vault-level access policies.

To make it easier to manage your vault, you can tag it.

To delete a vault, all of the files it contains must be deleted first.

Glacier Vault Lock

Allows you to deploy and enforce compliance controls on a vault, using a policy. A vault policy specifies controls, such as Write-Once-Read-Many (WORM).

A vault policy can be locked from future edits. Once locked, a vault policy is immutable.

Glacier Inventory & Glacier Jobs

Jargon - Glacier maintains a cold index of archives, called the inventory, which is updated every 24-hours

Whenever you want to retrieve a file from Glacier you must submit a Glacier job. ***The job is asynchronous and runs in the back-ground,*** behind the scenes, to deliver the requested files to you. You can ***configure Amazon SNS to create notifications*** once the job is finished.

For each job, Glacier maintains information about the job type, its creation date, the status of the job, its completion date, etc. As soon as the job completes, the files are available for you to download.

Glacier Access

There are 3 ways to access S3 Glacier:

1. Directly via the Glacier API or SDK;
2. Integrate a S3 life-cycle management policy with Glacier, or
3. Use a 3rd-party tool or gateway.

Uploading Files to Glacier

Uploads of files happen over the Internet. To upload a file:

1. create a vault;
2. create an access policy that controls the actions allowed inside the vault and then you attach that vault policy to the vault;
3. create the TAR or ZIP file that aggregates the files to be archived;
4. upload the archive file into the vault.

To upload the archive file, you can use:

- The SDK and invoke the Multipart Upload feature supported by the API;
- The AWS Direct Connect to upload files into Glacier from your corporate data center.

If you have a vast number of files to archive, you can use Amazon Snowball to ship your files to the AWS infrastructure and then upload them into Glacier.

3 Ways of Retrieving Files from Glacier

Standard

- The low-cost option used for getting files from a vault in just a few hours, between 3-5 hours.

Expedited

- Used for the occasional urgent access need to a small number of archived files;
- Data can be accessed within 1-5 minutes.

Bulk

- Used for retrieving petabytes of data;
- It takes 5-12 hours to retrieve the data.
- Each month, you can retrieve up to 5% of your data, calculated on a daily prorated basis, for free. If you retrieve more than 5% in any given calendar month, then you are charged a fee based on your maximum retrieval rate.

Best practice – place a daily retrieval policy on each vault, using the free daily prorated basis as the high-water mark.

AWS Import/Export Disk

AWS Import/Export Disk, using the Amazon internal high-speed network, supports the direct transfer of data onto and off of storage devices that you own and maintain.

The storage device is shipped from your data center, via standard shipping mechanisms, to the destination Region.

Import/Export Disk ***has an upper limit of 16 TB***. Import/ Export Disk ***can be used to move more data than you can get***

through an Internet connection in a reasonable period of time.

The data can be imported into S3, Glacier and EBS. The data can be exported from S3.

Encryption of data is optional, not mandatory.

Import/Export Disk jobs cannot be managed through the AWS Snowball console.

AWS Snowball

AWS Snowball is a network-attached storage (NAS) device (10Gbps network interface) with its own shipping container. You do not buy or maintain this hardware device.

Snowball ***can be used to export from, as well as import data into, S3. Provides PB-scale data transfer.*** A ***Snowball comes in 2 sizes: 50 TB or 80 TB.***

Each Snowball is protected by AWS KMS. Prior to transfer to the Snowball, all data is encrypted by 256-bit GSM encryption by the client. Encryption is enforced at rest and in transit. Jobs are managed through the Snowball console.

Once attached, you can transfer files from your on-premise file system to the Snowball. Snowball uses Amazon-provided shippable storage appliances shipped through UPS. The E Ink display shipping label shows the address where the Snowball will be shipped. Each Snowball is made physically rugged to secure and protect the storage device while in transit. You drop off the Snowball with UPS, no box required.

AWS Snowball Edge

AWS Snowball Edge is like the Snowball, but it transports up to 100TB of data.

The Snowball Edge hosts a file server and an S3-compatible endpoint that allows you to use the NFS protocol , S3 SDK, or S3 CLI to transfer data directly to the device, without specialized client software.

AWS Snowmobile

AWS Snowmobile is a secure Exa-byte scale data transfer service, driven to your site. With Snowmobile ***you can transfer up***

to 100 PB.

When you order a Snowmobile and it arrives at your site, AWS personnel connect a removeable high-speed network switch from the Snowmobile to your local network. The ***Snowmobile appears as network-attached data store.***

When transfer is completed, the Snowmobile is driven back to AWS where it is uploaded into the chosen AWS service, e.g. S3, Glacier, etc..

AMAZON DATABASE SERVICES

Amazon offers five database services:

1. Amazon Elasticache
2. Amazon DynamoDB;
3. Amazon Relational Database Services (RDS);
4. Amazon Aurora;
5. Amazon Redshift.

Data Form Follows Function

Most often people imagine that data is some independent thing, off by itself somewhere, inside a black box, under lock and key. The data does exist, physically, digitally, but its physical form and distribution must be determined by the functions which will compute that data. It is doubtful that American architect Frank Lloyd Wright expected his core architecture guideline to be applicable to digital data structures and databases as well.

The digital forms which an instance of a data type takes over time are dictated by the commands and queries which compute that data type, in that context in the business process. In terse geek: ***the algorithm dictates the data structure.***

Four Types of Data Machines

Nathan Marz has a four-fold model (he calls the Lambda Architecture) for defining and describing data machines. A global enterprise data architecture has, using Nathan M's schema as a starting point, five types of data machines:

1. Batch (and Graph)
2. Servicing;
3. Transactional;
4. Analytic;

As you'd expect based on their names, these machines function in distinctly different manners. However, what is not immediately apparent is that these machines are interdependent and complement one another. Within the AWS cloud, there are data services that correspond to the data machines listed above.

Command Query Responsibility Segregation (CQRS) Primer

A global information business most often needs a plurality of data forms which support queries. A global information business model needs a minority of data forms which support (transactional) commands.

The forms of data which support queries are not simple object-oriented forms into which an object-oriented language can easily implement a brute force 'put' statement (using dependency injection). Nor are those query forms always relations, or tables (which is the common term).

When a business requirement is documented as a use case, it becomes apparent when the business requires a command, and when the business requires a query. That evident and apparent phenomena is the basis of the CQRS principle (which addresses lots of design patterns).

The technologies which are horizontally scalable, and which operate on commodity hardware, are optimized for queries. For example, DynamoDB has a golden rule: 1 table for

1 query. That golden rule is in direct opposition to the object-oriented principle of polymorphism, in which a data structure can contain a variety of different objects/entities, and each of these types can be computed by a wide variety of functions. Polymorphism is great in Java, but it's worst in queries.

Amazon ElastiCache

ElastiCache is web service that functions as an in-memory cache. It simplifies the scaling, deployment and operation, of the cache.

2 products are currently available:

1. Redis and
2. Memcached.

Be aware that ElastiCache does not connect to or interoperate with your database service.

The ElastiCache only connects to and interoperates with your application services.

Amazon ElastiCache Benefits

Makes it easy to spin up a distributed cluster of in-memory cache.

Provides high performance and scalable caching.

Reduces administration of a distributed cache.

You can choose either Memcached or Redis cache services. ElasticCache supports the two different protocols used by Memcached and Redis.

If you migrate to ElastiCache, you need to change the cache's endpoint reference in your application configuration file.

ElasticCache:

1. Handles installation, patch management and monitoring;
2. Can automatically detect and recover from a cache node failure.

Cache Pattern Use Cases

It is important to keep in mind that in-memory cache has

very limited purpose and function. The function of cache is to hold frequently accessed static data in memory, so that reads of static data from disk are kept to a minimum.

Cache patterns include:

- Requests which return one-time-use data derive no performance benefit from in-memory cache.
- Requests which return many-time-used static data definitely improve read performance by using an in-memory cache service.

It is critically important to recognize that ***in-memory cache is not to be used to hold volatile data.***

ElasticCache has no mechanism to ensure transactional integrity, no mechanism to ensure that any object in cache is automatically kept in sync with its serialized digital representation persisted in storage as that object transitions through its life-cycle states.

The most sophisticated use of ElastiCache is in support of messaging, where the messages are immutable.

A popular use case for Elasticache is for the storage and management of web application session state data.

Application CQRS for In-Memory Cache

To use a distributed in-memory cache service, the application server must be built in conformance with the Command Query Responsibility Segregation (CQRS) enterprise integration pattern.

Every individual object instance must be fully aware of the individual states the controlling algorithm transitions it through, over its entire life-cycle.

Every individual object instance must be fully aware of when it is in a static and immutable state (those are the only states when it is in in-memory cache).

Every individual object instance must be fully aware of which states it transitions into, from which that object instance reads from cache.

Immutable In-Memory Cache

If an object in distributed cache is modified, then:

- Every individual cache object instance must be capable of persisting itself to permanent storage in full compliance with ACID constraints.
- Every individual cache object instance must be capable of recovering its state in the event of a application server failure, as well as in the event of a database service or a storage service failure.

Best practice - Do not attempt to modify objects in ElasticCache.

Using Static In-Memory Cache

Given a distributed in-memory cache:

- The CQRS application server is fully aware that it has received a request to read a uniquely identifiable instance of static data;
- The application server's request handler submits a request to the in-memory cache service for that identified instance of static data;
- If the application server's request handler receives an empty response from the in-memory cache service, the handler submits a request to the persistent data storage service;
- If the application server's request handler receives an non-empty response from the persistent data storage service, the handler returns the response to the client and then writes the new object instance into in-memory cache.

Amazon ElastiCache Memcached

Memcached is a multi-threaded in-memory key/value pair cache.

This means that the data structure of the objects in cache are not structurally compatible with a relation data structure managed by an RDBMs.

The combination of ElastiCache Memcached and Amazon DynamoDB is a best fit.

ElasticCache can elastically grow and shrink a Memcached cluster.

A Memcached cluster can contain up to 20 nodes.

When a Memcached instance is launched, the cache is devoid of content.

To improve read performance you can partition you cluster into shards.

Objects in Memcached are binary-large-objects (blobs).

The immutable information contained in an object blob is entirely up to you.

Every object blob in cache has a unique identifier.

ElastiCache supports Auto Discovery (your application does not manually need to connect to an individual node, it is aware of a list of nodes).

When using the provided client library, the application service can discover and connect to every cache node without needing to be aware of the physical cache topology.

Memcached offers no support for redundant data.

Refer to the AWS website for the supported version of Memcached.

Amazon ElastiCache Redis

Redis is an in-memory object store, that can function as a cache, as a message broker, or as a very primitive and rudimentary stateful database.

A Redis cluster is made up of 1 node.

Multiple Redis clusters can be organized into a Redis Replication Group.

Redis allows you to set-up redundant read replicas and to fail over from the primary replica in the event of a primary node problem or failure.

Redis supports up to 5 read replicas.

Only 1 node handles cache writes and the other 5 handle reads from cache.

When Multi-AZ is used, in the event of a failed primary node, a read replica can be promoted and become the new master node of the cluster.

Best practice – for best performance, place the application servers in the same AZs as the cache nodes.

Best practice – be certain to specify your preferred AZ during cluster creation.

Redis provides support for strings, lists and sets.

Redis provides support for sorting and ranking objects in cache.

Redis is able to persist objects in cache to disk, by making a snapshot.

A Redis snapshot is a full clone of the cache contents at a point in time and can be used to recover or to replicate cache.

The snapshot file is automatically stored by ElastiCache in Amazon S3.

A snapshot can be taken manually, or automatically based on a schedule which you configure.

Best practice – to minimize performance degradation of a Redis cluster, take a snapshot of a read replica and not of the primary node.

When a Redis Instance is launched it is devoid of content but can be initialized from a snapshot.

Redis can also function as a message broker, which supports the Publish and Subscribe enterprise integration pattern.

Refer to the AWS website for the supported version of Redis.

ElastiCache EC2 Instances

An ElastiCache cluster is made of multiple EC2 instances.

Adding new instance scales the cluster horizontally.

Increasing the power of an instance scales a node vertically.

Since Memcached is multi-threaded it can take full advantage of EC2 instances with multi-core CPUs.

There are many types of EC2 instances to choose from.

The size of memory can range from 555MB to 237GB but always check with the AWS website for the latest specifications.

Instances can be changed over time.

Access to ElastiCache Cluster

Access to the ElastiCache cluster is controlled by restricting inbound traffic, through the use of security groups.

When deployed inside an Amazon Virtual Private Cloud (VPC).

Each cluster node is assigned a private IP address within 1 or more subnets that you select.

Individual nodes can never be accessed via the Internet, or from EC2 instance outside the VPC.

On the subnet level, you can further restrict traffic by using network Access Control Lists (ACLs).

AWS Identity and Access Management (IAM) service is used to manage and control access to an ElastiCache cluster.

You define IAM policies per AWS Account.

Amazon DynamoDB

DynamoDB is a serverless proprietary NoSQL (Not Only SQL) data service, that has been available on AWS since January 2012. DynamoDB is a fully managed multi-master database that supports both key/value as well as document data models. A document is just a special type of key/value data structure.

DynamoDB:

- provides a consistent, single digit millisecond, latency, which scales horizontally,
- with built-in security,
- backup and restore and
- in-memory caching.

The DynamoDB service is ***purchased based on data throughput, not on data storage***.

The ***DynamoDB is Serverless***: there are no servers to provision, patch, or manage and no software to install, maintain, or operate. DynamoDB automatically scales tables up and down to adjust for capacity and maintain performance. Availability and fault tolerance are built in.

DynamoDB provides both on-demand and provisioned capacity modes so that you can optimize costs by specifying capacity per workload or paying for only the resources you consume.

Applications connect to the DynamoDB web service API end-point and ***submit over HTTPS requests*** to:

- Read and write items to and from a table;
- Create table;
- Delete table.

DynamoDB API accepts requests only in JSON format. You will use the AWS SDK to connect to DynamoDB and to interact with its tables and items. Languages and frameworks with a DynamoDB binding include Java, Node.js, Go, C# .NET, Perl, PHP, Python, Ruby, Haskell and Erlang.

DynamoDB exposes performance metrics that help users provision it correctly and keep applications using DynamoDB running smoothly, such as:

- Requests and throttling;
- Errors: ConditionalCheckFailedRequests, UserErrors, SystemErrors;
- Metrics related to Global Secondary Index creation.

These metrics can be tracked using the AWS Management Console, using the AWS Command Line Interface, or a monitoring tool integrating with Amazon CloudWatch.

If Auto Scaling is enabled, then the DynamoDB database will scale automatically. In addition, DynamoDB offers integration with Hadoop via Elastic MapReduce.

Additionally, ***administrators can request throughput changes*** and DynamoDB will spread the data and traffic over a number of servers using solid-state drives, allowing predictable performance. All data is stored on solid state devices (SDDs) and automatically synchronously replicated across multiple AZs in a Region.

In September 2013, Amazon made available a local development version of DynamoDB so developers can test DynamoDB-backed applications locally.

Amazon DynamoDB Use Cases

DynamoDB is a good fit for Use Cases that need low-latency data access at any scale, such as these:

- Mobile;
- Web;
- Gaming;
- Ad-tech;
- Internet of Things (IoT);
- Storing JSON Documents;
- Managing web application session data;
- Store metadata for S3 objects, etc.

DynamoDB can:

- handle more than 10 trillion requests per day and
- support peaks of more than 20 million requests per second.

Synchronous Replication & In-Memory Cache

For high durability and high availability, DynamoDB ***uses synchronous replication across multiple Availability Zones within an AWS Region.***

DynamoDB ***global tables replicate your data across multiple AWS Regions*** to give you fast, local access to data for your globally distributed applications.

For use cases that require even faster access with microsecond latency, DynamoDB ***Accelerator (DAX) provides a fully managed in-memory cache.***

ACID, Encryption and Backups

DynamoDB supports ACID transactions to enable you to build business-critical applications at scale.

DynamoDB encrypts all data by default and provides fine-grained identity and access control on all your tables.

You can create full backups of hundreds of terabytes of data instantly with no performance impact to your tables and recover to any point in time in the preceding 35 days with no downtime.

Immutable Information

Today, most computations write information 1 time and read that information N times.

Most new types of information of value today are immutable.

Consequently, the data structures that contain that immutable information are single-purposed, not general purposed.

The best practices of immutable information and single-purposed data structures dominate all use cases in which DynamoDB is a best fit.

Dynamo Data Model Tables

Don't imagine the relational data model, when you think of DynamoDB 'tables.'

A DynamoDB 'table' is an abstract data type that is better known by other names, such as:

- associative array,
- map,
- symbol table, or
- dictionary

In the DynamoDB data model, a table is a collection of items.

Items and Attributes

There are few nouns in the English language as ambiguous, as devoid of definitive meaning, as the word 'item.' It ranks alongside the noun 'thing.' Any phenomena, or part thereof, can be called an item, or just are rightly called a thing.

Each item:

- ***is a collection of 1 or more attributes.***
- ***has a primary key that uniquely identifies the item.***

Where a DynamoDB item is a (key, value) pair, such that

each possible key appears at most once in the collection. You can write an unlimited number of key/value items into a table.

There is a limit of 400KB on the size of the individual item.

An attribute is a name/value pair. A value can be a single value, or a set of values in which duplicates are not allowed. ***An item can have an unlimited number of attributes.***

Again, do not think in terms of the relational data model. A DynamoDB table does not have a pre-defined schema. Overtime, additional attributes can be accreted to an individual item. As the item schema changes, you must re-factor your application software to work with all of the different schemas that are present in the items in that particular table.

Best practice – Minimize the item schema variations within a given table. Over time, you can accrete new attributes onto an existing item. Because the application logic must support all schemas present in the table, that capability exponentially increases risk of failure.

Key/Value Pair Data Model Operations

An associative array, map, symbol table, or dictionary is an abstract data type composed of a collection of (key, value) pairs, such that each possible key appears at most once in the collection.

Operations associated with this data type allow:

- the addition of a pair to the collection;
- the removal of a pair from the collection;
- the modification of an existing pair;
- the lookup of a value associated with a particular key.

DynamoDB Data Types

Scalar – represents exactly 1 value. Four scalar types are supported:

- String – variable length characters, up to 400KB. UTF-8 Unicode is supported;

- Number – positive and negative numbers, with up to 38 digits of precision;
- Binary – binary data, images, compressed objects up to 400KB in size;
- *Boolean* – binary flag.

Null – a blank, empty, or unknown state. String, number, binary, Boolean cannot be empty.

Set – a unique list of 1 or more scalar values, all of the same data type. Three set types are supported:

- String set;
- Number set;
- Binary set.

Document – represent multiple nested attributes. Two types are supported and these types can be combined as well:

List – used to store an ordered list of attributes of different data types.

Map – used to store an un-ordered list of attributes of different data types.

Global Table

Global tables, internal to DynamoDB, automatically replicate your tables across your choice of AWS Regions. You simply select the Regions and DynamoDB handles all of the details for you.

Global table ensure data redundancy across Regions. A time-order sequence of changes is propagated to every Region where the table abides. They enable your application to be available, even in the event of isolation of a Region, or degradation of performance of a Region.

If an entire Region fails, you DynamoDB tables are available in another Region. This replication is transparent to you, allowing you to focus on your application business logic.

Primary Key

A DynamoDB table is not a relation! DynamoDB only requires that a 'record' stored in a 'table' only have a primary key attribute. ***The primary key uniquely identifies each item contained in the table.***

A 'primary key' points to 1 and only 1 item. The primary key of a DynamoDB table is the functional equivalent of the candidate key of a relation.

You do not need to know the attributes of the information you are persisting in storage, you do not need to know the characteristic properties of that entity, to persist an instance of that entity within the database.

2 Types of Primary Key

DynamoDB uses the primary key to distribute requests for items, as well as to support queries.

DynamoDB support 2 types of primary key:

Partition Key

- The primary key is a single attribute, with a value that is a hash. DynamoDB builds an unordered hash index on the primary key attribute.

Partition and Sort Key

- The primary key is made up of 2 attributes;
- Each primary key attribute is of type string, number, or binary;
- The 1st attribute is the partition key;
- The 2nd attribute is the sort key, or range key;
- Each item is uniquely identified by the combination of partition key and sort key.
- The combination of partition key and sort key of a DynamoDB table is the functional equivalent of the candidate key of a relation.

Secondary Indexes

When you create a primary key made of a partition key and a sort key, you gain the option of defining 1:N secondary indexes. ***The function of a secondary index is to support a particular query.***

You can query the table by referencing the secondary

index. You can query the table by referencing the combination of primary key and secondary index.

DynamoDB supports 2 types of secondary indexes:

Global Secondary Index

- This is a pair of partition key and sort key attributes that are different from the table's pair of partition key and sort key attributes;
- A global secondary index can created and destroyed at any time;
- A table can have 1:N global indexes.

Local Secondary Index

- The local secondary index re-uses the table's partition key but uses a different attribute as the sort key;
- You can only create a local secondary index when you create the table;
- A table can have 1 and only 1 local secondary index

DynamoDB updates all indexes whenever an item in the table is modified.

Single Purposed

Though secondary indexes can help make certain reads more performant, it is critically important to recognize that a key/value type table, or a document type, are never intended to support multiple use cases, nor multiple varieties of computations.

It is important to approach the design of key/value and document data structures with a healthy respect for their strengths as well as for their weaknesses.

A key/value data structure is write optimized and then for 1 and only 1 use case.

In contrast, a 1NF relation in an RDBMS can usually support a variety of different read use cases. The same table can be referenced in any number of different JOIN expressions. But, that is not the case with key/value or document data structures.

A particular key/value data structure is not a general-pur-

pose structure, as is a relation.

A particular key/value data structure is a best fit for 1 and only 1 read.

Ungoverned Data Redundancy

A JOIN logic is not supported in query expressions used with key/value data services. If different facts need to be joined, you must place those different facts – in the form of an attribute name/value pari into the same table.

This limitation naturally leads to redundant instances of the very same attribute name/value pairs being scattered across tables, with no mechanism available to keep them in sync. ***There is no mechanism by which to keep redundant attribute instances in sync because all attribute instances are understood to be immutable.***

Two Read/Write Capacity Modes

DynamoDB supports two read/write capacity modes for each table.

On-demand

- For workloads that are less predictable for which you are unsure that you will have high utilization, on-demand capacity mode takes care of managing capacity for you and you only pay for what you consume.

Provisioned

- Tables using provisioned capacity mode require you to set read and write capacity.
- Provisioned capacity mode is more cost effective when you're confident you'll have decent utilization of the provisioned capacity you specify.

You can switch between on-demand and provisioned capacity modes.

Provisioned Capacity

When you provision a DynamoDB table, you are required to estimate some amount of read and write capacity you expect will be required to support your workload.

Note – for a given table there will be 1 and only 1 write logical unit of work and 1 read logical unit of work.

UpdateTable Action

you configure the table to support the sustained, low-latency, response the use case requires.

Jargon - Capacity is defined in units of write tasks and in units of read tasks.

Ideally, the cardinality of the table is the low water mark for the write tasks.

The amount of read tasks will typically be 3-5 times larger than the write tasks.

Each HHTP request will consume some unit of capacity.

The larger the item size, the larger the capacity consumed.

The Read Consistency level effects capacity consumed, as well.

Updates to each secondary index consumes capacity units.

Amazon CloudWatch can be used to monitor DynamoDB capacity use and help you configure the table as needed for the workloads

Writing Items

Application connect to the DynamoDB web service endpoint and submit requests over HTTPS to read and write items, to create or delete a table. The ***DynamoDB web service API accepts requests in JSON format.***

DynamoDB's API supports 3 write actions:

PutItem

- Creates a new item, made of 1:N attributes;
- You can place conditional constraints that must be meet before the item is created;
- Will update an existing item.

UpdateItem

- Updates a existing item, based on the primary key, as replaces the attribute values;
- Also provide atomic counters, which allow you to

change a value and are guaranteed to be consistent across multiple concurrent requests;
- Will create a new item if the item does not already exist.

DeleteItem

- You use this action to remove an item from a table.

Reading Items

You can read an item after it is created, by invoking the GetItem action.

The ***GetItem action***:

- Allows you to use the primary key to retrieve an item
- If the table has a partition key and a sort key, then both must be used to retrieve the item
- By default, all item attributes are returned
- You have the ability to filter the collection of returned attributes

Each GetItem action consumes read capacity units, based on the size of the item returned and the read consistency level chosen.

By default, the GetItem action performs an eventually consistent read. You can select a ***strongly consistent read, which returns the most up-to-date version of the item*** and which consumes additional read capacity.

Read Levels

DynamoDB is a distributed database service, which distributes physical data across a Region. When an item is changed, that change has to be propagated across all copies of the item. It takes time – more than a second - to update all instances of a given item throughout a Region. Consequently, a read of an item right after it has been changed might not return the most up-to-date version of the item.

Eventual Consistent Reads

The default is eventual consistent reads. The response

might contain old, stale, attributes and values.

Strongly Consistent Reads

DynamoDB does support strongly Consistent Reads. If chosen, the response is guaranteed to contain the most up to date version of the item.

Batch Operations

DynamoDB allows you to manipulate more than 1 item per request.

BatchGetItem action

- Allows you to retrieve a batch of items;

BatchWriteItem action

- Allows you to batch together items to be created or updated;
- You can perform the operation on a maximum of 25 items per batch.

Searching Items

DynamoDB supports to search operations:

Query

- A ***search using only the primary key attribute values*** to find items in a table or in a secondary index;
- ***Requires a partition key attribute name and a distinct value to search***;
- You ***can optionally provide a sort key value and use a comparison operator*** to refine the results;
- Results are automatically sorted by primary key and are limited to 1MB;
- Use the Query search operation whenever possible to reduce capacity consumption.

Scan

- A scan ***reads every item in a table or secondary index and then it filters out values***;
- This can be a resource intensive operation;
- ***By default, the scan returns all attributes of every item in the table or index***;

- ***Items can be filtered using expressions***;
- The results are limited to 1MB, but you can page through the results in 1MB increments.

DynamoDB Security

All DynamoDB operations must be authenticated as a valid user or session.

DynamoDB support granular control over access rights and permissions for users and administrators. DynamoDB integrates with the AWS IAM service, which provides control over permissions using policies.

You can create policies to allow or deny specific operations on specific tables. You can also restrict access to individual items or attributes.

Applications which write and read a DynamoDB database must obtain a set of access control keys.

Best practice – do not store the access control keys in a configuration file. Instead, use the temporary or permanent IAM EC2 instance profiles to manage credentials.

Best practice – for mobile applications, use a combination of web identity federation with the AWS Security Token Service (AWS STS) to issue temporary keys.

In addition, DynamoDB offers Amazon VPC endpoints which are used to secure access to DynamoDB in your VPC.

DynamoDB Encryption at Rest

DynamoDB supports encryption at rest. Encryption at rest is fully transparent to the end user. DynamoDB uses AWS managed encryption keys stored in AWS KMS.

Amazon Relational Database Service (RDS)

RDS provides a partially (not fully) managed relational database server(s), which can be of a variety of proprietary as well as open source servers. In minutes, you can provision an RDS node that is:

- Highly secure;

- Highly available;
- Fault-tolerant;
- ***You cannot access the operating system of RDS Databases.***
- RDS handles administration tasks, such as:
- Backups;
- Software patches;
- Monitoring;
- Vertical scaling;
- Replication (with caveats).

RDS Endpoints and DB Instances

Amazon RDS exposes an endpoint to which client software can connect to and submit SQL command and query statements.

RDS does not provide a shell you can use to access the database server instance. You cannot use SSH to connect to a DB Instance. Access to certain RDBMS system privileges and tables is restricted and require advanced privileges to acquire.

A ***DB Instance is an isolated database environment deployed on a private network segment, in a single AZ.*** You can create 1:N DB Instances. In each DB Instance Engine, you can create 1:N physical databases.

Each DB Instance runs and manages a commercial or open source database engine, for example:

- MySQL;
- Oracle;
- PostgreSQL;
- SQL Server;

In a two-tier architecture, to ensure that traffic can flow from the database server to the web server create the database Security Group.

DB Instance Class

The ***DB Instance Class determines the CPU and memory resources*** available to the DB Engine. You can choose a class which best meets the needs of your workload. Independent of the class, you control the size and characteristics of storage used.

Amazon RDS will migrate you data to new DB instance class you have chosen.

DB Engine Parameter Group and Option Group

A DB Engine ***Parameter Group contains database engine configuration values*** which will be applied to 1: N DB Instances.

A DB ***Option Group specifies setting of features of the commercial or open source database service.***

Hosting the DB On-Site

Your responsibilities:

1. Application optimization;
2. Scaling database service;
3. High availability;
4. Backups;
5. DB Engine Software installation;
6. DB Engine patches;
7. OS Installation;
8. OS patches;
9. Server maintenance;
10. Rack and Stack;
11. Power and cooling.

Best practice – if you need full control of the database service, install the database service on an EC2 instance and manage it yourself, without any RDS operational benefits.

Hosting the DB Engine on EC2

Your responsibilities:

1. Application optimization;
2. Scaling database service;
3. High availability;
4. Backups;
5. DB Engine Software installation;
6. DB Engine patches;

7. OS patches.

AWS RDS responsibilities:

1. OS Installation;
2. Server maintenance;
3. Rack and Stack;
4. Power and cooling.

The application has operating system privileges on the relational database server.

Best practice - to configure this hosting model so that it is a highly available architecture, deploy two EC2 instances in a database server replication configuration using two different AZs.

Hosting the Database using RDS

Your responsibilities:

1. Application optimization.

AWS RDS responsibilities:

1. Scaling database service;
2. High availability;
3. Backups;
4. DB Engine Software installation;
5. DB Engine patches;
6. OS patches;
7. OS Installation;
8. Server maintenance;
9. Rack and Stack;
10. Power and cooling.

VPC and RDS

In order to host a database in a VPC using RDS, that ***VPC must have at least one subnet in at least two of the AZs where the RDS will be deployed.***

RDS Open Source Database Engines

MySQL

- versions 5.7, 5.6, 5.5 and 5.1;
- Community edition with InnoDB;
- Connect using MSQL Workbench;
- Multi-AZ deployments for high-availability;
- Read-replicas for horizontal scaling.

PostgreSQL

- versions 9.5.x, 9.4.x and 9.3.x;
- Connect using pgAdmin, or JDBC/ODBC drivers;
- Multi-AZ deployments for high-availability;
- Read-replicas for horizontal scaling.

MariaDB

- version 10.0.17;
- Supports XtraDB storage engine;
- Multi-AZ deployments for high-availability;
- Read-replicas for horizontal scaling.

RDS Commercial Database Engines

Oracle

- versions 11g, 12c;
- Connect using Oracle SQL Plus;
- Standard Edition One, Standard Edition and Enterprise Edition are supported.

Microsoft SQL Server

- Versions 2008 R2, 2012, 2014;
- Connect using SQL Server Management Studio;
- Express Edition, Web Edition, Standard Edition and Enterprise Edition are supported.

AWS does not support the DB2 database engine.

RDS Commercial Database Licensing

Commercial database servers require a license to operate.

AWS supports two licensing models:

License Included

- The license is held by AWS and is included in the DB Instance price.
- For Oracle, that is a Standard Edition One license.

- For Microsoft, that is an Express Edition , a Web Edition, or a Standard Edition, license.

Bring Your Own License (BYOL)

- You provide the license for the DB Instance.
- For Oracle, that is a Standard Edition One, Standard Edition, or Enterprise Edition, license.
- For Microsoft, that is a Standard Edition, or an Enterprise Edition, license.

DB Engine Storage Options

RDS is built using Amazon Elastic Block Storage (EBS). Storage options are dictated by the DB engine you have chosen. ***Storage can range from 4 to 16 TB and up to 30,000 IOPS.***

DB Engine Security

A database is a security mechanism, as it organizes a particular collection of particular facts, to which access is constrained. Every DB Engine enables you to create 1:N databases. Each database is isolated from all other databases managed by the DB Engine.

Every ***DB Engine grants and revokes permissions to specific databases, as well as to all of the particular database objects contained in those databases.***

In addition to the DB Engine security mechanisms

RDS Security

AWS RDS provides other security mechanisms as well:

- AWS Identity and Access Management (IAM) policies;
- Deploying the DB Instance with an Amazon Virtual Private Cloud (VPC);
- Use network Access Control Lists (ACLS) and security groups to limit traffic to the DB Instance;
- Connect to the DB Instance using SSL;
- Encrypt the data at rest and in motion, using Amazon Key Management Service (KMS);
- Native DB Engine encryption is supported as well.

Changing the DB Instance Type

Just like the EC2 type, you can change the DB Instance type.

The DB Instance type can be changed using the AWS RDS web console, or the AWS CLI, or the AWS SDK, or by using Lambda functions.

There is a small downtime during the change, therefore the change can be scheduled.

Amazon RDS is not integrated with Auto Scaling.

RDS Backups and Snapshots

RDS provides two backup mechanisms, which can be used in combination to protect your data:

1. Automated Backups;
2. Manual Snapshots.

Each application has its defined:

- Recovery Point Objective (RPO) - The maximum elapsed period of data loss that is acceptable in the event of a failure incident.
- Recovery Time Objective (RTO) - The maximum elapsed period of downtime that is acceptable during a recovery from backup to resumption of processing

The RPO and RTO are used together to determine how best to combine automated backups and manual snapshots in support of the Business Continuance and Disaster Recovery (BCDR) requirements.

Automated DB Instance Backups

RDS creates a storage volume snapshot of your entire DB Instance and all of its individual databases. RDS continually tracks changes to the databases and backs up your databases. ***Automated backups occur daily and can be configured to occur during a 30-minute backup window.***

When you create the DB Instance, you can set the backup retention period. ***By default, 1 day of backups are retained.***

The maximum retention period is 35 days. During the retention period you can restore your DB Instance by using the backup image to create a new DB Instance.

When you delete an DB Instances, all automated backups are deleted as well and are not available to be used for recovery purposes.

When Multi-AZ are configured, the backup is taken from the standby.

Manual DB Instance Snapshots

You can initiate a manual DB snapshot at any point in time, as frequently as you desire. ***During the snapshot storage I/O may be suspended*** while the data is being backed up, for the duration of the snapshot process.

You can restore a DB Instance from a snapshot image. The CreateDBSnapshot command is used from the RDS Console to create the snapshot.

When you delete an DB Instances, all manual backups are not deleted and are available to be used for recovery purposes.

Manual snapshots are retained until you explicitly delete them, using the DeleteDBSchapshot command from the RDS Console.

DB Instance Recovery

You cannot restore a DB snapshot to an existing DB Instance. ***You can only recover to a new DB Instance.***

After the restore process completes, only the default DB parameter group and security group are associated with the new DB Instance. ***You must associate custom DB parameter and security groups with the recovered DB.***

When automated backups are being taken, ***the RDS combines the contents of the DB Instances write-ahead transaction logs with the backup images, to restore the DB to a point in time,*** typically up to the last 5 minutes.

RDS Database Encryption at Rest

RDS ***supports encryption at rest mechanisms that are native***

to DB Engines. You can also encrypt and decrypt your database using AWS mechanism, such as KMS and CloudTrail, as well as SSL.

An RDS ***database can be encrypted only if the underlying EC2 instances supports DB encryption***. Encryption of an RDS database ***can be done when the database is created***. When you encrypt a database,***you encrypt its:***

- ***Instance storage;***
- ***Automatic backups;***
- ***Read replica;***
- ***Standby slave;***
- ***Snapshots.***

RDS ensures that the stores are encrypted.

RDS Monitoring

RDS sends all information metrics to Amazon CloudWatch and you can view those metrics in the RDS console, in the CloudWatch console, or via the CloudWatch APIs.

RDS offers 4 types of monitoring

Standard - Depending on the DB Engine, 15-18 metrics at 1-minute intervals. The usual metrics – CPU use, storage, memory, swap space, I/O latency, etc.

Enhanced - You get an additional 37 metrics, at lower level of granularity, at as low as 1 second intervals.

Event notification - You get event notification via Amazon SNS, when 17 different types of events occur within the DB Instance.

Performance insights - You get illustrations of the DB performance which help you analyze of any issues, e.g., an SQL statement, a particular user, etc.

RDS Multi-AZ

Amazon's use of the term 'high availability' in this context is misleading. For each type of DB engine, RDS allows you to ***setup an inaccessible slave instance of the DB, whose sole function is disaster recovery***.

Given the default where the DB Instance in a single Availability Zone, ***Multi-AZ uses synchronous replication to create a copy of that DB Instance in another AZ***.

The original DB Instance is called the primary and the copy is called the slave.

In addition to disaster recovery, the Multi-AZ configuration enables ***planned maintenance***, like OS patches or DB instance scaling, to be ***applied first to the standby***, prior to the master.

The slave instance does not enhance performance, ***the slave is off-line and cannot support commands or queries requested by the application***. As such, the availability of the DB instance is not enhanced, is not increased.

Multi-AZ Recovery

With Multi-AZ, the DB Instance becomes recoverable in a shorter window of time, relative to the other recovery mechanisms available in AWS.

RDS automatically monitors for and detects these events that ***cause failover:***

- ***Loss of availability of the primary AZ;***
- ***Loss of network connectivity to the primary DB;***
- ***Compute unit failure on the primary DB;***
- ***Storage volume failure on the primary DB;***

RDS automatically handles the failover from the primary to the slave due to any of these events:

Without human intervention, RDS automatically fails over to the slave;

The DNS name remains the same and just ***the CNAME is changed to point to the ex-slave*** and new primary.

Usability of RDS Read Replicas

Read replicas are a means of enhancing performance of an application by reducing the load on the main database. To enhance performance, the reads are handled by the replica. This adds elasticity to the application by scaling out the application reads (across the main and the replica). As the name declares read replicas do not support writes by the application.

However, if and only if the application was designed and build from day 1 to separate commands from queries, it is impossible to use this mechanism to any good effect. Since very few people are able to design an application before building it, very few people know about the CQRS pattern and even fewer have the skills required to use the pattern.

The CQRS requires a physical database that supports both commands as well as queries. If that is not the case, then there is no rational purpose in creating a read replica of the database. A read replica is intended to support queries which support application use cases.

OLTP application use cases are never the same as reporting or data warehouse use cases. The proposition that at a read replica of an application database is useable for analytic, reporting, or date warehousing, computations is an absurd, profoundly idiotic, notion. At best, at the very best, an RDS read replica can be used as a read data source for ETL processes. That is about it.

Scaling DB Engine Vertically and Horizontally

While some DB Engine can modestly scale vertically, virtually none can scale horizontally to any significant degree because none are based on a peer-to-peer architecture.

Vertical scaling

- Throw more hardware at the problem: more RAM, more CPUs, more powerful CPUs, enhanced networking, faster persistent storage devices, etc.

Horizontal scaling

- This is the notorious partitioning fantasy.
- The profoundly foolish premise is that the entire schema and every table contained within it, can easily have their tuples horizontally fragmented dynamically at runtime, without any loss of refer-

ential integrity, or risk thereof.

- If you set aside the highly complex DDL and DML programming that is required, the profound complexity introduced into the application to work with partitioning is not to be ignored.
- Each application thread must know precisely where in time and space it is executing relative to a particular tuple nested within a dynamically changing data model.
- Did I mention the critical need to recover the application and DB to a point in time, right before that failure event occurred?

Amazon Redshift

Amazon Redshift is based on PostgreSQL, which is based on Ingres, and ***uses columnar storage with a block size of 1024KB. Redshift is a fully managed petabyte-scale*** data warehouse service, for analyzing structured (in a relation/table) data.

Redshift is optimized for read queries. Redshift ***supports a 'standard' SQL and has an interface which is compatible with popular business intelligence tools.***

When a Redshift cluster is created, it is locked down by default so nobody has access to it. To grant access to the cluster, a Security Group must be associated with the cluster.

Redshift Use Cases

The sole use case for Redshift is data warehousing. This also goes by the brand name business intelligence. This is the same old Online Analytic Processing (OLAP) for which the relation data model and relational database services were never designed to support. RDBMS engines are built to support OLTP of relations, that is all. Redshift, however, uses columnar storage, not tabular storage.

Overall, data warehousing and business intelligence systems are not viewed by C levels as returning value on their investment. Today, data warehouses are viewed as being money pits and unless they are required to comply with laws and regulations are not considered worth pursuing.

Redshift Benefits

- Fast;
- Columnar storage;
- A data is automatically distributed across nodes
- The query is parallelized across several nodes;
- Cheaper – prices start at $1,000 per TB;
- Has multiple compression techniques;
- Data is compressed 3-4 times, which save on storage costs;
- Managed Service;
- Amazon administers the clusters, networking and operating system, patches, upgrading, backing up and restoring;
- Scalable clusters;
- Distributed architecture scales horizontally, out and in;
- Secure;
- Supports data encryption at rest and in transit;
- You can create an Amazon VPC to control access to Redshift;
- You can use AWS KMS and Hardware Security Modules (HSMs) to manage keys;
- Zone Map functionality - Keeps track of the min and max values of each block and enable you to skip over blocks devoid of the needed data.

Redshift Architecture

Redshift is a cluster, made of a Leader Node and up to 128 Compute Nodes.

The Leader Node

- Is the endpoint for SQL requests you connect to using JDBC or ODBC drivers, or Postgres drivers;
- Parses and optimizes the command or query state-

ment;
- Coordinates parallel SQL processing by distributing the SQL to the Compute nodes;
- Aggregates the result sets for a query returned from the Compute nodes;
- Returns the complete result set to the client application;
- Encrypts the data, compresses the data and runs the vacuum process and backup and restore tasks.

The Compute Node

- Process the raw data and return the results to the Leader node;
- Compute nodes communicate with each other while processing a query;
- Is divided into multiple slices;
- A slice is allocated a portion of a node's CPU, memory and storage;
- Slices process queries independently.

2 Redshift Cluster Types

Single-node Cluster

- There is only 1 node, which functions as both the Leader and Compute nodes;
- If that 1 node fails, the entire database goes down;
- A database snapshot is used to restore the database;
- Suitable to development and perhaps test environments.

Multi-node Cluster

- The Leader is a separate node from the Compute node(s);
- There is only 1 Leader node per cluster;
- When you create the cluster, you specify how many Compute nodes are needed;
- The data is automatically replicated among the Compute nodes, providing data redundancy;

- When a Compute node fails, it is replace automatically and the cluster automatically distributes data to it;
- Suitable for production environments.

Redshift DB Instance Types

Dense Compute (DC)

- Has SSD drives;
- For faster compute performance.

Dense Storage (DS)

- Has magnetic hard drives;
- For workloads with large data volumes.

Redshift Networking

You can choose the Availability Zone (AZ) in which the Redshift cluster will be created.

An Amazon Redshift cluster can be deployed into an Amazon Virtual Private Cloud (VPC).

A VPC is mandatory for all new cluster installations.

By using a VPC, the Redshift cluster is isolated from all other customers.

You can choose a cluster subnet group consisting of 1 or more subnets, which can be either in the private subnet or in the public subnet.

If you choose a public subnet, you can either provide your own public IP address, or have the Redshift cluster provide IP.

A Redshift cluster deployed in a private subnet is not accessible from the Internet.

The public or private subnet is only applicable to the Leader Node.

The Compute nodes are created in a separate VPC to which you have no access.

Redshift Enhanced VPC Routing

If you choose this option, then traffic for commands producing large data volume transfers – all COPY and UPLOAD traffic - are routed through your Amazon VPC. If enhanced VPC routing is not enabled, then Redshift routes traffic through the Internet, including traffic to other services in the AWS network.

Data Encryption at Rest and In Motion

You can choose to encrypt all of the data managed by Redshift. ***You can encrypt the data both at rest and in motion.***

When you launch the cluster, you enable encryption. Once you enable encryption on a cluster, you cannot disable encryption. If you launch a cluster and do not enable encryption, it remains un-encrypted during its ***life. Redshift uses AWS KMS customer default master key to encrypt Redshift databases.***

If you need to encrypt a cluster after it has been launched, then you must unload all of the data, enable encryption on the cluster and then upload all of the data back into the cluster.

For data at rest, ***Redshift uses AES-256 hardware-accelerated encryption keys to encrypt blocks of data and the system metadata for the cluster.***

You can manage encryption using AWS KMS, CloudHSM, or using your on-premise HSM.

For data in motion, you can use SSL to encrypt connections to the cluster.

Redshift Security

Like all other database engines, Redshift has its own security mechanism, which are common to relational database services.

You can also create IAM policies on IAM users, roles, or groups.

Data Loading

Redshift replicates all data within the cluster when it is loaded and also continuously backs up the data. Redshift ***attempts to maintain at least 3 copies of the data*** (the original and replica of the compute nodes and a backup in S3. Redshift can also synchronously replicate your snapshots to S3 in another Region for disaster recovery.

File-based Loading

- You load data files directly from S3;
- The most efficient and high-performance way to load Redshift tables;
- You can load CSV, JSON and AVRO encoded files into Redshift tables.

Amazon Kinesis Firehouse

- You can load streaming data or batch data directly into Redshift;
- You can insert, update and delete data via the Leader node using SQL commands;
- You can load and unload data via a Compute node using Redshift tools such as COPY or UNLOAD commands, or CTAS (create table as select);
- The COPY command is the recommend way to bulk load Redshift;
- A Compute node also supports data loading from DynamoDB, from EMR and via SSH commands.

In addition, data can be loaded directly into Redshift from Amazon DynamoDB, as text files from S3, and by using an SSH connection via an Elastic MapReduce (EMR) host.

Redshift Sort Keys

When you create a table, you can define 1 or more columns as the sort key.

When the data is loaded into the table, it is stored on disk in sorted order.

The query optimizer uses these facts when developing an execution plan.

The sort key increases the performance of MERGE JOIN statements.

Backup and Restore

Redshift take ***automatic snapshots of your databases in your***

cluster and saves them in Amazon S3.

Snapshots are incremental. The frequency of snapshots is either 8 hours or 5GB of block changes, whichever comes first. You can:

- define the retention period of the snapshots;
- turn-off automatic backups;
- take a manual backup, which can be retained as long as needed;
- configure Cross-Region snapshots and these can be automatically replicated to an alternate region;
- restore the entire cluster from a Cross-Region snapshot, which results in a new cluster of the original Instance type, in about 10 minutes;
- restore the entire database from a snapshot;
- restore an individual table from a snapshot.

Until you delete the Redshift cluster, Redshift provide free storage of snapshots that is equal to the storage capacity of the cluster. After that limit is exceed, you are charged for the additional storage at the normal rate.

Best practice – evaluate how many days automated snapshots need to be kept and configure their retention period accordingly and delete any manual snapshots that are no longer needed.

3 Data Distribution Options

KEY

- The slice is chosen based on a distribution key that is a hash of the defined column.

ALL

- Distributes a copy of the entire table to the first slice on each node;
- Helps to optimize JOINs;
- It increases the amount of storage consumed;
- Can be useful with small tables (like a dimension table) that participate in JOINs with much larger

tables (like fact tables) and which are infrequently modified.

EVEN

- Data is distributed across all slices, in a round-robin distribution;
- Useful for small dimension tables, for tables that do not participate in JOINs or GROUP BY clauses, or not used in aggregation computations.

Vacuum and Analyze

You need to perform regular maintenance by running the VACUUM command.

You need to reorganize data loaded into Redshift and reclaim space after deletions.

You need to keep statistics up to date so that the query optimizer can create accurate execution plans.

You update statistics by running the ANALYSIS command.

AMAZON HIGH AVAILABILITY (HA)

In AWS, there are two corner-stones, there are two building blocks, of all high availability (HA) design patterns, and they are the:

1. EC2 Instance, and the
2. Amazon Elastic Load Balancer (ELB).

In AWS, to have HA requires at a minimum two EC2 instances deployed into 2 different AZ.

There are a good variety of on-premise as well as cloud HA design patterns, where each good HA architecture variation is valid and robust relative to the Use Case it is intended to support. Within the 'Reliability Pillar' chapter a few cloud HA architectures are examined.

As an example of variation, in one HA architecture imagine that there are EC2 instances hosting an application, that these instances are deployed into multiple subnets, where each subnet is located within a different AZ, and where these EC2 instances are placed behind a single ELB. Or, in a mutation of that variation, 2 ELBs front that same configuration of EC2 instances.

Despite the sometimes significant differences in their resource and service configurations, all HA architecture rests upon the same two corner-stones. However, where, when, how we configure and deploy those 2 building blocks, as well as other additional AWS resources and services, is dictated by the Use Case.

This writer argues that there is an invisible ground on which these 2 building blocks are arranged, which actually dictates the HA design pattern: what gets built, when, where, and how. Why a particular HA design pattern is adopted must be dictated by the Return on Investment (ROI), which underlies the Use Case for which the HA design pattern is being considered.

That Use Case ROI cannot be allowed to be invisible to the HA architects, least their geek passions run hog wild and they over build a luxurious behemoth. Only throw as much HA stuff at the Use Case as the ROI limits, and never more. HA is really expensive to analyze, design, build, deploy, operate, trouble-shoot, and business disaster recover. And that good news only applies when the HA solution is not being subjected to a DDoS attack.

No worries, its mostly all good; not all good, just mostly good. Joking aside, as will be shown, AWS provides numerous other resources and services that significantly improve the quality of life with HA architecture. As the old(est) guy in the room, I remember in the early 1990s rolling by hand (and pushing out to physical hosts deployed around the planet) all of the HA configurations that can now be accomplished in moments by using the AWS Management Console. Not that you want to use that tool to manage HA solutions given the AWS CloudFormation service. But it needs to be acknowledged just how much easier HA is in 2019. Anyway, the writer digresses. Back to the main event.

In HA architectures the stuff gets complicated quickly, so HA is where the IT herd gets thinned quickly down to a small minority. HA architecture is sophisticated and demands a top-shelf development and operations culture, i.e., daily the culture functions in Information Management Maturity (IMM) levels 4 or 5. A culture at IMM level 3 can evolve to manage HA architecture solutions, but cultures at IMM levels 1 and 2 are too primitive, are unable, to function in the complex HA space/time. So levels 1 and 2 cultures, fallback, please – the universe invented HA SMEs, so farm-out the HA Use Case to them.

AWS HA Services

AWS defines availability and high-availability as: 'Availability specifically refers to the amount of time your system is in a functioning condition ... 100% minus your system's downtime. High Availability (or HA) is about ensuring that your application's downtime is minimized as much as possible without the need for human intervention. It views availability not as a series of replicated physical components, but rather as a set of system-wide, shared resources that cooperate to guarantee essential services.'

A small number of highly effective AWS services provide support for high availability:

- Auto Scaling;
- Elastic Load Balancing;
- CloudWatch;
- Amazon Route 53.

Auto Scaling

When you start an EC2 instance, you are billed for 1 full hour of running time. For certain instance types, AWS has a billing model based on paying per second, along with pay per hour.

Auto Scaling is a service that enables you to scale EC2 capacity horizontally, based on the known conditions that you set.

With Auto Scaling, you ***use events (known conditions) to provision EC2 instances on demand when needed and released when no longer needed.***

Best practice - scale out quickly, scale in slowly.

Principle - unless the system/application is designed and built to scale horizontally, according to known conditions,

Auto Scaling is not usable by that system/application.

Auto Scaling integrates seamlessly with Elastic Load Balancing (ELB) to horizontally scale the EC2 instance behind the load balancer.

The default maximum EC2 instances that can be launched in 1 Region, by 1 AWS Account, is 20.

Resource limits can be raised, as their defaults are intended to limit race conditions that cause unintended high billing charges.

Best practice – when there is a requirement to store session state information and Auto Scaling is used, store the session state information in DynamoDB.

Auto Scaling Benefits

The benefits of Auto Scaling:

- Dynamic horizontal scaling of a system/application;
- 'Best user experiences' rules/logic-based scaling;
- Health Check and fleet management; configure health checks; maintains desired EC2 instance 'fleet' capacity;

Auto Scaling can be used with other services, such as:

- EC2 Container Service (ECS);
- Elastic Map Reducer (EMR) cluster;
- AppStream 2.0 instances;
- DynamoDB.

Auto Scaling Group

Auto Scaling has components that you configure. ***Auto Scaling requires an Auto Scaling Group,*** where you ***define the logic that governs when/how EC2 instances will be launched as well as terminated*** with a given group/collection.

An Auto Scaling Group can span multiple AZs in a Region. An Auto Scaling Group cannot span Regions, it can only be a part of 1 Region.

In turn, ***the Auto Scaling Group requires a:***

1. ***Launch Configuration and;***
2. ***An optional Scaling Policy.***

The Auto Scaling Group is a collection of EC2 instances managed by Auto Scaling.

The Auto Scaling Group must have a:

1. Name;
2. Minimum number of EC2 instances that can be in the group;
3. Maximum number of EC2 instances that can be in the group.

An Auto Scaling Group can use either On-Demand (the default) or Spot Instances but not both.

To manage Spot Instance, you must specify a maximum bid price in the Launch Configuration. To change the bid price, you must create a new Launch Configuration and associate it with the group.

An instance added to an Auto Scaling Group should be in a running state. The added instance will be automatically registered with the ELB attached to the group.

Best practice - use a stateless EC2 instance type that can be spun up quickly can be healthy quickly and able to accept traffic quickly within, can more gracefully exit from, an Auto Scaling Group.

A classic use case: Auto Scaling Group can be used to roll-out a patch/upgrade at scale, easily.

Optionally, you can specify desired capacity (the # of instances that the group must have running at all times). The default desired capacity is the minimum number of EC2 instances specified for the group.

How to Create an Auto Scaling Group

You can access Amazon EC2 Auto Scaling by signing into the AWS Management Console.

Choose EC2 from the console home page and then choose Auto Scaling Groups from the navigation pane.

You can also access Amazon EC2 Auto Scaling using the

Amazon EC2 Auto Scaling API, which is a Query API.

These requests are HTTP or HTTPS requests that use the HTTP verbs GET or POST and a Query parameter named Action.

If you prefer, there are AWS SDKs, sample code, tutorials and other resources for software developers. If you prefer, the AWS Command Line Interface (CLI), or the AWS Tools for Windows PowerShell.

Launch Configuration

The Launch Configuration is a template used to create new EC2 instances and which contains these details:

1. Configuration name;
2. Amazon Machine Image (AMI);
3. EC2 instance type;
4. Security Group (of the VPC in which the Auto Scaling Group launches the EC2 instances. The security group for your load balancer must allow it to communicate with registered targets on both the listener port and the health check port.);
5. Instance Key Pair;
6. Identity and Access Management (IAM) instance profile;
7. ***UserData***, storage attachment, etc.

Once you create a Launch Configuration and associate it with an Auto Scaling Group ***you cannot edit the Launch Configuration.*** If the launch configuration needs to be changed, a new launch configuration must be created, and that Auto Scaling Group must be updated with the new launch configuration.

It is due to the Security Group that an Auto Scaling Group is limited to 1 VPC and in turn to 1 Region, as well as be able to exist in multiple Availability Zones (AZs) as may be needed.

An Auto Scaling Group can have 1 and only 1 Launch Configuration, at a given point in time.

When the Auto Scaling Group is associated with a new launch configuration, each new EC2 instance references the new launch configuration.

Best practice - by changing the Auto Scaling Group's Launch Configuration, the new EC2 instances launched in the group can be made to vertically scale up or down.

When a Launch Configuration is disassociated from an Auto Scaling Group, there is no impact on the running EC2 instances.

A Launch Configuration can be associated with 1:N Auto Scaling Groups.

The default maximum of Launch Configurations per Region is 100.

Auto Scaling Health Check

To determine if a given EC2 instance is or is not running, at periodic points in time a health check is taken of EC2 instances running within a Auto Scaling Group.

When Auto Scaling discovers an unhealthy EC2 instance, it terminates that instance and launches a new instance. When an unhealthy instance is being replaced, the Auto Scaling Group does not wait for the cooldown period to complete the scaling action.

Auto Scaling Cooldown Period

There is the potential that scaling in and scaling out activities can overlap. The cooldown period is a configurable feature of the Auto Scaling Group. The purpose of the cooldown period is to help ensure that the Auto Scaling Group does not launch or terminate additional EC2 instances before the previous scaling activity takes effect.

The Auto Scaling Group waits for the cooldown period to elapse before resuming scaling activities.

Lastly, the cooldown period is not supported for scheduled scaling policies.

Attaching an EC2 Instance to an Auto Scaling Group

The following criteria must be satisfied when attaching an EC2 instance to an Auto Scaling Group:

1. The EC2 instance is not a member of another Auto Scaling Group;
2. The AMI used to launch the EC2 instance must exist, and
3. The EC2 instance must be in the running state.

Auto Scaling Group Scaling Policy

An auto scaling group scaling policy is a set of CloudWatch metric thresholds that dictate when to add or remove EC2 instances form the autoscaling group.

Maintain Current Instance Levels scaling

- Configure Auto Scaling to maintain a minimum count of EC2 instances running at all times.
- This is the default Auto Scaling Policy/plan.
- Best use case: steady state workloads that need a specific count of running EC2 instances.

Manual scaling

- You specify the change in the maximum, minimum, or desired capacity to the Auto Scaling Group.
- Auto Scaling manages the process of launching and terminating the EC2 instances in that Auto Scaling Group that are needed to maintain the desired capacity.
- Best use case: to handle an infrequent but planned, event.

Scheduled scaling

- A pre-know and a predictable, when you will need to increase or decrease EC2 instances in an Auto Scaling Group
- A function of recurring time, date and place.

Best use cases: end of week, end of month, end of quarter, end of year, automated test workloads.

3 Ways to Scale Dynamically

Simple scaling - Increase or decrease the current capacity of the group based on a single scaling adjustment.

Step scaling - Increase or decrease the current capacity of the group based on a set of scaling adjustments, known as step adjustments, that vary based on the size of the alarm breach.

Target tracking scaling - Increase or decrease the current capacity of the group based on a target value for a specific metric. This is similar to the way a thermostat can be used to maintain the temperature.

Simple and Step Scaling

With simple and step scaling policies, you:

1. choose scaling metrics (e.g., CPU utilization; disk read, disk write, network in, network out, etc.);
2. choose threshold values for the CloudWatch alarms that trigger the scaling process, as well as
3. define how the Auto Scaling group is to be scaled when a threshold is in breach for a specified number of evaluation periods.

A Simple Policy requires that you create 2 policies:

- 1 policy for scaling out, or increasing the group size;
- 1 policy for scaling in, or decreasing the group size;

A Step Policy allows you to scale in/out per exact capacity, or by count of instances, or by percentage change in capacity.

Best practice - use step scaling policies instead of simple scaling policies, even if you have a single scaling adjustment.

Target Tracking Scaling

With a target tracking scaling policy, you select a scaling metric and set a target value.

Amazon EC2 Auto Scaling creates and manages the CloudWatch alarms that trigger the scaling policy and calculates the scaling adjustment based on the metric and the target value.

Use the Amazon CloudWatch Logs Agent Installer to install the Agent on the EC2 instance and to configure that Agent.

The CloudWatch alarm references the Scaling Policy by ***Amazon Resource Name (ARN).***

The scaling policy adds or removes capacity as required to keep the metric at, or close to, the specified target value.

In addition to keeping the metric close to the target value, a target tracking scaling policy also adjusts to the changes in the metric due to a changing load pattern.

Best practice - If your scaling metric is a utilization metric that increases or decreases proportionally to the number of instances in the Auto Scaling group, use a target tracking scaling policy.

Dynamic Scaling and Session State

When EC2 instances are dynamically scaled up and down, in and out, it is critically important to maintain the state information of the user session.

If session information is maintained in the EC2 instance and that instance fails, you lose that information.

If session information is maintained in the EC2 instance and even 1 user session is connected to the instance then the instance cannot be taken down.

Best practice - maintain user session information in DynamoDB, so that EC2 instances (targets) can scale up and down, in and or, dynamically.

Auto Scaling – EC2 Termination Policy

To ensure that the Auto Scaling works smoothly, gracefully, you have to decide exactly how each EC2 instance in the Auto Scaling Group will be shut-down/terminated. A termination policy determines the order in which the instances will be terminated.

When an EC2 instance is terminated it is automatically deregistered from the ELB (if integrated with Auto Scaling) and waits for a grace period, during which any open connections to that instance will be drained. When the grace period expires, the instance is terminated.

If the EC2 Termination Policy of the auto scaling group is suspended, the ReplaceUnhealthy and the ScheduledActions are affected.

Best practice - terminate an instance that is close to billing an hour.

Auto Scaling Group Lifecycle Hooks

When an EC2 instance joins an Auto Scaling Group, the lifecycle of an EC2 instance becomes more complicated than usual. Based on your BPM EC2 instances in an auto scaling group may require custom action when they are launched or terminated by the Auto Scaling Group. Each Auto Scaling Group can have multiple, but a limited number of, lifecycle hooks.

For example, a custom action can 'pause' an instance for a specific period of time (1 hour by default) or until you decide to proceed. While an instance is paused, it cannot complete its startup sequence. While an instance is paused, you can configure the instance as needed, i.e., install and configure software.

An EC2 instance in an auto scaling group that is waiting to completion of a lifecycle hook action is in a reported as being in a Pending:Wait state. After the custom action completes, the instance enters the Pending:Proceed state. When the startup sequence completes entirely, the instance enters the InService state.

Auto Scaling integration with ELB

When Auto Scaling is integrated with ELB, these two things happen:

1. When an EC2 instance is launched, it is automatically registered with ELB.
2. When an EC2 instance is terminated it is automatically deregistered from the ELB .

Auto Scaling is capable of doing Elastic Load Balancer (ELB) health checks as well (e.g., hardware failure; system performance degradation, etc.).

When integrated with ELB, Auto Scaling balances the EC2 instances behind the ELB, even across multiple AZs (as when the ELB runs across multiple AZs)

Auto Scaling Best Practices

Principle: it is important to know when Auto Scaling is changing the count of EC2 instances.

Best practice - configure Amazon Simple Notification Service (SNS) to deliver a notification (as an HTTP or HTTPS POST, an email message, or as a message posted on an Amazon Simple Queue Service (SQS) queue) whenever Auto Scaling changes the count of EC2 instances.

Best practice - avoid bursting (starting and stopping EC2 instances too quickly) in ways which degrade ROI.

Best practice - before adding it to an Auto Scaling Group, carefully consider if a bootstrapped, if a stateful, EC2 instance is a 'good fit with,' ought to be launched from, an Auto Scaling. Probably not!

Best practice - schedule a cool down period during which scaling activities in the Auto Scaling Group are suspended. The period defines how long to wait before starting or stopping a new instance.

Best practice – when an application is scaling up and down multiple times within an hour this can be due to the scale down threshold being set too low. Raise the scale down threshold and see if that helps optimize costs.

Elastic Load Balancing (ELB)

ELB is a service that provides a high-availability virtual load balancer. An ELB intercepts network traffic from clients (that make requests) and services (that respond to requests). The ***ELB automatically distributes incoming network traffic*** across applications, microservices and containers, hosted ***across a group of EC2 instances, in 1:N AZs, in 1 Region.*** An ELB cannot be used to distribute network traffic across Regions.

For each request that a host client makes through a load balancer, the load balancer maintains 2 connections:

- 1 connection with the host client that made the request and
- 1 connection with the EC2 instance behind the ELB that is handling the request.

ELB in Amazon VPC only supports IPv4 IP addresses.

ELB in EC2-Classic supports both IPv4 and IPv6 IP addresses.

Principle – only if a system/application is designed and built to operate with a load balancer, can ELB be of benefit to that particular system/application.

ELB ***uses Perfect Forward Secrecy to offer SSL/TLS cipher suites.***

You create an ELB by using the Amazon Management Console, as well as by using the AWS Command Line Interface (CLI).

ELB and the OSI Model

ELB supports routing & load balancing of these traffic to EC2 instances:

- HTTP
- HTTPS
- TCP
- SSL

The Application Layer #7 uses the HTTP and HTTPS protocols, from the client application on the host to the load balancer and from the load balancer to back-end EC2 instances.

The Transport Layer #4 uses the TCP connection between the client application on the host and the back-end EC2 instance through the load balancer.

The Transport Layer #4 is the lowest layer in the OSI model that the ELB can configure.

The SSL protocol is implemented as a transparent wrapper around the HTTP protocol and is used to encrypt data transmitted over the Internet. In terms of the OSI model encryption belongs in the Presentation Layer #6, however, SSL implements encryption in Session Layer #5.

Advantages of ELB

- Works with VPC to securely route traffic internally between application tiers.
- Configure Security Groups for ELB that control incoming and outgoing network traffic to the instances.
- Supports integrated certificate management, SSL decryption and port forwarding.
- Is able to terminate network traffic at the ELB (to avoid having to run CPU-intensive decryption on EC2 instances).
- Helps mitigate distributed denial-of-service (DDoS) attacks. A DDoS is a large-scale DoS attack where the perpetrator uses more than one unique IP address typically on different networks.
- Provides lots of predefined security policies.
- Provides a stable, single, Canonical Name (CNAME) record entry point for Domain Name System (DNS) configuration;
- Best practice - always reference the ELB by its DNS name, never by its IP address.
- ELB:
- Can be integrated with Route 53 for DNS failover;
- Supports both Internet-facing and internal application-facing load balancers;
- Allows you to expose only Internet-facing public IP addresses of EC2 instances;
- Supports health checks of EC2 instances, to ensure that network traffic is not routed to unhealthy or failing EC2 instances;
- Can automatically scales in and out, horizontally, based on resource utilization metrics collected by CloudWatch;
- Highly available (HA). Internally and transparent

to you, AWS deploys multiple load balancers in a separate ELB VPC, that spans multiple AZ;

- Can support HA systems/application deployed across multiple AZs;
- Seamlessly integrates with Auto Scaling to scale in and out the EC2 instances behind the ELB;
- Provides native support for microservices and container-based applications. Instances can be registered with multiple ports, allowing requests to be routed to multiple containers on the same instance;
- uses dynamic port mapping as its means to automatically register EC2 instances.

ELB Access Logs

ELB access logs are used to help analyze network traffic patterns, as well as to trouble-shoot network traffic issues.

By default, ELB access logs are not enabled. When you ***enable ELB access logging*** you ***choose which S3 bucket the logs will be placed.***

It is important to know that ***by default the ELB's access logs contain only the IP address of the load balancer itself.*** The ELB access logs ***can contain the time a request is received, its client IP address, latencies, request paths, and server responses.***

In addition, ***the back-end server access logs contain only the protocol used between the server and the load balancer.*** However, depending on the use case, the ELB can be configured to manipulate the header fields of the HTTP requests and HTTP responses that it intercepts, and by so doing capture critically important information about those requests and responses.

HTTP requests and HTTP responses use header fields to send information about the HTTP messages. The HTTP message header fields are colon-separated name-value pairs that are separated by a carriage return (CR) and a line feed (LF). A standard set of HTTP header fields is defined in RFC 2616, Message Headers, included in that set are the following header fields:

X-Forwarded-For - The X-Forwarded-For request header helps you identify the IP address of a client when you use an HTTP or HTTPS load balancer. Because load balancers intercept traffic between clients and servers, your server access logs contain only the IP address of the load balancer. To see the IP address of the client, use the X-Forwarded-For request header. Elastic Load Balancing stores the IP address of the client in the X-Forwarded-For request header and passes the header to your server.

X-Forwarded-Proto - The X-Forwarded-Proto request header is used to identify the protocol (HTTP or HTTPS) that a client used to connect to your load balancer. ELB stores that information in the header and passes the header along to your server.

X-Forwarded-Port - The X-Forwarded-Port request header is used to identify the destination port that the client used to connect to the load balancer.

ELB High Availability

Internally and transparent to you, AWS deploys multiple load balancers in a separate ELB VPC, that spans multiple AZs. When a load balancer is a single point of failure and it fails, the system/application behind it goes off-line until the problem is repaired. When network traffic increases/decreases and the load balancer needs to scale horizontally/vertically, how is that managed?

ELB solves these problems. ***ELB is always deployed across multiple AZs. You can register 1:N Auto Scaling Groups with the same ELB.*** You do not have to do any high-availability (HA) configuration or management of the ELB.

6 Types of ELB Load Balancers

AWS supports these types of load balancers:

1. Internet-Facing;
2. Internal;

3. HTTPS;
4. Network;
5. Application;
6. Classic.

Internet-Facing Load Balancer

An Internet-Facing Load Balancer takes requests from hosts located in the Internet and distributes these requests to back-end EC2 instances that are 'registered' with the ELB. ***Internet facing ELBs are best provisioned within public subnets.***

When configured, the load balancer is given a public DNS name, that hosts in the Internet use to send requests to the system/application back-end located behind the ELB.

The function of the DNS servers is to resolve that public DNS name to the IP address of the ELB virtual load balancer.

Also called an external load balancer.

You need to create the Internet-facing load balancer in a public subnet within the VPC.

Internal Load Balancer

In multi-tier systems/applications is often beneficial to load balance between the tiers of the system/application.

An Internal Load Balancer routes traffic to EC2 instances running in the private subnets of a VPC.

You need to create the Internal load balancer in a private subnet within the VPC.

HTTPS Load Balancer

The HTTPS Load Balancer uses the SSL/Transport Layer Security (TLS) protocol for encrypted connections (aka, SSL offload).

Enables traffic encryption between the ELB and the hosts in the Internet that initiate HTTPS sessions, as well as for connections between the ELB and the backend system/application.

ELB provides security policies that have predefined SSL negotiation configurations to use to negotiate connections between hosts in the Internet and the load balancer.

To use SSL, you must install an SSL certificate on the load balancer, which it uses to terminate the connection and then decrypt requests from hosts in the Internet, before sending these requests to the back-end EC2 instances.

Optionally, you can choose to enable authentication on the back-end instances.

Server Name Indication (SNI) is not supported by ELB.

Therefore, if you deploy multiple websites on a fleet of EC2 instances behind the ELB with 1 single SSL certificate you need to add a Subject Alternative Name (SAN) to the certificate for each EC2 instance (to avoid site users seeing a warning message when the site is accessed).

Network Load Balancer

The Network Load Balancer (NLB) or the TCP load balancer, acts in the Transport Layer #4 of the OSI model. The NLB support both TCP and SSL, distributing requests across the registered targets in its AZ only.

This is a connection-based load balancing model. The client connection is always bound to a server connection, which results in every request being bound to an EC2 back-end instance. Can handle requests across EC2 instances, containers and IP addresses based on IP data.

As they are received, the NLB handles all request packets and forwards them to the back-end. The NLB does not examine a packet, does not change a packet. The NLB makes no change to the request header.

The back-end EC2 instance can see the client-side source IP address. There is no X-Forwarded-For headers, Proxy Protocol prepends, source or destination IP address, or ports to request.

Before You Can Create an NLB

- Decide which Availability Zones you will use for your EC2 instances.
- Configure your virtual private cloud (VPC) with at

least one public subnet in each of these Availability Zones.

- These public subnets are used to configure the load balancer.
- You can launch your EC2 instances in other subnets of these Availability Zones instead.
- Launch at least one EC2 instance in each Availability Zone.
- Ensure that the Security Groups for these instances allow TCP access from clients on the listener port and health check port within your VPC.

How to Create an NLB

- Open the Amazon EC2 Console.
- On the navigation bar, choose a Region for your load balancer.
- Be sure to select the same Region that you used for your EC2 instances.
- Step 1: Select a Load Balancer Type;
- Step 2: Configure Your Load Balancer and Listener;
- Step 3: Configure a Security Group for Your Load Balancer;
- Step 4: Configure Your Target Group;
- Step 5: Register Targets with Your Target Group;
- Step 6: Create and Test Your Load Balancer.

Application Load Balancer

The Application Load Balancer (ALB) works on the Application Layer #7 of the OSI model ***and supports HTTP and HTTPS (HTTP/2), as well as WebSockets protocol***. With ALB you can register an EC2 instance which has different ports multiple times and can support applications that run within containers.

When a packet arrives at the ALB, it's request header is examined and then decides what to do next. Behind the ALB, connections are pooled in a back-end server and when a request arrives at the ALB, it forwards them using connection pooling.

The request header can be modified by the ALB, a header containing the X-Forwarded-For header containing the client IP address (when you use an HTTP or HTTP load balancer).

Content-based routing – if you application has multiple servers – the ALB can route to a specific server per the content of the request.

Host-based routing – you route a client request based on the Host field of the HTTP header.

Path-based routing – you route a client request based on the URL path of the HTTP header.

- A number of decisions have to be made before you create an ALB:
- Decide which two Availability Zones you will use for your EC2 instances.
- Configure your virtual private cloud (VPC) with at least one public subnet in each of these Availability Zones.
- These public subnets are used to configure the load balancer.
- You can launch your EC2 instances in other subnets of these Availability Zones instead.
- Launch at least one EC2 instance in each Availability Zone.
- Be sure to install a web server, such as Apache or Internet Information Services (IIS), on each EC2 instance.
- A web page hosted by that web server can be used to support the health check process of the EC2 instance.
- Ensure that the Security Groups for these EC2 instances allow HTTP access on port 80.

- A number of decisions have to be made before you create an ALB:
- Decide which two Availability Zones you will use for your EC2 instances.
- Configure your virtual private cloud (VPC) with at least one public subnet in each of these Availability Zones.
- These public subnets are used to configure the load balancer.
- You can launch your EC2 instances in other subnets of these Availability Zones instead.
- Launch at least one EC2 instance in each Availability Zone.
- Be sure to install a web server, such as Apache or Internet Information Services (IIS), on each EC2 instance.
- A web page hosted by that web server can be used to support the health check process of the EC2 instance.
- Ensure that the Security Groups for these EC2 instances allow HTTP access on port 80.

How to Create an ALB

Open the Amazon EC2 Console. On the navigation bar, choose a Region for your load balancer. Be sure to select the same Region that you used for your EC2 instances.

- Step 1: Select a Load Balancer Type;
- Step 2: Configure Your Load Balancer and Listener;
- Step 3: Configure a Security Group for Your Load Balancer;
- Step 4: Configure Your Target Group;
- Step 5: Register Targets with Your Target Group;
- Step 6: Create and Test Your Load Balancer.

AWS Classic Load Balancer

The AWS Classic Load Balancer supports the classic EC2

instances.

It supports both NLB and ALB and therefore operates at layers #4 and #7 of the OSI model.

A Classic LB is always Internet-facing load balancers.

You can host only 1 back-end application behind the Classic LB.

To host multiple application, you have to use DNS to resolve the back-end applications.

Preparing the VPC and EC2s for a Classic LB

Prepare Subnets for Your Load Balancer

- To ensure that CLB can scale properly, verify that each subnet used by the CLB has a CIDR block with at least a /27 bitmask (for example, 10.0.0.0/27) and has at least 8 free IP addresses. CLB uses these IP addresses to establish connections with the EC2 instances.
- Create a subnet in each Availability Zone where you want to launch instances. Depending on your application, you can launch your instances in public subnets, private subnets, or a combination of public and private subnets.
- When you create a load balancer, you must add one or more public subnets to the load balancer.
- If your EC2 instances are in private subnets, create public subnets in the same Availability Zones as the private subnets with your instances;
- You will add these public subnets to the load balancer.

Prepare Security Groups

- You must ensure that the load balancer can communicate with your EC2 instances on both the listener port and the health check port.

ClassicLink

ClassicLink enables your EC2-Classic instances to communicate with VPC instances using private IP addresses, provided that the VPC security groups allow it.

If you plan to register linked EC2-Classic instances with your load balancer, you must enable ClassicLink for your VPC and then create your load balancer in the ClassicLink-enabled VPC.

Before You Can Create a Classic LB

- Complete the preparation of the VPC and EC2 instances for the Classic LB.
- Launch the EC2 instances that you plan to register with your load balancer.
- Ensure that the Security Groups for these instances allow HTTP access on port 80.
- Install a web server, such as Apache or IIS, on each instance, enter its DNS name into the address field of an Internet-connected web browser and verify that the browser displays the default page of the server.

How to Create a Classic LB

- Open the Amazon EC2 Console.
- On the navigation bar, choose a Region for your load balancer.
- Be sure to select the same Region that you used for your EC2 instances.
- Step 1: Select a Load Balancer Type;
- Step 2: Define the Load Balancer;
- Step 3: Assign Security Groups to the Load Balancer in a VPC;
- Step 4: Configure Health Checks for Your EC2 Instances;
- Step 5: Register EC2 Instances with Your Load Balancer;
- Step 6: Tag Your Load Balancer (Optional);
- Step 7: Create and Verify Your Load Balancer.

ELB Target Groups and Target

A Target Group is a logical grouping of targets behind a load balancer. A target can be an EC2 instance, a microservice, or a container-based application for an ALB, or can be an IP address for an NLB.

EC2 instances can be registered with the same target group using multiple ports. A single target can be registered with multiple target groups.

The target group is a Region construct. The ELB target group can also be associated with the Auto Scaling Group. Target Groups can exist independently from the load balancer. You can keep adding resources to a target group.

Best practice - when a combination of on-demand and spot instances are deployed behind an ELB, create two separate Auto Scaling Groups: one group of the on-demand instances and another group for the spot instances. Next, both of the auto scaling groups are registered with the same ELB.

ELB Listeners

The ELB intercepts network traffic between host interfaces in front of the ELB and the services running behind the ELB.

Each EC2 instance (target) behind an ELB has a listener port and a health port.

An ELB can be configured to do health checks using inbound TCP port 80. However, the Security Group in which the EC2 instance is launched needs to allow that specific inbound traffic. If the ELB is so configured, but the Security Group does not allow that inbound traffic (i.e., it blocks that traffic), all instances will appear to the ELB as 'OutOfService.'

Each load balancer has 1:N listeners configured for HTTP on port 80. A listener is a process that checks for connection requests.

Every listener is configured with a protocol and a port # for use by a front-end connection (with a host in the Internet, with a client application) and a protocol and a port # for use by a back-end connection (to EC2 instances behind the load balancer).

Best practice - for HTTP and HTTPS listeners ***enable the keep-alive option in the kernel settings of the EC2 instances.*** When enabled keep-alive allows the load balancer to reuse connection to the back-end EC2 instance, thereby reducing its CPU utilization.

Best practice - make sure that the value assigned to the keep-alive time period is > the idle connection timeout configured on the ELB.

For both NLB and ALB listeners, the ports between 1 and 65535 are supported.

You can use WebSockets with HTTP, HTTPS and TCP listeners.

ALBs provide native support for HTTP/2 with HTTPS listeners.

Using HTTP/2, you can send up to 128 requests in parallel.

The ALB converts these to individual HTTP/1.1 requests and distributes them using a round-robin routing algorithm.

ELB Rules

An ELB Rule is a logical link between a listener and target group and consists of a condition and an action. Rules are used to forward a request to a specific target group.

When you create a listener, by default it has a rule, which is forward, which forwards the request to the target group, has no conditions attached to it and has the lowest priority. A listener has 1:N rules.

When a request meets the conditions of the rule, the associated action is taken, the request is forwarded to the target.

There are ***2 types of rule conditions***:

1. ***Host***;
2. ***Path***.

Each rule has a priority attached to it.

The rule with the highest priority is executed first, the one with the lowest priority is executed last.

When path-based routing is used, the rule must be specified in the path pattern format, which is case sensitive, can be up to 128 characters in length.

You can have up to 10 different sets of ELB rules, which means you can host up to 10 back-end application using ELB.

The Interplay of Rules and Targets

When a request is received by the ALB:

- The ALB checks the priority order from the listener rule to determine which rule to apply.
- Once it decides which rule to apply, the ALB selects a target from the target group and applies the action of the rule using a round-robin algorithm.

The routing is performed independently of each target group and it doesn't matter if the target is registered with multiple target groups.

When a request is received by the NLB:

- The NLB selects a target from the target group for the default rule, using a flow hash algorithm, based on the protocol, source IP address, source port, destination IP address and destination port.

When a request is received, the Classic LB:

- Selects the least outstanding request's routing algorithm for HTTP and HTTPS listeners and
- Selects a registered instance using the round-robin routing algorithm for TCP listeners.

Configuring ELBs

The configuration of the ELB can be changed by using the Amazon Management Console, as well as the AWS Command Line Interface (CLI).

Many aspects of ELB behavior can be configured:

- Idle Connection Timeout;
- Cross-Zone Load Balancing;
- Connection Draining;
- Proxy Protocol;

- Sticky Sessions;
- Health Checks;

Idle Connection Timeout

For each of the 2 connections that the ELB makes per client application request, the ELB manages an idle timeout. An idle timeout is triggered when no data is sent over the connection for a specified period of time called the idle timeout period. After the idle timeout period elapses after no data having been sent the ELB closes the connection.

If an HTTP request does not complete within the idle timeout period, the ELB closes the connection, even if data is being transmitted. By default, for both connections, the Idle Connection Timeout is set to 60 seconds.

Best practice - to long running activities (e.g. file uploads) through the ELB, the Idle Connection Timeout needs to be increased.

Cross-Zone Load Balancing

When the EC2 instances behind the ELB are deployed across multiple AZs, Cross-Zone Load Balancing is used to ensure that request traffic is routed evenly across all back-end EC2 instances.

Cross-zone happens across the targets and not at the AZ level.

Cross-Zone load balancing can:

- Dampen the need to deploy the same # of EC2 instances in every AZ.
- Improve the system/application's ability to handle failure of 1:N EC2 instances.

When a client cache's DNS lookups, requests incoming to the ELB can favor 1 AZ over another, thereby creating an imbalance. Cross-zone can reduce the impact of that imbalance created by the clients.

There is no additional bandwidth charge for cross-zone traffic, so there is no charge for data transfers across multiple

AZs.

Cross-zone is useful with ALB across multiple AZs.

Best practice - for higher fault tolerance, maintain the same # of EC2 instances in every AZ.

Best practice – given a minimum required 4 EC2 instances and an ELB, for higher fault tolerance and high availability, maintain 2 EC2 instance in 3 AZs. If you loose an AZ, the minimum required 4 instances are running.

Connection Draining

Connection Draining ensures that the load balancer stops sending requests to EC2 instances that are deregistering or that are unhealthy, while keeping the existing front-end connection with the client open and thereby completing in-flight requests made to those EC2 instances.

Specify a maximum time period that the load balancer keeps connections alive before reporting the instance as deregistered.

The maximum time period ranges between 1-3,600 seconds. The default is 300 seconds.

When the maximum time period limit is reached the load-balancer closes connections to the deregistering instance.

If the EC2 instance is part of an Auto Scaling Group and connection draining is enable on the ELB, and a scale-in event occurs, the event will wait for inflight requests to complete for 300 seconds before terminating an instance.

Proxy Protocol

When the ELB load balancer uses either TCP or SSL for both the front-end and the back-end connections, the load balancers forwards to the request header as is to the back-end EC2 instance.

If you enable Proxy Protocol, a human-readable header is added to the request header, with connection information such as:

- Source IP address;

- Destination IP address and
- Port #s.

The modified request header is then sent to the back-end EC2 instance.

Best practice - when the ELB is itself behind a Proxy Server which modifies the request header information content, give careful consideration before enabling Proxy Protocol.

Sticky Sessions

By default, the ELB route requests to the EC2 instance with the smallest load.

Sticky Sessions enable the ELB to bind a client application session (known as session affinity) to a specific back-end EC2 instance.

An advantage of this is that the EC2 instance can cache the user data locally for better performance.

Ensures that all requests sent from a client application are routed to the same EC2 instance.

ELB creates a session cookie called AWSELB that maps the client application session to the EC2 instance.

Best practice - if your system/application uses a session cookie, configure ELB such that the AWSELB session cookie follows the duration specified by application's session cookie.

ELB Health Checks

Each EC2 instance (target) behind an ELB has a listener port and a health port. ELB supports periodic Health Checks that test the status of every back-end target or target group registered with the ELB:

- The status of a healthy EC2 instance is ***InService***.
- The status of an unhealthy EC2 instance is ***OutOfService***

If an EC2 instance registered with the ELB fails a health-check, the ELB marks the instance as OutOfService, and stops sending new requests to that instance.

For each ELB health check, we define:

- the duration of time between health check events, as well as the amount of time to wait for a health check response from an EC2 instance.
- the threshold for the # of consecutive health check failures before an EC2 instance is marked as unhealthy.
- a list of successful response codes used by the targets.

Health Check helps redirect traffic away from unhealthy/ failed targets/target groups.

ALB supports HTTP and HTTPS health checks, while the NLB supports TCP health checks.

The ELB TCP health check is a Ping (a network layer ICMP connection attempt). The ELB TCP health check only detects if the EC2 instance is healthy. The TCP protocol cannot detect is the web service is up and running.

The ELB HTTP/HTTPS health check is a periodic web page GET request. Note, if that web page is not provisioned on the target EC2 instance, the health check will fail.

It is not possible for the ELB to use the UDP protocol to perform health checks.

ELB Using Multiple AZs

ELB uses multiple AZs, so if 1 AZ goes off-line, there is no impact to the ELB and traffic will be routed via a load balancer in another AZ.

The DNS will route the traffic via a different AZ.

If you system/application is deployed only into 1 AZ and it uses ELB and that 1 AZ goes off-line then your system/application fails but not ELB.

Best practice - use multiple Availability Zones (AZs) when building a system/application that uses ELB and Auto Scaling.

Changing the ELB IP Address

1 CNAME is beneficial when running multiple services, like HTTP/HTTPs, TCP and SSL, on different ports from a single IP

address. Each record has a type (name & #), an expiration time (time to live), a class and type-specific data. CNAME records must always point to another domain name, never directly to an IP address (which if an IPv4 IP Address is a type A resource record).

When a DNS resolver encounters a CNAME record while looking for a regular resource record, it will restart the query using the canonical name instead of the original name. If the resolver is specifically told to look for CNAME records, the canonical name (right-hand side) is returned, rather than restarting the query. The canonical name that a CNAME record points to can be anywhere in the DNS, whether local or on a remote server in a different DNS zone.

If the IP address of the ELB ever changes, then only 1 record is changed in 1 place within the network: in the DNS A record of the ELB.

ELB Security Techniques

An ELB is typically configured to allow inbound access on port 443 (SSL). However, depending on the use case, that may not be sufficient.

Use case – a host interface (which has a unique IP address) is sending malicious requests to the web application located behind the ELB.

Only network ACLs let you provision a deny rule. To deny all traffic from a host interface, add a rule to the subnet Network ACL where the ELB resides.

ELB Best Practices

Best practice – there is the requirement to be able to modify the configuration of the ELB, and often only on a one-time-basis (not on-going). To provide access to the ELB create an IAM Role and attach a policy that allows modification access/privileges.

Amazon Route 53

Amazon Route 53 is a fully managed pay-as-you-go ***Region***

independent, Tier 0 DNS service that has a 100% availability service-level agreement. AWS manages the infrastructure, it's *fault tolerance, high availability*, and *auto-scaling, queuing and polling*, operating system upgrades, deployments, etc.. Route 53 is ***capable of providing DNS services to a VPC that spans multiple Regions and can distribute workloads across Regions.***

The service is called Route 53 because DNS servers respond to queries on the User Datagram Protocol—or UDP—port 53. Route 53 is one of our only services that has a 100% availability service-level agreement.

The Route 53 service ***preforms these tasks***:

Domain name registration

- Route 53 is automatically configures as the DNS for the domain and a hosted zone is created for the domain. You add resource records to its zone file to define how Route 53 responds to DNS queries.
- A private hosted zone is used to route traffic for a domain within a VPC.
- A public hosted zone is used to route traffic on the Internet for a domain and its subdomain(s).

DNS Service

- Maps domain names to IP addresses; complies with DNS standards; uses User Datagram Protocol (UDP) and its responses are limited to 512 bytes in size. You can transfer domain services to Route 53 without having to also use Route 53 to register the domain name.

Health Caching

- AWS automatically sends requests every 30 seconds to your applications to verify that they are reachable, available and working.

Amazon Route 53 does not charge for alias queries to CloudFront distributions, Elastic Beanstalk environments, ELB load balancers, or S3 buckets.

If there is a need to point a domain name at a VPC ELB in Route53, you need to configure an ALIAS record set for the ELB

that points to a type 'A' record.

If you are using Route 53 for a web site hosted in S3, the S3 bucket name must be the same as the domain name.

Route 53 Routing policy

After creating the resource records, you choose a routing policy that determines who Route 53 handles DNS queries.

The following types of routing policies are supported by Route 53:

Simple

- This is the default policy, used when a single resource instance is present in the domain.

Weighted

- Used when there are multiple resource instances that perform the same function present in the domain.
- Each resource record is assigned a relative value.

Latency-based

- Used to route traffic based on the lowest network latency for the end user.
- Can be created for EC2 instances, with or without an Elastic IP address, as well as for ELB load balancers.
- You must specify the name, type, and AWS Regions, when creating the policy.

Failover

- An active-passive failover, in which the surviving instance absorbs all of the traffic.

Geolocation

- Routes traffic based on the geolocation of the requesting client.
- Can be created by continent, by country, or by state in the USA.

If you do not set up a default resource record set, a 'no answer' response is returned for queries from IP addresses that cannot be mapped to geographic locations.

If resource record sets overlap geographic regions, priority goes to the smallest geographic region.

Route 53 Health Checks

Route 53 health checks can be used for any endpoint which can be accessed via the Internet. Hence, Route 53 is an ideal tool to use for monitoring those endpoints.

You configure a Route 53 health check that monitors an endpoint that you specify either by IP address or by domain name. At regular intervals, that you specify, Route 53 submits automated requests over the Internet to verify that the endpoint is reachable and functioning. This feature can be also be to monitory endpoints inside you on-premise system.

AWS APPLICATION INTEGRATION

The capacity of any application to be integrated is extremely limited. Rarely is an application designed or built to be integrated with any other application. Applications most often support an industry standard interface, e.g., JDBC,REST, but the presence of these APIs does not mean that the behaviors of the application, the information managed by the application, can be integrated with any other application.

The security contracts, the service contracts, as well as the data contracts, supported by an application are idiosyncratic, are not common expressions. For example, does the application's data contract support General Data Protection Regulation (GDPR) governance and compliance. Or given a security contract, is the identity of an end user established by an IdP that supports OpenID Connect (OIDC) or does the application require an Active Directory compatible SAML?

Application integration is complex with sizeable variations and incompatibilities and is therefore very challenging and are the reasons why most cannot be accused of being done well.

Big Balls of Mud

The goal of software engineering is to maximize cohesion.

An application might start off in life with a single purpose, with maximized cohesion, but inevitably over time the application is tortured to act in ways that it was never initially intended to. Instead of improving the 1 thing it did well, the application now attempts 9 different things each more or less to poor effect.

Given a typical application and any other typical application, their brittle integrations are most often tightly mingled shotgun affairs of calls and scheduled dependencies. The resulting mélange of application behaviors is called the Big Ball of Mud.

The one certainty about big balls of mud is that they can only scale vertically and only after great struggle and to limited effect. Big balls of mud had other balls of mud placed inside them, stuck onto them, and mostly in the unsightliness places and in the worst of times. Given any attempt to improve one ball of mud other balls of mud suffer.

Loose Coupling

Points of application integration are called couplings. The other goal of software engineering is to minimize coupling, also called loose coupling.

Service Oriented Architecture

Service Oriented architecture (SOA) and micro-services are nothing new, despite the new rebranding. Distributed processing of information has its inherent problems (which is, after all, why TCP/IP was invented way back when). Moreover, under the best of conditions, distributing information processing gives rise to inescapable hurdles, barriers, and traps.

A good SOA instance 'maximizes cohesion and minimizes coupling.' This means a good SOA instance does 1 thing very well, while exposing a stateless RESTful API. These features enable client services to 'build to the interface,' without concern for what goes on inside the little black box somewhere over there. Consequently, it is at the service, the data, and the security, contract interfaces where data architecture manifests (or is absent without leave).

Unfortunately, most SOA architectures lack a decent data architecture for the simple reason that their architects like to pretend that distributed processors can be optimized without regard for the persistent data they compute. As such, SOA architects are effective at defining the service's task management, state transitions, and work-flows, as well as the data structure that is a best match to the service's algorithm(s).

SOA Contracts

Each SOA service enforces a security contract, and at least 1 of these 2 types of contracts:

1. Service
2. Data

Over time, as business processes evolve, a given SOA service maintains existing contracts over existing interfaces, while simultaneously supporting new versions of those contracts over new interfaces. Of course, it is best to deprecate older versions of an interface whenever feasible.

Security Contract

A security contract interface constrains and governs access to both service and data contracts interfaces (e.g., available at a URL endpoint) to only authenticated and authorized sessions, in accordance with governance rules and regulations established by the authority over the domain in which the session arises and is present.

It is not sufficient that access be constrained:

1. Access must be audited,
2. A defense against cyber-attacks must be adopted, and
3. Remediation steps (including notifying system users) must be actionable.

Service Contract

A good service contract interface is stateless, and does 1

thing very well, and only 1 thing. That 1 thing is most often a query for information, else it's a command. When the request is a command, use of the service contract alters the (impermanent/permanent) state of the data machine in a deterministic manner.

Data Contract

A good data contract interface is stateless, and the data machine remits 1 dataset, in the structure, format, and encryption, best suited to the client's algorithm.

Microservice

In its most basic form, a microservice is a SOA service that maximizes cohesion and minimizes coupling. When you both maximize cohesion and minimize coupling the service naturally gets small, really small, microscopic even when compared to big ball of mud.

AWS Application Integration Services

AWS Application integration is old school, while serverless applications are new school. Now, fall back and let's drop a groove or two of some of that old school stuff.

There are far too many possible combinations of AWS application integration services to do them justice inside a paragraph. To express those potentials in a few sentences, imagine a lowly EC2 instance that hosts a simple web service. From a host interface in the Internet, an authenticated end user is able to upload a MPEG4 file (e.g., a captivating image of their pet rock, sitting up) that will, unbeknownst to the end user, end up becoming an ambiguated object within an S3 bucket. When the file is uploaded via the web page, the file becomes a message. That message is written onto an SQS queue. Safe somewhere off on another EC2 instance in the VPC, there is a worker-bee process that periodically awakens and reads a message off the queue and using an IAM role writes that message (now in the form of an encrypted object) through the S3 API and into an S3 bucket in a Region in which the worker-bee toils. The worker-bee is not done with its chores, however. As soon as the write completes, the worker-bee deletes the message from the SQS queue, and then creates an email message that is transmitted using SES. With its tasks now successfully completed, the worker-bee goes back to the SQS and just like a busy bopping buzzing bee asks the proverbial question that is all about its sole purpose in life: 'please, may I have some more?' In nature, the life-span of a worker bee is two weeks. And, the length of the life-span of a queen bee, well there's a big difference. Just ask Alexa.

AWS Application Integration includes:

- Amazon Simple Workflow Service (SWF)
- AWS Step Functions
- Amazon Simple Queue Service (SQS)
- Amazon Simple Notification Service (SNS)
- Amazon MQ (Apache ActiveMQ)
- Amazon API Gateway
- Amazon Simple Email Service (SES)

In that the Amazon SWF, AWS Step Functions and Amazon MQ are not covered by either the CF or the CA curriculum, they are not covered in this manuscript. Lastly, the Amazon API Gateway is covered in the AWS Serverless Application chapter of this manuscript.

Amazon Simple Queue Service (SQS)

Certification test hint – vocabulary and rhetoric are clues into the meaning of a statement or thought. When the word 'decoupling' is present in an AWS certification test question the best interpretation: the service to select is SQS, unless a specific business requirement that calls for SWF.

A time-tested and proven technique to ensure loose coupling between components and applications is to queue used to exchange messages between the various parts of the system, asynchronously. ***Amazon Simple Queue Service (SQS) is a fully managed message queueing service*** able to scale to millions of messages.

SQS messages are:

- ***Guaranteed to be delivered at least once (can be more than once);***
- ***Can live in the queue for a maximum of 14 days;***
- ***Can be in JSON, XML, or unformatted text.***

Of note, ***SQS is able to coordinate on-premise servers with EC2 instances launched in an AWS VPC.***

An SQS message can contain 256KB of text (in any format) and is generated by one part of the system for consumption by another part of the system. The queues are the repositories of the messages, where they wait to be processed. SQS can support 1:N concurrent readers and writers on the same queue. ***It is critically important that the application ensure that a delete command is issued to SQS after processing the message.***

The features and benefits of SQS are similar to SNS, however SQS is a pull service and SNS is a push service. The SQS supports two types of queues:

- Standard - offers at least once delivery and best effort ordering.
- FIFO (first in first out) - allows you to order messages that aren't ordered programmatically. The FIFO queue offers exactly once processing and duplicates are not introduced. The throughput limit of the FIFO is up to 300 sends, receives, or deletes per second.

Amazon SQS offers a free tier! New and existing customers can receive 1,000,000 queuing requests for free each month.

Amazon Simple Notification Service (SNS)

The Amazon Simple Notification Service (SNS) is a pub-sub service that enables you to communicate by sending notifications to subscribers. With SNS, you can create a uniquely named topic and then control access to it by defining policies that determine which publishers and subscribers can communicate on a given topic.

A publisher sends a message (the maximum size is 256KB) to a topic (a.k.a., access point) that they created and own, or to which they have been granted permission. SNS then matches that messages to a list of subscribers of that topic and delivers the message to each subscriber. SNS guarantees that all subscribers to a topic receive all published messages and that they each receive the same message at least once, but message order is not guaranteed nor can a message be recalled.

At present SNS supports these subscriber types:

- Email, plain or JSON
- Web ports 80 or 443
- Short message service
- Amazon SQS
- Mobile push messaging and
- AWS Lambda function

SNS does not support the Real Time Messaging Protocol (RTMP), however, CloudFront does support RTMP for distribution of live media.

Amazon Simple Email Service (SES)

The Amazon Simple Email Service (SES) is a pay-as-you-go email *sending* service that helps digital marketers and application developers send marketing, notification and transactional emails. SES interface supports the Simple Mail Transfer Protocol as well as the AWS SDK. With SES, emails can also be received, and these incoming emails at automatically delivered to an S3 bucket.

AWS SERVERLESS APPLICATIONS

In AWS there are a variety of serverless services, e.g., SNS, SQS, S3, etc., that can be used to build and to integrate applications. Today there are numerous serverless AWS services, such as SNS, SQS, Glue, Kinesis, etc.. However, not all serverless services are used to construct serverless applications. As usual, the various AWS serverless services easily interoperate with each other to construct applications that span multiple serverless services. In the context of AWS Serverless Applications the focus is on AWS Lambda which is used to develop and operate AWS Serverless Applications.

In both prior and present architectures, the AWS solution contains a Virtual Private Cloud (VPC), a suite of EC2 instances and various AWS backend services the majority of which are and have been compliant with legislative governance as well as being certified as compliant, e.g., HIPAA; SOC; ISO 9001; etc.. Such cannot be the case with all serverless applications.

In a serverless application, the first component abstracted away is the VPC; replaced by a temporary IAM Role allowed or denied specific actions in response to specific events.

The second component abstracted away is the EC2 instance class; replaced by an immutable and inaccessible Linux AMI instance that is represented as a unit of sliding cost called the CPU. Gone as well are those AWS resources that can be attached to the EC2 instance: the EBS, the ENI, the ELB, etc.. Neither can you configure network performance or log or monitor the serverless application or collect its performance metrics.

Given the absence of VPC, EC2 instance administrator access/control, encrypted persistent storage, etc., an AWS Serverless application will in the near term remain incapable of being certified as compliant with specific governance legislations. However, most any business process models (BPMs) not involved in matters of compliance are most often suitable candidates as serverless applications. In fact, the common place web service could be entirely built from Lambda functions if those functions were available over the network as serverless API endpoints (hence, the AWS API Gateway).

Serverless Application as Container

The key to understanding serverless applications is to stop thinking in terms of a big ball of mud. Instead, think in terms of a container that you can configure to support an on demand or a scheduled execution of an action.

To configure a container that supports an activity, a use case containing key performance indicators (KPIs) with the means to verify and validate success as well as failure, and where the task(s) contained in the use case have their inputs and outputs identified and defined, is required.

In its simplest definition, a serverless application is a type of solution where AWS, not the client, manages the infrastructure needed by the container and its function. In AWS, these services are used to create serverless applications:

AWS Lambda
AWS API Gateway

AWS Lambda

As defined by AWS, '*Lambda is a fully managed service* that runs stateless code in response to an event or on time-based interval.' AWS Lambda manages the infrastructure, it's *fault tolerance, high availability*, and *auto-scaling, queuing and polling*, operating system upgrades, deployments, etc.

By design, a Lambda function cannot support the HTTP/HTTPS protocol nor can a Lambda function interpret an HTTP request: an AWS Lambda compatible event must be in JSON format. AWS created AWS Lambda to handle most any AWS service events, e.g., an object is uploaded into an S3 bucket, a CloudWatch log is delivered, a DynamoDB item is updated, handle a request to the API Gateway, etc.. Prior to AWS Lambda to handle most AWS service events required use of other AWS services, e.g., SNS or SQS, which added additional complexity and cost to the management of AWS service events.

Reflecting its origins, AWS services have built-in AWS Lambda functions: Amazon DynamoDB, Amazon S3, Amazon Kinesis and AWS Config. Other AWS services have built in triggers that connect to Lambda functions: Amazon CloudWatch, AWS CodeCommit and AWS CloudFormation. Lastly, a client-built backend application can invoke a Lambda function.

In general terms, how Lambda handles an AWS service event is similar to how a BPM handles a business service event: an action is taken in response to an event, unscheduled or scheduled. Once the BPM process is conceived as a microservice, the implementation of that BPM process to a suite of orchestrated Lambda functions is not too far of a stretch.

A Lambda Function

As it is expressed, the use case task is an action that can fail or can succeed. To take an action requires authorization and valid inputs, and where success as well as failure are represented as output. In the cloud, it is easy to take the next step and call the business action a function.

A BPM may execute a function on a scheduled basis or, on-demand in response to an (service) event. In Lambda, 0:N instances of each function can run at the same time. In Lambda, each function is assigned a unique immutable ARN and handles a specific event (represented as a JSON object) that is the known cause of a neutral, positive, or negative, feedback loop (that can be associated with a positive/negative ROI).

If all goes well the action/function succeeds, otherwise the action/function fails. This is the most common algorithm and is present in most any process in most any BPM. Moreover, most actions in most BPM processes can be measured to determine their return on investment (ROI) per event action incident per loop.

When a function/action is implemented on-premise it is effectively impossible to measure its ROI, over its life-time, or at points therein. In addition, attempts to modify an existing function/action are impaired by tight coupling.

However, in the AWS serverless application space, each time the function runs in a container and that container is monitored and logged, for which you are charged a fee. By summing the fee that AWS charges every time the function executes, the ROI that that function delivers to the shareholder(s) can be established.

The AWS Lambda buyer decides how much CPU will be allocated to their function/container when it executes, which partially determines the cost to execute the function one time. The best practice still is to refrain from CPU intensive computations unless they cannot be avoided. At present, AWS does not support allocating GPU resources to a Lambda function.

In AWS serverless applications each function is a chunk of stateless programming language statements (within a 'container') that must complete execution using pre-allocated memory, between 128MB up to the maximum of 3GB, at an allocated fee.

By default, the Lambda function is allocated 512MB of memory for its use, but if the function exceeds the maximum allowed it is automatically aborted by AWS Lambda. In AWS Lambda, the fee charged for each execution of the function is per its pre-allocated memory fee (whether or not all of the pre-allocated memory is or is not consumed by the function when it ran). The AWS Lambda function completes in 100 milli-seconds to 15 minutes maximum, but if the function exceeds the maximum allowed it is automatically aborted by AWS Lambda.

At present, AWS Lambda supports Python, Java, Node.js, C# or .NET Core, and Go. A Lambda function is a ZIP file that contains a chunk of stateless programming language statements. In addition to the programming statements that execute the task/function, the Lambda function contains all other libraries that the function requires: access the AWS API, the AWS CLI, the AWS SDK, or other programming language libraries.

To run, a Lambda function must be associated with an IAM Role that defines allow/deny permissions. To unit test a Lambda function requires the use of AWS Lambda.

The transparency of function ROI provided by serverless applications can inhibit the development and operation of big balls of mud. In the serverless application a function that fails to deliver the required ROI has nowhere to hide. The transparency of function ROI provided by serverless applications can inhibit the development and operation of big balls of mud. In the serverless application a function that fails to deliver the required ROI has nowhere to hide.

Perhaps the greater benefit of serverless applications is the absence of the need to depend on highly skilled human resources capable of effectively deploying and operating the VPC, the EC2s, etc., That significant consideration is not relevant with a serverless application. The challenge of acquiring highly skilled human resources capable of delivering viable and robust software (small chunks though they must be) still remains, for the time being.

Given a big ball of mud on-premise, invariably composed of tightly coupled applications, the prudent adoption of Lambda functions makes it easier to deconstruct a big ball of mud hard-wired to infrastructure and resurrect the processes imprisoned within it as uncoupled microservices that succeed or that fail to deliver their ROI.

The function code can be imported into AWS Lambda as an object stored in an S3 bucket or in a compressed format as a Zip file. How often the function is going to run can be scheduled. If the function is an action in response to an event, the identity of the event source is specified. Each function requires pre-allocated memory that it needs as well as a timeout period: these must be specified. If the function needs to access a resource then the VPC it is contained within must be specified.

AWS API Gateway

AWS Lambda cannot handle HTTP requests directly from the Internet. ***The AWS API Gateway is used to create an HTTP endpoint*** that allows an HTTP request to be mapped to an AWS Lambda function by converting the request into a JSON object. ***You define which standard HTTP request methods*** (i.e., GET, POST, PUT, PATCH, DELETE, HEAD, and OPTIONS) ***are supported at by the AWS resource at the endpoint.***

The API Gateway is fully managed, has its own cache (used for storing responses) is capable of handling 100,000s of concurrent requests and provides an ideal way to access AWS services via their APIs. Access to the API Gateway itself is under control of IAM permissions as is permission to perform required actions supported by the AWS service's API. In addition, to enhance protection against DDoS attacks the API Gateway can be integrated with CloudFront.

SECURITY PILLAR

'Fools rush in where angels dare to tread.'
Anonymous
'At all speeds, maintain a distance of 2 seconds between you and the vehicles in front of you.'
Motorcycle Driving Instructor

When solving a system requirement, security is a best first thought on-premise as well as in the cloud. If chapters were ordered in linear sequence based on risk this security chapter is #1. However, this chapter is placed later in the manuscript because without understanding the cloud environment it is impossible to perceive its vulnerabilities or to appreciate the precautions that are always necessary therein (at all times).

When the TCP/IP protocol runs over a physical network that brings its own specific security exposures. When the HTTP/HTTP protocol runs, on a TCP/IP network, that brings its own specific security exposures. When either network protocol is exposed to host interfaces present in the Internet that brings its own specific security exposures. When data is in motion or at rest that brings its own specific security exposures. Take that entire bundle of risk and move it to another dominion on this planet and there will be another set of security exposure. All of these security exposures, as well as others, have to be successfully mitigated. The security mitigation strategies supported by, the resources and services available from, AWS are the topic of this chapter (a chapter that does not stand apart from all other chapters in this manuscript).

As a system engineer, it is critically important to analyze each resource and service (to be and that is) present in a system, to assume responsibility to ensure that security mitigation precautions are in place as warranted by the BPM and are part of daily life on-premise as well as in the cloud.

Two Types of Permissions

'When doing battle, seek a quick victory.'

Sun Tzu

AWS supports two types of permissions:

1. **User-based, and**
2. **Resource-based.**

The Distributed Attack Horizon

"It ain't over 'til it's over"

Yogi Berra

Per AWS 'the goal of the Security pillar is to keep the impact of any type of failure to the smallest possible area.' To keep things small, really small, is the goal.

There is a folk saying that goes: an ounce of prevention is worth a pound of cure. The weight of that assertion takes on mammoth proportions in the context of cloud solutions exposed to the Internet and thereby accessible by members of the general public. True, not all solutions in the cloud are directly exposed to network traffic sourced from hosts present in the Internet. Nevertheless, because they are based on TCP/IP and HTTP/HTTPS protocols, particular types of security risks are inherent to cloud-based solutions.

On-premise or in the cloud, all systems have an attack horizon, have a surface consisting of security, data and service, contracts provisioned by the systems, e.g., the Application Programming Interface(s) (APIs). The attack horizon is not just the public-facing API methods but includes the chains of internal methods calls linked to those public methods. And as always, there is the interface of the native/guest operating system (OS) which hosts the APIs. The OS is also part of the attach horizon. When recognized in all its aspect, ***an attach horizon is a multi-layered structure***, is a stack, e.g. LAMP (Linux, Apache web server, MySQL, PHP), is at minimum ***all of the layers of the OSI Model***. Moreover, since the system is distributed, so also is its attack horizon distributed.

It may seem inappropriate to think of the system's APIs as its attack horizon but that is how knuckleheads who trespass in other party's systems look at things. And, if you are to avoid a predatory animal, such as a hacker, you need to understand what their instincts, intentions and talents are. These understandings are needed to perceive things from the hackers' viewpoint, to get inside the skin of the beast and feel how it feels and come to grips with how it moves.

Being able to see the hackers' viewpoint does not require that one also believes that that viewpoint has integrity. Like all systems, that hacker viewpoint can be readily hacked. This reasoning ability is similar to boxing skills, to knowing when to block and when to punch, above as well as below the belt, accepting that there is no umpire watching and there are no rules to restrain the moves available to both combatants. As you can infer, this boxing is not happening in a ring, it is on the street and it is not coming down after giving mutual consent.

To a malevolent hacker a system is like a home with doors and windows, in which other people keep their valuables. Since every window is made of glass, all homes can be broken into by a knucklehead determined to misappropriate other peoples' stuff. In this analogy, the glass is the public-facing APIs, the end-points, present in and across all stacks that make up the system.

At present, as in the past, in most places, most of the time, it is not possible to stop the acts of a determined hacker who has deep skills, there are preventative measure that can be taken, as well as actions in response to a discovered security breach/

attack event.

An 'after the fact' measure can only hope to minimize the probability of a repetition of that particular security breach/ attack event. This gesture can be a dance intended to ward off lightening striking the same spot twice. In practice, this gesture is like putting an icepack over an eye after it has been punched. Yes, the icepack reduces the swelling, but the eye is likely still unable to see in present time that same punch that landed successfully in the past. Unless you have the imagination, it is hard to see where the punch is coming from, let alone see it coming within the tiny time window in which it both executes and lands on target.

If you have had the responsibility for a system which contains items of high value, then there has been cause in your professional life to learn the best practices appropriate to secure computing, operating in a single office space, or operating around the entire planet. Without that influence in your life there is likely no reason for you to know about security practices. That general lack of knowledge puts hackers at a great advantage.

The ultra-best perspective of a computing system is as a virtual machine which has parts and where each part moves into, through and out of, states in which the properties and relationships of those parts are changed. To hold that perspective in mind requires knowledge of the whole and of the parts, as well as knowing their state transitions (at least, the collection of state transitions that have the highest monetary value to the business process model (BPM)). The states which are treasuries of highest value warrant the highest investment in security practices and technologies.

History does hold many important life lessons, however, one of its' more important lesson is vigilance: to remain focused in the present moment in which all security attacks/ breaches occur. To minimize the probability of a successful system breach there are numerous resources, services and best practices at our disposal, so that we do not foolishly leave our guard down while present in the public arena, while running a system over the Internet.

This boils down to discovering and knowing which resources, services and best practices to use when, where, why and how. And then designing, developing and running tests intended to penetrate your system, intended to breach the security measures implemented by the system as a whole as well as in each of its parts (that has an API or is a command process), in both development and production environments. The goal is to discover the points in the system that are vulnerable to attack. Whatever does destroy it in this generation can also be used to make the system stronger in the next generation. If an internal team does not inspect their own system along these lines, the system remains exposed only to the people who are now hacking it.

Whether a system is on-premise, in the cloud, or is a hybrid, security is a matter of managing risk inherent in the nature of the system and balancing the probable mitigation of the resulting damages. Nevertheless, running a system in the cloud does have its own particular bundle of risk, e.g., TCP/IP and HTTP/HTTPS over the Internet.

The good news is that the AWS clients are not abandoned to the wolves in sheep's clothing always on the prowl. AWS provides the resources and services that help manage risk and mitigate the impact of security breach/attack events. It is up to the AWS client to understand and command the tools to use, how, when, where and why.

DDoS Attacks

A common place and notorious security attack on HTTP-based applications is the Distributed Denial of Service (DDoS). The attack is distributed in that there are simultaneous attacks taken by a combination of a number of digital agents, running on hosts that are usually present in different domains. Invariably the IP address of these digital agents are invalid, just like the phone numbers used by the criminals who manipulate the public phone systems.

When a denial of service attack is single hosted, it is called a DoS.

Perhaps the most well-known DDoS event was the one that happened on during the first days when the US federal government's Obama-care website was available to the public. The overt purposes of a DDoS attack is to consume network bandwidth, computing resources, etc. at levels which interrupt access to the application by legitimate end users.

However, as is often the case, over-cycling a system in whole or in its parts invariably opens cracks in time through which malevolent code can be injected, un-noticed, into the system's components. These pernicious nasty clumps of bytes are called Trojans (unlike the prophylactic which prevents diseases, these filaments introduce viruses into the system). The alien code is used for different nefarious purposes, such as extracting valuable personal identity information (PII), misappropriation of assets from financial accounts, taking command of an application or of a host computer/virtual machine.

To manage the risk presented by DDoS attacks, AWS makes the following recommendations to its clients:

- Secure your applications with AWS services
- Safeguard exposed resources
- Minimize the attack surface
- Evaluate soft limits and request increases ahead of time
- Learn normal behavior and
- Create a plan for attacks

There is a flavor of DDoS that uses the same connectionless protocol (that runs at the Transport layer of the OSI Model), called the User Datagram Protocol (UDP), which DNS uses. These types of DDoS attacks go by the names UDP-floods and SYN floods. To defend against these types of DDoS, AWS recommends fronting you application with an Elastic Load Balancer (ELB) that implements the classic load balancer which only supports valid Transmission Control Protocol (TCP) requests and drops invalid requests.

Another defense against DDoS attacks is the adoption of Amazon CloudFront. Like ELB components, CloudFront has TCP request filtering capabilities and it also has HTTP request filtering capabilities. CloudFront can also drop invalid requests.

There is also Amazon WAF, which is used to set up rules for handling HTTP request. The WAF rules function as a firewall that is able to drop requests based on IP addresses, HTTP headers, HTTP body, or uniform resource identifier-or URI-strings, that are known to cause problems for the web application.

To safeguard exposed resources is a matter of keeping the count of exposed resources to an absolute minimum, while adopting VPC best practices for controlling inbound and outbound network traffic.

To minimize the solution's attack surface, you keep the number of endpoints, the security contracts that include a service contract and or a data contract, to an absolute bare minimum. Doing so is never a challenge when the application/service API is designed to maximize cohesion – to have a thing do 1 thing and do it well. Clearly to be able to design an API that has maximized cohesion requires that you know how to engineer software for a single well-defined use case.

AWS Security Design Principles

Regardless of the scope of a use case, whether the solution will be on-premise or in the cloud or a hybrid, system security needs to be strengthened. AWS advocates several system security design principles:

For each entity (digital and human), implement strong system identity that is restricted to least privileges, where authorization for each action/interaction is required. In addition, enforce 'separation of duties,' decrease reliance on long-term credentials, and centralize system privilege management.

Trace, monitor, and audit, entity actions/interactions in real-time, using alerts and alarms where needed. To take this to the next level, integrate trace logs and action/interaction metrics so that incidents can be responded to in an informed manner asap.

A computing system is a layered construction, i.e., OSI model, in which the surface and edges of each layer are an attack horizon. Therefore, security controls over all resources and services present in each layer are needed.

Security attacks are automated, therefore automated security mitigation components, not human resources, are best able to scale rapidly and securely in a cost-effective manner. For example, a security hardened AMI golden image is automatically used for each EC2 instance launched in an Auto Scaling Group. In addition, CloudFormation templates (under software management control) that embody security best practices can be used provision VPCs.

Data in motion and at rest is protected (which usually includes data encryption, as well as data backup and recovery). In addition, direct human access to information is kept to an absolute minimum.

Be prepared for security events/incidents and align your organizational response requirements accordingly, in a timely manner. The best way to prepare for a security event is to practice on simulated events and use the feedback from these events to optimize the response.

Shared Responsibility Model

In the cloud, security responsibility is shared between AWS and the client.

AWS is responsible for securing the cloud infrastructure, i.e., hardware, software, networking and AWS data centers.

The client is responsible for the security and compliance of everything that they put on the cloud infrastructure and which they connect to in the cloud infrastructure.

AWS Responsibilities

AWS acknowledges the following security responsibilities:

Physical security of the data center

- Logs and audits the employees who access the data center, employee duties are segregated, employees with physical access to the data center have no access to the AWS Management Console, surveillance video systems are used, fire detection and suppression systems are installed, electricity is supplied to each data center redundantly, Uninterruptable Power Supply (UPS) provides backup power, the climate is controlled.

Network security

- Use of redundant firewalls, monitors and controls internal and external network traffic, protects against activities such as detecting and blocking port scanning, inbound ports are blocked by default, unauthorized intrusion attempts are controlled, IP spoofing is not allowed and packet sniffing is ineffective.

Amazon EC2 security

- AWS has root access to the host operating system (OS) (on which the EC2 instance is launched) and is responsible for securing the OS. These activities are logged and audited. AWS does not have access to the EC2's guest OS or to the instance itself. AWS provides a mandatory firewall (in the form of a Security Group) that denies network traffic inbound to the EC2 instance.

Highly available data center

- All AZs are active at all times. Every AZ has redundant infrastructure to provide fault-tolerance.

Configuration management

- AWS installs configuration management software on the hardware in its data centers. All updates are done in a manner that does not impact the client. All changes are authorized, logged, tested, approved and documented. AWS notifies clients, via email and the Management Console, of configuration changes that can potentially impact them.

Disk management

- AWS manages disks and prohibits clients from accessing each other's data. Clients have no direct access to the raw disk devices on the host computer. All disk drives are wiped prior to use.

Storage device decommissioning

- AWS uses DoD 5220.22-M and NIST 800-88 to wipe off all data from a storage device. After being wiped, the device is degaussed and then physically destroyed.

Client Responsibilities

Per AWS, the client has the following security responsibilities:

Authentication and AWS account management

- The client is responsible for the authentication of all AWS accounts and the users of their applications and their permissions.

VPC configuration

- The client is responsible for the VPCs that they create. The client controls access to the VPC and to the AWS resources and services present therein.

VPC Firewalls

- The client is responsible for the Security Groups that control network traffic to and from EC2 instances, as well as the Network Access Control Lists (NACLs) that control network traffic across their VPCs.

Management of EC2 instance guest OS

- The client has full root access and administrator control of the guest OS running on their EC2 instance, its accounts, services and applications. This includes OS patches as well.

Service configuration

- The client is responsible for managing the deployment and configuration of their applications and services.

Application management

- Includes encrypting data, application end users and their privileges, all application layer security and compliance requirements, e.g., SOX, HIPPA, PCI, etc. compliance

AWS Security Mitigation Techniques

AWS advocates that you adopt five (5) mitigation techniques that are intended to minimize the attack horizon of you cloud solution:

1. Identity and access management
2. Detective controls
3. Infrastructure protection
4. Data protection and
5. Incident response

The intent of these security mitigation techniques is to shrink the solution's attack horizon and abort the attempts by knuckleheads to penetrate the system's horizon. To that end, AWS provides numerous resource and services to help you manage security and mitigate the impact of security breach/attack events.

Under the category of detective controls includes the tools and services used to enable tracing and monitoring of network traffic and API calls, using event driven alerts, conducting audits of AWS account activities as well as changes to AWS resources or service use.

Infrastructure protection include firewalls, of course but this topic includes all types of resources provisioned to create the solution. For example, the client controls the guest operating system of each EC2 instance that they launch and each of these instances must be secured as needed. There are contexts in which the high availability AWS services, e.g., Auto Scaling, Elastic Load Balancer, etc., prove to be highly resilient when under attack.

There is a folk saying: the best laid plans of mice and men often go astray. The modern version of this saying is shit happens. After the milk is spilled it has to be cleaned up. A response to a security breach involves cleaning up the system by filling in the cracks and wholes that were exploited by the knucklehead during the event, that enable the breach to happen in the second place (in the first place, the hacker exists, therefore shit happens).

The incident response usually involves other remediation activities that do not directly involve the component of the system but involve the practices of the people working within the system established by their management. Unless management has defined security policies, they cannot be established. When policies regarding personal identity information are ambiguous and ill-defined, the probability of security breaches is a near certainty, if not already a current and ever-present event.

AWS Security Detective Control Services

AWS provides these detective control services:

- AWS Config
- AWS CloudTrail
- AWS CloudWatch
- AWS GuardDuty

The AWS Config, CloudTrail and CloudWatch services are covered in the Operational Excellence dimension.

Amazon GuardDuty

Amazon GuardDuty is a security threat detection service that is uses machine learning and rules sets to enrich threat detection. GuardDuty identifies activities that can be tied to a compromised AWS account, EC2 instance, as well as a malicious reconnaissance, e.g., unusual API calls, network traffic outbound from an EC2 instance to a known malicious host interface or domain, suspicious DNS queries, etc.

Amazon GuardDuty is enabled and accessed through the AWS Management Console and, like many other AWS services, GuardDuty can be customized by the client. You can add your own:

- ***threat lists*** - a list of known malicious IP addresses, data around which GuardDuty focuses upon.
- ***trusted IP lists*** - whitelisted IP addresses, data around which GuardDuty ignores.

Amazon GuardDuty has its jargon as well. The AWS account that enables GuardDuty is referred to as the 'account.' A GuardDuty account can invite other account to enable GuardDuty. When another account accepts your invitation and enables GuardDuty, your account is designated as the 'master account,' and the other added accounts are designated a your 'member accounts.' The master account can view and manage GuardDuty on behalf of its member accounts. It is possible to connect all of your AWS accounts and workloads in this manner and thereby monitor them in a single console.

The term is 'data source' retains its usual meaning in GuardDuty. The data source is the originating location of a set of data. GuardDuty is all about detecting and analyzing unauthorized and unusual activity around data. To that end, GuardDuty continually analyzes and processes data, at scale, from:

- The originating location of a set of data;
- CloudTrail event logs
- VPC flow logs and
- DNS logs.

GuardDuty uses the term 'finding' to refer to a potential threat that it has discovered in, has inferred from, the data set. A finding has a detailed description of the security threat issue and all findings are displayed in the console.

When a threat is detected, GuardDuty can use actionable

alerts, which can be integrated into event management and workflow systems or can trigger AWS Lambda functions purposed for remediation of prevention.

AWS Security Infrastructure Protection Services

AWS provides these infrastructure protection services:

- Amazon Virtual Private Cloud (VPC)
- Amazon Inspector
- AWS Shield
- AWS WAF

Amazon Inspector

The inspection of a system to discover its points that are vulnerable to attacks is an ounce of prevention that is worth a pound of cure. Even given access to security subject matter experts in the stacks used in your system, a manual process is time consuming and error prone. To help their clients with their need to inspect their applications, AWS provides the Amazon Inspector service.

When you look at the Inspector service, it is like CloudFormation and so many of other AWS services, it is the exact type of service that AWS needs to solve AWS devops problems, that was developed for internal use but which also meets a set of needs that are shared widely by their clients. In a real sense, these types of services were at one point in time dogfood that AWS teams ate before being placed into wide release to the general public.

Amazon Inspector is rules-based and contains 100s of rules related to security compliance standards and known vulnerabilities. AWS continually refines that set of rules. When the Inspector completes, a report is produced, in which the discovered vulnerabilities and violations are prioritized based on severity.

The following information and more, is contained in an Inspector report:

- The assessment run start time, end time and status;

- The identity of the EC2 instance accessed;
- The name and severity of the issue;
- The description of the issue and
- Some recommended step(s) to be taken to remedy the issue, etc.

AWS Shield

The AWS Shield is available in 2 versions:

1. AWS Shield Standard and
2. AWS Shield Advanced.

AWS Shield provides additional security threat protections at OSI Model layers #3, #4 and #7.

AWS Shield Standard

AWS Shield Standard service is built into all AWS services, is always 'turned on,' and at no additional cost to the customer, provides in real-time security threat detection and mitigation in OSI Model layers #3 and #4, against cyber-attacks, such as SYN floods, UDP floods and reflection attacks. No additional costs, no time or effort, as required to gain the benefits delivered by AWS Shield Standard.

AWS Shield uses a combination of signatures of network traffic, network traffic anomaly algorithms and other secret-sauce techniques to detect unauthorized network traffic.

AWS Shield Standard does provide some protection against layer #7 DDoS protections, but its' strength is in the arena involving the most common, most frequent network and transport layer attacks. If AWS Shield Standard is integrated with AWS WAF, then a more robust and resilient OSI Model layer #7 protection against DDoS attacks, SQL injection, content web scrapers, etc., can be attained. Beyond the pay-as-you-go charge for using AWS WAF, there is no additional charge incurred by integrating these two (2) services.

AWS Shield Standard is frequently integrated with Elastic IP, ELB, CloudFront and Route 53 to enhance security protection and attack mitigation. The mitigation techniques are applied automatically by AWS Shield and do not require human intervention to initiate, do not require the involvement of AWS Support. Since layers #3, #4 and #7 attacks consume AWS resources and services, these attacks can result in spikes in charges to the client.

AWS Shield Advanced

Unlike the standard version, AWS Shield Advanced is only available at an additional pay-as-you-go charge to the client. As expected, Advanced provides stronger, more sophisticated, mitigation techniques around DDoS attacks, intended to enhance the protection of EC2 instances with an Elastic IP address, ELB load balancers, CloudFront content distributions and Route 53 hosted zones.

Some of the premium benefits the client gains from Advanced include the following:

To assist you, you have access to a 24x7 DDoS AWS response team.

You have access to in-depth, advance, real-time metrics and reports that provide visibility in the attack, while it is ongoing.

DDoS attack detection and mitigation on layers #3, #4 and #7.

You can create your own rules to mitigate layer #7 attacks. A custom rule might automatically block unauthorized network traffic, can trigger a response to a specific incident, etc. The 24x& DDoS team is available to assist client with the development of their custom rules on layer #7 attacks.

At no additional charge, you can integrate Advance with AWS WAF at no additional charge.

Cost protection that absorbs spikes in charges for AWS resources and services created by a DDoS attack.

If appropriate, during a large-scale DDoS attack, Advanced with automatically deploy your Network ACLs (from where they are located within your VPC and near your EC2 instances) to the border of your AWS network (which itself is capable of handling the large volume of network traffic, well beyond the capacity provided by a client solution).

AWS Web Application Firewall (WAF)

The AWS Web Application Firewall (WAF) is just what its name suggests: a firewall service that protects a web application. WAF can be deployed with and protect CloudFront, an Application Load Balancer type ELB, or with Amazon API Gateway. The WAF protects these AWS services by filtering the requests sent over the network to these applications for common security exploits that can effect system availability, can consume resources excessively, as well as compromise the security of the system.

The WAF rules are centrally defined by the AWS client (at any stage of the system's lifecycle) and are capable of blocking or allowing (for a specific application) HTTP requests based on IP addresses, HTTP headers, HTTP body, or URI strings (i.e., SQL injection attacks; cross-site scripting). A custom WAF rule can be easily created and deployed quickly in response to changing request patterns. An WAF rule used in one application can be shared and used to protect other applications as well.

To gain the benefits of WAF the AWS client is not required to make an upfront commitment. The AWS client pays for WAF based on how many rules that they deploy and how many HTTP requests that WAF handles. To automate security mitigation, an AWS client is also able to connect a CloudWatch alarm to a WAF rule.

AWS Security Data Protection Services

AWS provides these data protection services:

1. Amazon Macie
2. AWS KMS
3. AWS CloudHSM
4. Amazon S3

5. Amazon EBS

Amazon Macie

Currently available only in the US West and US East Regions, Amazon ***Macie is a fully managed security service used to enhance data discovery and classification, as well as data security***. Macie uses machine learning (ML) (i.e., Natural Language Processing (NLP) methods) to automatically discover, classify and protect your ***data present in Amazon S3***. Macie provides a dashboard and continually monitors data access activity (by persons, applications and AWS services) and analyzes these for anomalies (relative to historical patterns), which if discovered a detailed alert is generated.

AWS Key Management Service (KMS)

The AWS Key Management Service (KMS) is a managed and highly available multi-tenant cryptosystem for managing symmetric cryptographic keys used to encrypt data.

Basically, the KMS service is used to encrypt data. KMS is implemented in a two-tier key hierarchy that uses 'envelope' encryption. This means that KMS is a storage, management and auditing solution that works both directly within your application as well as across the AWS services and recourses that you provision in your cloud environment.

The cryptographic key is the core resource in KMS, which is called a ***Customer Master Key*** (CMK), or master key for short. The CMK is used by KMS to encrypt and decrypt up to 4KB chunk of data, directly inside KMS. An un-encrypted CMK cannot be exported from KMS.

CMKs can be either ***customer-managed keys*** or ***AWS-managed keys***. A customer-managed key is one that you import into KMS from you own key management infrastructure. AWS takes ownership of the customer-managed keys. Ownership in this limited context means that AWS maintains the trusted root of authority on the key, does not allow the customer-managed key to leave KMS, nor will the customer-managed key be lost, misplaced.

KMS keeps track of the CMK used to make 1:N KMS ***data key***. KMS uses a data key to encrypt and decrypt volumes of data larger than 4KB, which occurs outside of KMS, in the AWS customer's application. An un-encrypted data key can be exported from KMS. Unlike the data key, a CMK is not directly accessible by the client.

Each unique AWS service, each unique data item, is encrypted with a unique key (which KMS keeps track of). If a piece of encrypted data or service is later compromised by an action, only that piece of data is compromised, because a different key is used in each case no others are compromised.

To make the data key, KMS uses a process called ***envelope encryption***. When you request that the KMS create a data key, a CMK is used to encrypt the data key and returns both a disposable plaintext and an encrypted ciphertext version of the data key to you/SDK. The plaintext data key is used to encrypt the data, while the ciphertext data key is stored near the encrypted data. Later, the ciphertext data key is used to decrypt the data. Best practice is to dispose of the plaintext data key asap. The disposed plaintext data key can be retrieved later, granted suitable permissions and by providing the ciphertext data key.

A KMS master key:

- Is used to encrypt, decrypt and re-crypt, data;
- can be used to generate random numbers useable by cryptographic applications;
- can be used to generate data keys that can be exported from KMS in plaintext, or encrypted (under a master key);
- is protected by FIPS 140-2 validated cryptographic modules;
- can create master keys that can never be exported from KMS;
- is used based upon policies that you define, for a 'context' which you also define.

KMS automatically maintains a trusted root authority over each master key. KMS supports the following management activities with master keys:

- Create, describe and list master keys (with a description and a unique alias is desired);
- Enable and disable master keys;
- Temporarily disable master keys;
- Re-enable master keys;

Each AWS service is provided with a default-key that is usable only with that service, but you can create a custom-key for use with a given AWS service.

- Automatically rotate the keys on an annual basis;
- Create and view permission grants and access control policies for master keys;
- Enable and disable automatic rotation of the cryptographic material in a master key;
- Import cryptographic material into a master key;
- Tag you master key for easier identification, tracking and categorizing;
- Create, delete, list and update aliases (friendly names assigned to the master keys);
- Delete master keys;

KMS enables you to maintain control over which IAM users and roles can:

1. use the keys and
2. gain access to the encrypted data.

KMS is seamlessly integrated with most other AWS services, e.g., CloudFormation, EBS, S3, RDS, Redshift, EMR, etc.

KMS is also integrated with AWS CloudTrail and provides encryption key usage logs that help with auditing, regulatory and compliance needs. When integrated with CloudTrail, all requests to use KMS keys are logged, therefore it can be known which IAM user/role used which key and when IAM user/role used it.

In turn, CloudTrail delivers its logs to an S3 bucket that you designate.

KMS is accessible from the AWS Management Console and the KMS Restful API (by using the AWS SDK or AWS CLI with a given CMK). Left to run automatically, in the background, KMS manages the CMKs and data keys used by AWS resources and services. But, access to KMS, particularly through the its API, involves something that AWS calls the ***encryption context***. The same encryption context is required to decrypt (or decrypt and re-encrypt) the data. When using the API, a set of key-value pair is used by KMS as an additional authenticated data used to authenticate encryption. Is the encryption context provided to decrypt is not an exact, case-sensitive match, the request to decrypt fails.

AWS Cloud Hardware Security Module (CloudHSM)

The AWS ***CloudHSM service is a scalable, dedicated (single-tenant) hardware security module appliance used to store security keys.***

Cloud HSM that ***protects cryptographic keys by using a dedicated tamper-resistant hardware device, located within your VPC***. Some corporate, contractual and regulatory compliance requirements specify strict cryptographic key management and explicitly require such hardware devices to be used, both on-premise as well as in the cloud.

Currently, CloudHSM are Luna SA 7000 HSM appliances from SafeNet, Inc. These appliances are designed to meet Federal Information Processing Standard 140-2 and Common Criteria EAL4+ standards. As ***a managed service***, AWS handles the patches to and backups of the device.

There are no upfront fees with CloudHSM. After you turn it on and until you turn it off, ***you are charged an hourly-fee, or partial hour fee***.

Lastly, ***CloudHSM manages both symmetric and asymmetric cryptographic keys***.

AWS Security Incident Response Services

AWS provides these incident response services:

1. AWS IAM
2. AWS CloudFormation

Both of these services are covered elsewhere in this manuscript.

COST OPTIMIZATION PILLAR

All solutions have their price point (i.e., their cost), which when the system varies outside of, market forces ensure that its fate is doomed. Delivering a solution in the form of system or application architecture is not an academic discipline. Even though a delivered system/application embodies engineering principles and best practices that ensure it is viable and robust, if that system/application cannot be developed/operated within range of its price point then it is doomed.

All systems, all applications, all organizations, all teams have a price point outside of which they are doomed. Inside that price point – inside that Goldie Lock Zone – all teams, all organizations, all applications, all systems survive, and some even thrive. At a minimum, cost optimization is about survival in a harsh market.

As Darwin pointed out, there are natural forces at play that ensure the extinction of any organism that depletes the resources present in its environment. To survive, the organism must maintain a balance with its environment, with its reality. In reality capital is limited and the capacity of the system/application to support reality – its capacity to output a positive return on investment (ROI) - determines its survivability, determines its fate. That rule applies to all forms of organization: for-profit as well as not-for-profit.

The Goldie Lock Zone is very easy to reach and maintain. The Goldie Lock Zone is cost optimized and is not ambiguous. A use case is a narrative story that has no capacity to be tested in reality whenever it is devoid of key performance indicators (KPIs). All use cases devoid of a capacity to be tested by reality exist outside of the Goldie Lock Zone, are doomed.

In the Goldie Lock Zone, each use case has KPIs that shareholders use to verify and validate (a given part of) the delivered system/application and are thereby able to transparently determine its ROI.

ROI is most often a matter of balancing consuming how much of a resource at what price and for how long: a duration in which capital is acquired, capital is grown, capital is preserved, otherwise the system/application is doomed.

KPIs have the effect of ensuring that capital is not wasted on unneeded costs or suboptimal resources. Consequently, KPIs continually test the solution for its capacity to support reality and therefore the use case team is capable of being held responsible to right-size the supply of resources so that they match demand (in the real world). The use case team is able to function over time at that level because the KPIs are a benchmark by which they are kept aware of what the resources they are buying and how much they are paying for those resources.

Most importantly, without KPIs per use case there is no basis (in reality) upon which to measure cost optimization. It is folly to monitor and track the supply and cost of resources over time when there is no basis upon which to measure cost optimization.

Cloud Cost Model

An on-premise use case is no different than a cloud use case in that both are doomed whenever that fail to optimize cost. However, in the cloud the cost model is different than the on-premise cost model, specifically how the resources are supplied, and at what cost, are radically distinct.

In the cloud you pay as you go, every step you take, every move you make, every breath you .... This is known as the 'consumption model.'

In the cloud, several fixed costs (a.k.a., capital expenses) associated with the on-premise infrastructure including facilities, hardware, licenses and maintenance staff do not exist.

In the cloud you gain access to managed services and to serverless applications.

In the cloud you can at most any moment stop consuming resources that you are not using, a free choice which can stop the fees that you pay the cloud vendor.

In the cloud the resources and services that you consume are monitored and tracked, and you are charged a fee that you can increase or can decrease depending upon the requirements of your business process model (BPM). Consequently, in the cloud it is much easier to determine overall efficiency and the cost associated with delivering the system/application. Those cost measurements can be used to both budget as well as understand gains/losses in acquiring, growing, preserving, capital.

AWS Cost Optimization Features

To optimize cost you have to understand the costs of a system/application. To help you, AWS provides various tools. A key cost optimization tool is the lowly cost allocation tag. No AWS resource to too small or too large to be assigned a cost allocation tag. The cost allocation tag is used to tag all AWS resources. In turn, a collection of cost allocation tags can be grouped into a cost center tag that helps consolidate AWS fees and charges. AWS provides:

The Cost Explorer that reveals and identify patterns of spending on AWS resources over time. AWS allows you to pre-purchase resources – in the form of Reserved Instances – to help reduce costs.

Auto Scaling to help you match the supply of AWS resources to their demand without overspending for those resources.

Amazon CloudWatch alarms and the Amazon Simple Notification Service (SNS) to warn you if you exceed or are forecasted to exceed you budget.

AWS Trusted Advisor to inspect your AWS environment and find opportunities to reduce cost and to eliminate unused/under-used resources.

Cost Optimization Design Principles

AWS advocates the following 5 design principles that help you optimize cost of AWS resources and services:

1. Adopt the consumption model;
2. Measure overall efficiency – understand how the costs of AWS resource and services directly affect business output, and gain understanding of how increases/decreases in output related to AWS costs;
3. Reduce expenses relative to on-premise operations – the primary focus and effort involves the business processing requirements, and not on IT infrastructure;
4. Analyze and attribute expenditures – until on-premise IT environments, it is exceedingly simple and easy to accurately identify the cost of a system/application as well as how it is being used. These material facts enable you to measure ROI and provide the basis on which to optimize the cost of AWS resource and services.
5. Use managed services – reduce cost of ownership by using managed services (which AWS is responsible for operating and maintaining) at cloud scale.

AWS Pricing Model

In the AWS pricing model, 3 things have the greatest impact on your costs, that drive your costs, and where the consumption of each is under your complete control:

1. Compute;
2. Storage, and
3. Outbound data transfer – you can transfer data into AWS at no charge (but there are exceptions for which fees are charged by AWS), you can transfer data between AWS services within the same Region at no charge. However, AWS charges for aggregated outbound data transfer.

Since you control the 3 things that have the greatest impact on your costs, each of these 3 things are used by you to optimize cost and are therefore the most important cost factors for you to master.

Moreover, the AWS pricing model conforms to a utility pricing model as well:

1. Pay for what you use (i.e., the consumption model; you are able to lower variable costs);
2. Pay less when you reserve (e.g., Reversed EC2 instances; reserved RDS capacity);
3. Pay less when you use more, and
4. Pay even less when AWS grows.

AWS Outbound Data Transfer Fees

Understanding and optimizing compute and storage costs are straight-forward but outbound data transfer takes significantly more effort to understand and to optimize. ***Data can be transferred from AWS outbound to the public Internet. And data can be transferred outbound internally between AWS resources and services.***

Each month, AWS aggregates outbound data transfer across:

1. VPCs;
2. EC2 instances;
3. S3 buckets;
4. RDS instances;
5. SimpleDB;
6. SQS queues, and

7. SNS.

And the aggregate outbound data transfers there is a charge that appears on your monthly statement as 'AWS Data Transfer Out.' In line with the consumption model, long-term contracts are not required to consume the 7 AWS resources and AWS services listed above.

Here are the outbound data transfer fees that you can optimize:

1. AWS charges an outbound data transfer fee, based on which Region the data is located within, when you *transfer data out of AWS to the public Internet.*
2. AWS does not charge an outbound data transfer fee when you use the EC2 instance's private IPv4 address to *transfer data within an AZ.*
3. AWS charges an outbound data transfer fee when you use the EC2 instance's a public or Elastic IPv4 address or IPv6 address to *transfer data within an AZ.*
4. AWS charges an outbound data transfer fee when you use the EC2 instance's a public or Elastic IPv4 address or IPv6 address to *transfer data into AWS.*
5. AWS charges an outbound data transfer fee when you *transfer data between AWS services located in the same Region, but in different AZs.*
6. AWS charges an outbound data transfer fee when you *transfer data within a Region inbound to an EC2 instance from an AWS service that is not located in the same AZ as the EC2 instance.*
7. AWS charges an outbound data transfer fee when you *transfer data between AWS services.*
8. AWS charges an outbound data transfer fee when you *transfer data between AWS Regions* (and where those fees are Region based).
9. AWS does not charge an outbound data transfer fee when you *transfer data into a Region from any AWS services in any other Region.*

To optimize cost it helps to design solutions that avoid outbound data transfers for which you will be charged higher fees. The fee to transfer data between Regions is the most expensive compared to intra-region data transfers. Outbound data transfer are more expensive than intra-AZ data transfers. And, use private IPv4 addresses as opposed to public or Elastic IPv4 addresses or IPv6 addresses.

AWS Cost Management

AWS Cost Management includes these areas:

- Cost-Effective Resources
- Matched Supply and Demand
- Expenditure Awareness
- Optimizing Over Time

AWS Cost Management Cost-Effective Resources

AWS offers these cost-effective resources:

- AWS Free Tier Account
- Reserved Instances
- Cost Explorer

AWS Free Tier Account

To encourage the adoption of Amazon Web Services, Amazon offers you a Free Tier account that provides you with hands-on experiences with AWS resources and services. The Free Tier account expires 12 months after you sign up and includes:

- EC2 t2.micro instance for up to 750 hours per month.
- 1 GB of Amazon QuickSight Super-fast, Parallel, In-memory, Calculation Engine—or SPICE—capacity. Amazon QuickSight is a cloud-powered business analytics service.
- 750 hours of Amazon RDS per month.
- GB of standard storage from Amazon S3 (up to 20,000 get requests and 2,000 put requests).
- 1 million free AWS Lambda requests per month.

Some services have non-expiring offers that continue after your 12-month term.

You will not be charged unless your usage exceeds the limits of the AWS Free Tier, or if you use services that are not included in the AWS Free. Fortunately, you are able to enable a billing alert when as pre-defined charge threshold if exceeded.

AWS Billing and Cost Management

The AWS Billing and Cost Management service:

Enables to you ***forecast future resource/service usages and fees*** to help you plan and budget costs.

Monitors you usage of AWS resources and services and provide the most up-to-date cost and usage information.

Use to pay your AWS bill.

The AWS Billing and Cost Management service is configurable. You can select a custom time period within which to view you cost and usage data, on a monthly or daily level of granularity. You can also group and filter cost and usage information to help you analyze the trends of cost and usage information (over time) in a variety of useful ways and use that information to pin-point identify and optimize costs.

To help you visualize the usage and cost data, the services provides these graphs:

Spend Summary – shows last month's costs, the estimated costs for the current month to date, and forecast of the costs for the current month.

Month-to-Date Spend – shows the usage of the tops AWS services and their proportion of the costs.

Lastly, the AWS Bills page lists the costs you incurred over the past month for each AWS service with a breakdown by Region and AWS account.

AWS Cost Explorer

The AWS Cost Explorer is a free tool ***used to view charts of your costs for up to the last 13 months and forecast how much you are likely to spend of the next 3 months.*** You can get started immediately analyzing your costs by using with the set of default reports (which are listed below) and you can create your own custom cost reports as well. You can save these reports and measure your actual progress toward your goal. And, like the Billing and Cost Management service, with the Cost Explorer you can select a custom time period within which to view you cost and usage data, on a monthly or daily level of granularity. You can also group and filter cost and usage information to help you analyze the trends of cost and usage information (over time) in a variety of useful ways and use that information to pin-point identify and optimize costs.

Included in the default reports are:

- ***Monthly Costs by AWS Service***
- ***EC2 Monthly Cost and Usage***
- ***Monthly Costs by Linked Account***
- ***Monthly Running Costs***
- ***Reserved Instance (RI) Reports***

AWS Cost and Usage Report

To support cost and usage optimization at the lowest level of granularity, AWS provides the cumulative Cost and Usage Report. This report contains line items of each AWS product, usage type and operation, as well as their unique combinations, that your individual AWS account consumed over time, aggregated by the hour or by the day.

Each update is cumulative, and each version of this report includes all line items and information contained in previous versions. The intra-month reports are estimates of usage and cost, are subject to change as usages change, which AWS finalizes in the end-of-month version of this report. Applying refunds, credits, or support fees, can cause a finalized end-of-month report to be updated to reflect your 'final' end-of-month charges.

You specify the S3 bucket that AWS delivers the report files to and which AWS updates up-to 3 times a day. The Cost and Usage Report in an S3 bucket can be queried by Amazon

Athena, it can be downloaded from the S3 console and the report can be uploaded into Amazon Redshift as well as Amazon QuickSight.

Calls to the AWS Billing and Cost Management API can create, retrieve, and delete a Cost and Usage Report. The Cost and Usage Report is available on the Reports page of the AWS Billing and Cost Management console, 24-hours after you create it.

However, if the consolidate billing feature in AWS Organizations is used then this report is only available to the master account (from whom other member accounts can obtain their report).

AWS Cost Management Matched Supply and Demand

For matched supply and demand, AWS provides the Auto Scaling Service, which is covered elsewhere in this manuscript. Please refer to the table of contents.

AWS Cost Management Expenditure Awareness Services

AWS provides these expenditure awareness services:

- Amazon CloudWatch
- Amazon SNS

These services are covered elsewhere in this manuscript. Please refer to the table of contents.

Optimizing Over Time

AWS publishes documents on this topic at its training website and also provides the AWS Trusted Advisor service, which is covered elsewhere in this manuscript. Please refer to the table of contents.

Total Cost of Ownership (TOC)

At the financial center of the decision to use cloud resources and services is the total cost of owning and operating a system/application in the cloud, verses on-premise, verse an on-premise-cloud hybrid.

In the cloud, unlike on-premise (and hybrids), several CAPEX inherent to on-premise and hybrids (e.g., maintenance staff, facilities, software licenses, hardware, etc.) are not present in the cloud. Unlike in the cloud where scaling up or down is simple and you pay only for what you use, scaling down on-premise does not reduce CAPEX and scaling up on-premise involves long delays.

Despite the CAPEX differences, and given the technical differences, the fairest way to compare a cloud solution with an on-premise (or hybrid) is to use the Total Cost of Ownership (TOC) tool. The TOC captures the total direct as well as indirect costs of owning as well as operating a system/application in AWS.

AWS TOC Calculator

The AWS TOC is a tool you use to help reduce the TOC, the money invested in the capital expenditures for AWS resources and services. The AWS TOC allows you to estimate the cost saving when using AWS and gives you the option to modify assumptions to meet your business needs. The AWS TOC does provide a set of report that might be used in presentations to the C-levels. The AWS TOC can be reached at this URL https://awstcocalculator.com/

AWS Simple Monthly Calculator

The AWS Simple Monthly Calculator is a tool that you can use to estimate the cost of running a solution in the AWS Cloud, based on estimated usage. This calculator will help you determine how adding a new AWS resource or server will impact your overall bill. The AWS Simple Monthly Calculator can be reached at this URL https://calculator.s3.amazonaws.com/index.html

AWS Budgets Dashboard

The AWS Budgets dashboard provides you with the ability to set a budget for AWS resource and service usage or costs.

Budgets can be tracked for a start and end date of your choosing, at a monthly, quarterly, or yearly time period. When your actual usage and cost exceeds you set budget amount (or AWS forecasts that they will be exceeded) you will receive an alert. And, when your actual usage and costs drops below the budgeted amount you also receive an alert to that effect. Budget alerts are sent vial email or an SNS topic, and are available for EC2 instances, RDS, Redshift and ElastiCache.

Budgets can be created and monitored from the AWS Budgets dashboard or via the Budgets API.

OPERATIONAL EXCELLENCE PILLAR

"No use lying, no use joking, everything is broken."
Bob Dylan

I don't think that Bob ever worked in IT devops, but his rhyme describes that environment very well. When you build your first machine, application, database server, distributed microservice, Hadoop cluster, etc., the process is one of trial and error where most individual acts are at first mostly errors. That process repeats itself in multiple nefarious forms large and small, until you have arrived at a viable and robust solution. The nature of the process is one of discovery, of discovering why what works, how, and when. And, like all surviving explorers, you take notes along the way and make maps of the domain, particularly in the form of scripts that automate the construction and deployment of the machine, application, server, microservice, cluster, etc., which in-turn are kept under source code control, unit tested, continuously integrated, etc.. No use lying, no use joking, if there ain't no script then it is broken.

The operational excellence pillar of the AWS Well-Architected Framework focuses on how to design a solution that will be provisioned into a runtime production environment. Now, it is important to take full notice of the implicit point:

operational excellence originates in the solution design phase. If the architecture of the solution is badly designed then operational excellence cannot be achieved – first fix the underlying causes of the operational problems, and only then aspire to excellence. For big balls of mud, it is seldom if ever technically possible, or cost effective, to fix their inherent problems.

AWS defines excellence along three (3) 'planes:'

1 Control plane – creates the resources;

2 Data plane – uses the resources, and

3 Management plane – configures the resources.

In turn, business success in each of operational plane is determined by 3 factors, for which there are corresponding best practices:

Effective preparation required to support the BPM running in the AWS cloud.

The successful operation of a workload is measured by the use case's Key Performance Indicators (KPIs);

The timely evolution of operations required to sustain the BPM.

In the sections of the manuscript that follow, each of those 3 factors of operational excellence are investigated, and all AWS resources and services related to that factor are explored, and their best practices are introduced in context. It is important to recognize that the same AWS recourse or service can appear in multiple factors, as well as in multiple pillars. Where a service or resource supports multiple pillars that is due to the bundle of features and present in the product as well as the benefits that the product delivers. For example, Amazon Elasticsearch is an Analytics product. However, when Elasticsearch is used to analyze the logs of your services it becomes a support tool in operations.

As the 3 factors are described above, each is tied, as the need to be, to the BPM. For a system architecture to be rated successful in has to support the BPM, which means that the BPM must be understood in order to produce a well-architected solution (on the ground or in the cloud).

Whatever the most important part of the BPM implemented in the system are, whatever they are, both the operations team(s) and the system themselves have to be able to respond effectively and efficiently to the requirements of the BPM. The architecture has to deliver the outcomes required by the BPM, when, where, and how.

That statement is easier to write that to achieve across a team, particularly given the American penchant for ambiguity – a penchant only useful for stampeding crowds. At a minimum, the processes with the highest priorities have to be identified. Next, adequately protected. And then ensured to be able to be changed over time.

Operational Excellence Design Principles

Unfortunately, manually creating and configuring infrastructure is typical and common-place on -premise. Aside from being error prone, manual process are not easily repeated and are hard to reproduce.

The preferred solution is to automate these tasks and steps by creating a script and automating the execution of that script. That script (which provisions, terminates and configures resources) can serve as documentation of the infrastructure. And like good software, the infrastructure code is easily extended, is testable, and is reusable.

AWS advocates the following design principles used to achieve operational excellence in the cloud (which is key to ensuring reliability):

1 Perform operations using code – define your infrastructure in code (and managed as software), perform operations in code, and automate their execution by triggering them in response to system events;

2 Automate documentation changes – in the AWS cloud, the creation and updating of infrastructure documentation can be automated;

3 Make frequent, small, reversible changes – design and operate the infrastructure so that its components can

be updated regularly;

4 Refine standard operations procedures frequently – as the BPM and the infrastructure evolve, evolve your procedures to ensure that they are viable and effective;

5 Anticipate failure, as it can happen – test and practice your business continuance and disaster recovery procedures;

6 Learn from all operational failures.

Infrastructure as Code

AWS uses the phrase 'infrastructure as code' to describe how we can define our infrastructure programmatically, as code. This is a significant shift in mindset from the traditional manual processes that are common-place in IT shops. And of course, with infrastructure as code it is required that the code be managed as software. You also gains similar benefits as that from software.

The infrastructure code is testable, is updateable, and is reusable, and repeatable.

AWS Operational Excellence Preparation Resources and Services

To prepare for operational excellence, AWS advocates these tools and services:

- AWS Support
- AWS Management Console
- AWS OpsWorks
- AWS Systems Manager
- Amazon EC2 Run Command
- AWS Config
- AWS CloudFormation
- VPC Flow Logs
- AWS CloudTrail
- Amazon CloudWatch

AWS Support Tiers

AWS offers 4 different tiers of support, with differing services:

1. Basic;
2. Developer (fees charged);
3. Business (fees charged) and
4. Enterprise (fees charged).

All AWS Support plans include an unlimited number of support cases, with no long-term contracts. With the Business and Enterprise tiers, you earn volume discounts on your AWS Support costs, as your AWS charges increase.

Support Severity

AWS support uses the following severity chart to set response times.

Critical - the business is at risk. Critical functions of an application are unavailable.

Urgent – the business is significantly impacted. Important functions of an application are unavailable.

High - important functions of an application are impaired or degraded.

Normal - non-critical functions of an application are behaving abnormally, or there is a time-sensitive development question.

Low – there is a general development question, or desire to request a service feature.

Basic Support

- Customer Service & Communities
- 24x7 access to customer service, documentation, whitepapers and support forums.
- AWS Trusted Advisor
- Access to the 7 core Trusted Advisor checks and guidance to provision your resources following best practices to increase performance and improve security.

- AWS Personal Health Dashboard
- A personalized view of the health of AWS services and alerts when your resources are impacted.
- Alerts and remediation guidance when AWS experiences events that may impact you.
- You can set alerts across multiple channels, e.g., email, mobile notifications.

Developer Support

- Enhanced Technical Support
- Business hours email access to Support Engineers
- Unlimited cases / 1 primary contact
- Case Severity / Response Times
- General guidance: < 24 business hours
- System impaired: < 12 business hours
- Architectural Guidance
- General

Business Support

- Enhanced Technical Support
- 24x7 phone, email and chat access to Support Engineers
- Unlimited cases / unlimited contacts (IAM supported)
- Case Severity / Response Times
- General guidance: < 24 hours
- System impaired: < 12 hours
- Production system impaired: < 4 hours
- Production system down: < 1 hour
- Architectural Guidance
- Contextual to your use-cases
- Programmatic Case Management
- AWS Support API
- Third-Party Software Support
- Interoperability & configuration guidance and troubleshooting

- Proactive Programs
- Access to Infrastructure Event Management for additional fee.

Enterprise Support

- Enhanced Technical Support
- 24x7 phone, email and chat access to Support Engineers
- Unlimited cases / unlimited contacts (IAM supported)
- Case Severity / Response Times
- General guidance: < 24 hours
- System impaired: < 12 hours
- Production system impaired: < 4 hours
- Production system down: < 1 hour
- Business-critical system down: < 15 minutes
- Architectural Guidance
- Consultative review and guidance based on your applications
- Programmatic Case Management
- AWS Support API
- Third-Party Software Support
- Interoperability & configuration guidance and troubleshooting
- Proactive Programs
- Infrastructure Event Management
- Well-Architected Reviews
- Operations Reviews
- Technical Account Manager (TAM) coordinates access to programs and other AWS experts as needed.
- Technical Account Management
- Designated Technical Account Manager (TAM) to proactively monitor your environment and assist with optimization.
- Training
- Access to online self-paced labs

- Account Assistance
- Concierge Support Team

Technical Account Manager

The Technical Account Manager:

1 Acts as your 'voice in AWS' and serves as your advocate.

2 Uses business and performance reviews to provide proactive guidance and insight into ways to optimize AWS.

3 Orchestrates and provides access to technical expertise inside AWS.

4 Provides access to resources and best practice recommendations.

Infrastructure Event Management

Infrastructure Event Management includes:

- Through pre-event planning and preparation, provides a common understanding of event objectives and use cases.
- Resource recommendations and deployment guidance based on anticipated capacity needs.
- Dedicated attention of the AWS Support team during an event.

Provides the ability to immediately scale down resources to normal operating levels post-event.

The Concierge Service

The Concierge Service:

1 Provides a primary point of contact to help manage AWS resources.

2 Personalized handling of billing inquiries, tax questions, service limits and bulk reserve instance purchases.

3 Direct access to an agent to help optimize costs to identify underused resources.

AWS Management Console

Accessing, managing, and administering AWS resources and service is supported by a simple and easy to use web-based user-interface (UI), called the AWS Management Console. The Management Console can be used to manage all aspects of your AWS Account, from monitoring your fees to managing identity credentials and their permissions. In addition, all functions available in the Management Console are also available in the AWS API and CLI.

The Management Console is also a great way to discover the many AWS resources and services that are available to you. The easy to use and simple UI of each resource and services makes them available for your use in just a few clicks and after filling in a few text boxes.

AWS OpsWorks

The AWS OpsWorks is a configuration management service that lets you configure and operate an application in the AWS cloud. By using Puppet or Chef, AWS OpsWorks lets you define the application architecture and configure software and resources using templates.

Puppet and Chef are outside the scope of this manuscript.

AWS Systems Manager

The AWS Systems Manager is a free service that helps you automatically create system images and configure Windows and Linus OS, to apply OS patches, and to collect software inventory. AWS Systems Manager allows you to define and track system configuration, to inhibit unauthorized variations from standards, and to maintain OS and software compliance.

AWS Systems Manager is designed for the AWS cloud, but it can be extended into your on-premise environment as well.

Amazon EC2 Run Command

Amazon EC2 Run Command is used to automate common EC2 administrative tasks. This tool supports a Shell scripts and commands on Linux and PowerShell commands on Windows. These commands can be run under specific IAM identities. For easy auditing, all commands are centrally logged to the AWS CloudTrail. You can use Run Command from the Amazon EC2 Console to configure the instances without having to login to the instance, i.e., no need for SSH of RDP. This tool is also accessible from the AWS Management Console, the AWS CLI, and AWS SDK.

AWS Config

The AWS Config is a free rules-based service that helps you assess, monitor, audit and evaluate the configurations of your AWS resources. AWS Config continually monitors and records the configurations of your AWS resources and helps you automate the evaluation of changes to configurations as well as drill down into the details of those changes. When a change is detected, and SNS notification can be sent to you for your review/response. Overall, AWS Config can significantly simplify compliance auditing, security analysis, change management and operational troubleshooting.

AWS Config and CloudTrail Integration

AWS Config and CloudTrail can interoperate. For example, there is a need to identify when a VPC Security Group Rule is changed, added or deleted, for which affected EC2 Instances, and by whom. Working together, CloudTrail and AWS Config can provide details on who made what change and what changes were made. CloudTrail provides the AWS API call history which enable security analysis, and resource change tracking. AWS Config provides a detailed view of the configuration of the AWS resources (in an account). This includes how the resources are related to each other, and how they were configured in the past, so that changes in the configuration through time can be established.

AWS CloudFormation

The AWS CloudFormation is a free service used to launch,

configure and connect AWS resources. CloudFormation treats infrastructure as code and does so by using JSON and or YAML formatted templates.

AWS does not charge a fee for using CloudFormation. You are charged for the infrastructure resources and services created using CloudFormation.

CloudFormation enables you to ***version control your infrastructure*** and is also a ***great disaster recovery option***.

CloudFormation Template

The AWS CloudFormation template is used to define the entire solution stack, as well as runtime parameters. You can reuse templates to set-up resources consistently and repeatedly. Since these templates are text files, it is a simple matter to use a version control system with the templates. The version control system will report any changes that were made, who made them, and when. In addition, the version control system can enable you to reverse changes to templates to a previous version.

Best practice – use a version control system to manage the CloudFormation templates.

An AWS CloudFormation template can be created using a code editor. But, they can be easily created using the drag-n-drop CloudFormation Designer tool, available in the AWS Management Console. The Designer will automatically generate the JSON or YAML template document.

AWS Resources and Services for Operating Most Excellently in the Cloud

To operate most excellently in the cloud, AWS advocates these services:

- VPC Flow Logs
- AWS CloudTrail
- Amazon CloudWatch

VPC Log Flows

The Amazon VPC Flow Logs enable you to capture information about IP traffic going to and from network interfaces in your VPC.

You can create a flow log for a VPC, a subnet, or a network interface and it will be monitored.

Each network interface has a unique log stream.

Log streams contain flow log records, which are log events that consist of fields that describe the traffic for that network interface.

VPC Flow Log captures accepted and rejected traffic flow information for all network interfaces in the selected resource.

The information that's captured by the flow logs can help you troubleshoot why specific traffic is not reaching an instance, which in turn can help you diagnose overly restrictive security group rules.

You can also use flow logs as a security tool to monitor the traffic that is reaching your instance.

You can create alarms to notify you if certain types of traffic are detected and you can also create metrics to help you to identify trends and patterns.

The flow data is stored and published to a log group in Amazon CloudWatch logs.

After you create a VPC Flow Log, you can view and retrieve it using CloudWatch.

There are no additional charges for using Flow Logs. But, CloudWatch charges apply.

AWS CloudTrail

CloudTrail is the de-facto AWS service that can log and monitor all API calls (AWS management console activities, CLI commands and arguments, SDK calls and input parameters,) that enter AWS ***made by a given AWS Account, what acts they did, when they did those acts and from where they acted.***

Best practice – ensure that CloudTrail logging is enabled on each AWS Account.

For a given AWS Account, CloudTrail enables:

- ***Governance,***
- ***Compliance,***
- ***Operational Auditing, and***
- ***Risk Auditing***

CloudTrail can be used to support external compliance audits, by providing evidence how data is being transmitted, processed and stored in AWS. CloudTrail helps track changes to AWS resources, support compliance with rules and with troubleshooting operational problems.

CloudTrail typically delivers log files 15 minutes after the API call and can publishes new log files every 5 minutes. To validate CloudTrail log files, AWS uses SHA-256 for hashing and SHA-256 with RSA for digital signing of the file.

The ***CloudTrail console displays the event history of a Region, over the past 90 days.***

The CloudTrail logs can be saved to S3, can be sent to CloudWatch and to CloudWatch Events. AWS Account trail log files delivered to S3 are encrypted by S3, using SSE-S3 keys. You can choose to use SSE-KMS encryption if needed.

For a given Region, you can send the account trails to a central account and from which analysis across the accounts is supported. The central account controls access to the logs as well as their distribution.

You can create up to 5 account trails per Region. You can create a trail that applies to all Regions and record the log files for each Region.

You can configure an SNS notification when a CloudTrail log file is written into an S3 bucket.

Best practice – configure an SNS notification when a CloudTrail log file is written into an S3 bucket.

If, after enabling CloudTrail, if it is disabled or changed then CloudTrail, or CloudWatch Logs, or CloudWatch Alarm, can be used to detect that change and to then send an SNS notification.

Best practice – once CloudTrail is enabled, use CloudTrail, or CloudWatch Logs, or CloudWatch Alarm to detect if CloudTrail is later disabled or changed, and to then send an SNS notification to the appropriate party.

Amazon CloudWatch

Amazon ***CloudWatch is a service that monitors your EC2 instances, and it collects and processes raw data into readable, near real-time metrics.***

CloudWatch (is a distributed system that) ***integrates with AWS IAM, collects and manages metrics about your existing system, application, and custom, log files***. CloudWatch ***gives you visibility into resource use, application performance, as well as monitor operational health, create rules and alarms and troubleshoot operational health***. CloudWatch ***can examine logs for specific phrases, values, or patterns.***

CloudWatch provides > 100 types of metrics and you can create your own metrics. Using CloudWatch's Free Tier, the frequency of metrics update is 5 minutes. If a shorter interval is needed, you will have to pay extra.

EC2 instances publish their CPU utilization, data transfer, and disk usage metrics to CloudWatch. The EC2 instance does not publish memory utilization by the instance.

AWS has no visibility into:

- events that are visible to the operating system of the EC2 instance.
- your system/application specific-events.

CloudWatch Logs

CloudWatch Logs are used to monitor and troubleshoot systems/applications by using your existing system, application and custom, log files. CloudWatch Logs is ***a managed service that collects and keeps your logs***. CloudWatch can aggregate and centralize logs, across multiple sources.

CloudWatch can use S3 or Glacier to store your logs. By default, metrics data is retained in S3 for a 2-week period.

Best practice – in this use case, due to an application bug, the EC2 instance must be rebooted. Ensure the bug event is captured in the application log. CloudWatch Logs can be used to monitor that application log for the error keywords, create an alarm, and then restart the EC2 instance.

How to Publish Logs to CloudWatch

Logs can be published to CloudWatch using these means:

- CloudWatch Logs Agent;
- AWS CLI;
- CloudWatch Logs SDK;
- CloudWatch API – allows programs/scripts to PUT metrics (a name-value pair) into CloudWatch, which can then create events and trigger alarms.

You can also export logs data to S3 for archiving, for analytics, or stream the logs to Amazon Elasticsearch Service or to Splunk and other 3rd party tools.

Monitoring and Metrics

CloudWatch monitoring of and metrics are available for:

1 Auto Scaling;
2 Elastic Load Balancing;
3 Amazon SNS;
4 Amazon EC2;
5 Amazon ElastiCache;
6 Amazon Elastic Block Store (EBS);
7 Amazon DynamoDB;
8 Amazon Elastic MapReduce (EMR);
9 Amazon EC2 Container Service (ECS);
10 Amazon Elastisearch Service;
11 Amazon Kinesis Streams;
12 Amazon Kinesis Firehose;
13 AWS Lambda;
14 Amazon Machine Learning;
15 AWS OpsWorks;

16 Amazon Redshift;
17 Amazon Relational Database Service (RDS);
18 Amazon Route 53;
19 Amazon Simple Queue Service (SQS);
20 Amazon S3;
21 Amazon Simple Workflow Service (SWF);
22 Amazon Storage Gateway;
23 Amazon WorkSpaces;
24 Amazon CloudFront;
25 Amazon CloudSearch;

CloudWatch Custom Metric

CloudWatch can measure CPU usage, disk I/O, and network operations. But, CloudWatch is not able to measure everything about everything. There is one very important thing that needs to be measured but which CloudWatch does not measure: EC2 Instance Memory Usage.

To measure EC2 instance memory usage you need to be add a custom metric in CloudWatch. However, the custom metrics are only available with the Linux AMI. A Perl script is used to monitor and capture the custom metric (memory usage, swap usage, disk use). It is the CloudWatch Agent installed on the EC2 instance that operates the custom metric Perl scripts.

The standard CloudWatch usage charges apply to your use of custom metrics Perl scripts.

CloudWatch Events

A CloudWatch Event is aware of operation changes in an AWS cloud environment as they are occurring and generates a stream of information. A CloudWatch Event delivers a near real-time stream of system events that describe changes in AWS resources in an environment. CloudWatch Events use simple rules that match events present in the stream, and routes those matched events to one or more target functions or streams, which take a corrective action in response as needed. CloudWatch Events can be scheduled to automated actions that are triggered at certain times using cron (the OS tool) or rate expressions.

CloudWatch Alarms

A CloudWatch Alarm monitors a single metric over a period of time that you specify ***and performs 1:N actions based on the value of the metric relative to a given threshold over a number of time periods***. For example, an alarm can represent a reboot of an EC2 instance, or the scale-in and the scale-out of instances in an Auto Scaling Group.

An Alarm has these states:

- ***OK***;
- ***ALARM***;
- ***INSUFFICIENT_DATA***.

You can set up rules and an action can be taken whenever a change is detected. For example, a CloudWatch alarm action can be used to automatically stop, terminate, reboot, or recover and EC2 instance. Stop and terminate can be used to optimize cost savings when an instance does not need to be run. Reboot and recover actions are used when an instance is impaired.

When the alarm changes state, ***the action is a SNS notification*** that is quickly sent to a target you choose:

- A Lambda function;
- An Auto Scaling Policy;
- An SNS queue;
- An SNS topic;
- A Kinesis Stream;
- A built-in target.

Each AWS Account is limited to 5,000 Alarms.

2 Levels of Monitoring

Basic Monitoring

- ***No charge.*** Sends data points to CloudWatch every 5 minutes for a limited # of preselected metrics.
- Basic monitoring ***only monitors and captures hyper-***

visor level metrics. It does not monitor operating system metrics, such as memory use or disk space use.

Detailed Monitoring

- *For a charge*, sends data points to CloudWatch every 1 minute for a metrics.
- For an additional charge, supports aggregation of metrics across AZs in a given Region.
- You obtain metrics through the CloudWatch API by performing an HTTP GET request.

CloudWatch Logs Agent

Use CloudWatch Logs Agent to stream your existing system, application and custom, log files from EC2 instances, AWS CloudTrail and other AWS services.

The CloudWatch Logs Agent is available on Linux and Windows EC2 instance types.

Use the Amazon CloudWatch Logs Agent Installer to install the Agent on the EC2 instance and to configure that Agent.

View CloudWatch Graph and Statistics

Use CloudWatch Dashboard(s) to view different types of graphs and statistics of the metrics you collect. For example, in a graph you can view the CPU use, and can see its trend over time.

During operational events, the Dashboard can act as a playbook that provide guidance about how to respond to specific incidents.

RELIABILITY PILLAR

AWS defines reliability in a few ways:

'the probability that an entire system, including all hardware, firmware and software, will satisfactorily function for a specified period of time'.

'the ability of a system to recover from infrastructure or service failures, dynamically acquire computing resources to meet demand and mitigate disruptions such as misconfigurations or transient network issues.'

The goal of reliability is to minimize the impact of failure events. This goal is accomplished in a manner similar to software engineering, i.e., an ounce of prevention is worth a pound of cure: you understand that the method/function can and will fail in a variety of ways, each of which needs to be handled in an automated manner.

The common way to measure reliability is Mean Time Between Failure (MTBF) but can also be evaluated using Recovery Time Objectives (RTOs) (i.e., the time that your business is down during an outage) and Recovery Point Objectives (RPOs) (i.e., the amount of data that will be lost). As will be shown, the combination of RTO and RPO is a practical way of evaluating, as well as comparing and contrasting, the reliability of a given design.

Reliability Design Principles

AWS advocates several design principles to enhance reliability of your solution:

1. Testing recovery procedures
2. Automatically recover from failure
3. Scale horizontally to increase aggregate system availability.
4. Stop guessing capacity
5. Manage change in automation

As will be shown, AWS offers numerous resources and services that both directly and indirectly enhance reliability.

Areas of Reliability

AWS partitions reliability into 3 areas:

1. Foundations
2. Change Management
3. Failure Management

AWS Reliability Foundations Services

The AWS reliability foundations services include:

1. AWS IAM
2. Amazon VPC
3. AWS Trusted Advisor
4. AWS Shield

The AWS IAM, VPC and Shield are covered elsewhere in this manuscript. Please refer to the table of contents.

AWS Trusted Advisor

At no charge, every AWS account has access to the AWS Trusted Advisor. Accessed from the AWS Management Console, the AWS Trusted Advisor helps AWS customers improve security and performance. It's prominent focus is on:

- Service Limits
- Security Groups
- Specific Ports Unrestricted
- IAM use
- MFA on the AWS Root Account
- Find under-utilized resources

The AWS Trusted Advisor provides customers with easy

access to a variety of important performance and security recommendations. As reported by AWS, the most popular recommendations involve:

- Cost optimization
- Security
- Fault tolerance
- Performance improvement; and
- Service checks
- The AWS Trusted Advisor is also a source of best practices that cover:
- Service limits;
- Security group rules that allow unrestricted access to specific ports ;
- IAM use;
- MFA on the root account;
- S3 bucket permissions;
- EBS public snapshots, and
- RDS public snapshots.

For AWS clients who have purchased the Business or Enterprise Support plans there are additional checks and guidance available.

AWS Reliability Change Management Services

The AWS reliability change management services include:

- AWS CloudTrail
- AWS Config
- Amazon CloudWatch – this is the AWS service that is key to ensuring reliability.
- Auto Scaling

The above services are covered elsewhere in this manuscript. Please refer to the table of contents.

AWS Reliability Failure Management Services

The AWS reliability failure management services include:

- AWS CloudFormation
- Amazon S3

- Amazon Glacier
- AWS KMS

The above services are covered elsewhere in this manuscript. Please refer to the table of contents.

Reliability Design Patterns

In the AWS cloud there are 4 common reliability design patterns:

1. Backup and Restore
2. Pilot Light Architecture
3. Fully Working Low-Capacity Standby Architecture
4. Multi-site Active-Active Architecture

For each of these design patterns, their preparation and disaster recovery phases will be explain, and then their RTO and RPO will be described.

Backup and Restore

The best that can be said of reliability based on backup and restore best practices is that the approach minimizes costs (i.e., you pay fro storage of the backup images), as well as being a simple solution that is easy to get started with.

Preparation Phase: Level 0 backup images of each component of the system have to be taken, and incremental backup images taken subsequently. These backup image files are stored in S3. To be able to restore the system 'know how' covering these matters are mandatory and must also be documented: which AMI to use/build; restoring from a backup image; configuring the deployment; smoothly switching over to the recovered components.

Disaster Recovery Phase: restore failed component(s) from their backup images, launch required infrastructure, switching over to the recovered/launched components.

RTO: this takes as long as it take to restore from backup and then launch and switch over.

RPO: since the last time the backup image was made.

Pilot Light Architecture

A typical Pilot Light Architect has an on-premise system (the primary) which the DNS service (e.g., Amazon Route 53 points to). And in the AWS cloud, you have a secondary system, that includes a replicate database that is a mirror image of the on-premise database and the other application components are also present in the cloud but they are all minimally provisioned resources.

Preparation Phase: though the other application components are provisioned in the cloud they are not running (other than the data replication processes). Of course, backups are being taken on a regularly scheduled basis and recovery procedures must be fully documented and well known.

Disaster Recovery Phase: when the primary fails, the components in the cloud are automatically up-scaled and launched. The DNS service is then changed to point to the backup system now running in the AWS cloud.

RTO: the time it takes to detect the primary system failure and the automated provisioning of the secondary system in AWS cloud.

RPO: this depends on the frequency of data replication between the primary and the secondary.

Fully Working Low-Capacity Standby Architecture

In the fully working low-capacity standby architecture there are two running systems, the fully provisioned primary and a low-capacity secondary, to which the DNS server is distributing requests to. In this example, the low-capacity secondary is running in the AWS cloud.

Preparation Phase: the low-capacity secondary must be designed and built to auto-scale horizontally.

Disaster Recovery Phase: immediately begin to failover to the secondary, the low-capacity secondary is auto-scaled to match the capacity of the now-failed primary system, and the DNS server is changed to point only to the AWS cloud secondary system

RTO: as long as it takes the secondary to scale-up to primary capacity.

RPO: directly dependent on the type of data replication system being used.

Multi-site Active-Active Architecture

In the multi-site active-active architecture, there is a primary system and a secondary system which have the same capacity and can take the full processing load at any moment.

Preparation Phase: data replication is happening between the primary and the secondary.

Disaster Recovery Phase: immediately failover by having the DNS server point only to the secondary.

RTO: as long as it take to failover.

RPO: directly dependent on the type of data replication system being used.

Reliability Best Practices

AWS recommends the following reliability best practices:

1 Start simple and work towards more complex automation;
2 Be certain to take full backups of the AWS solutions;
3 Incrementally improve the RTO and RPO on an ongoing basis;
4 Exercise and practice disaster recovery procedures.

PERFORMANCE EFFICIENCY PILLAR

'We'll see that the sweet spot for clear high-level thinking about algorithm design is to ignore constant factors and lower-order terms, and to concentrate on how an algorithm's ***performance scales with the size of the input.***'
Tim Roughgarden

When the solution architect designs and builds according to the above guardrails, each piece of software and configuration code they design, create, test and deploy has a firm foundation upon which to realize performance efficiency in a manner that is validated and verified. Rarely is the first version of the code the fastest (and robust as well as viable) version. It takes time, effort, and good quality measurements to both attain as well as hold onto performance gains. The devils are in the details, and performance efficiency is often a dance with the devil(s) – some of whom it is futile to negotiate with, while there are others that respond well to alternative methods, techniques, and tools.

AWS defines performance efficiency as: 'the ability to use computing resources efficiently to meet system requirements and to maintain that efficiency as demand changes and technologies evolve.'

To attain performance efficiency it is required that you:

1. Best fit networking, computing, storage, and databases to the use case;
2. Continually review your 'best fit' decisions by using benchmarking and load tests that verify and validate the components chosen as well as their features;
3. Continually monitor the system, and seek out areas where the system is under-performing, and where performance is degrading;
4. Be prepared to change your solution, including removal of technologies, to achieve required performance.

Performance Efficiency Design Principles

Performance efficiency is lost when we enter the 'rob Peter to pay Paul' zone. Past a certain point, no more good effect can be realized given the limitations of resources and services, at their current price point. A gain in performance in one component can result in the degradation of 1:N other parts of the system, that can result in the system as a whole becoming non-performant. The devils are in the details.

AWS advocates several performance efficiency design principles, certain of which are cloud specific:

- Democratize advanced technologies – instead of having to master difficult low-level engineering know-how to deliver a solution and then building from scratch, learn to consume a service that already supports the requirements.
- Go global in minutes – quickly provision your solution into multiple Regions located around the globe.
- Use serverless architecture – have AWS manage your infrastructure and focus on the business processing requirements.
- Experiment more often – test and evaluate new designs in a virtual environment that offer the po-

tential to enhance performance.
- Mechanical sympathy – choose the technology that is a best fit to the processing requirements.

Areas of Performance Efficiency

AWS has these areas of performance efficiency:

1. Selection
2. Review
3. Monitoring
4. Trade-offs

AWS Performance Efficiency Selection Services

AWS offers these performance efficiency selections:

- Amazon EBS
- Auto Scaling
- Amazon S3
- Amazon RDS
- Amazon DynamoDB
- Amazon VPC
- Amazon Route 53
- AWS Direct Connect

All of these selections are covered elsewhere in this manuscript. Please refer to the table of contents.

AWS Performance Efficiency Review

Computing is all about life-long learning. This area is suggests that we do our homework, over and over again and again, ...

AWS Performance Efficiency Monitoring Services

AWS offers these performance efficiency monitoring services:

- Amazon CloudWatch
- AWS Lambda

Each of these selections are covered elsewhere in this manuscript. Please refer to the table of contents.

AWS Performance Efficiency Trade-offs

In the AWS cloud, performance efficiency trade-offs often involve these services:

- Amazon CloudFront
- Amazon Elasticache
- AWS Snowball
- Amazon RDS

All of these selections are covered elsewhere in this manuscript. Please refer to the table of contents.

AWS LOOSE ENDS

The following are a loosely associated bundle of items that are good to know and which also appear on the certification exams.

AWS Training Portal

When you purchase a class from AWS Academy or from one of its partners, the class instructor provides that student to a self-registration link they us to begin the setup process that provisions access to class content. The class curriculum includes lectures, lab content and knowledge assessments and is available with Quiklabs.

AWS Educate

AWS Educate is Amazon's global initiative to provide comprehensive resources for design, building, deploying and operating AWS cloud solution. The topics cover the entire range of AWS resource and service categories.

Like AWS Free Tier, AWS Educate provides a benefits and free services. To create you AWS Educate account, go to this URL https://aws.amazon.com/education/awseducate/

ABOUT THE AUTHOR

In the spring of '85, out of the blue, while finishing an undergraduate degree in Geology (and planning that fall to enter graduate school to study Mineral Economics), the writer's first computer was dropped on his work desk along with the assignment to create a program that estimated the ownership and operating expenses of surface and subsurface mining equipment. Back then, in the dark ages, no one had a computer on their desk, or certainly no one owned their own computer. Before that moment, the writer had never touched a computer, or had seen a computer. At that time, given 80% of others in Geology were out of work, the machine placed on my desk was better than their alternatives.

That micro-computer was a brand-new proto-DOS HP-85, with a tiny key-board, a 4" green monitor, and it ran applications you write in a language called BASIC. I literally did not know what a CPU was, what RAM was (ram was a barnyard animal, right?), what an operating system was, what a programming language was, etc.. Thirty days later the bug-free program ran in under 5 minutes, completing the work a Geologist accomplished in one week using a hand-held HP calculator.

Rather than be run over by the gathering herd of machines, that fall the writer switched disciplines entered graduate school to study information systems. In the fall of 1985, the writer's first personal computer was a 10MHZ CPU, 16KB of RAM, a 14" black-n-white TV as a monitor, with a dial-up modem cartridge, used to connect to a VAX 11-780 running BSD Unix 4.3 and INGRES, on which ran an application written in C code using double pointer indirection. In the following spring, my next computer had 12 MHZ with 32 KB and man was it fast, really, really fast!

Since earning a Master of Science (MS) in 1987, and working in pure and applied research, the author has been developing and operating globally distributed systems since 1990, first using varieties of UNIX, and then Windows NT, and then Linux, and now there off-spring. The author has worked with a mixture of on-premise and since 2007 a mixture of cloud platforms: first with proto-Azure while an employee at the Microsoft Center of Excellence, then in 2012 using Amazon Web Services (using Hadoop and Redshift), followed in 2015 using Google Cloud Platform (GCP).

Prior to the first week of February 2019, this author had no interest in acquiring either AWS or AWS Academy certifications. I had worked with AWS, as with Azure, without certifications needed. It was only due to an unexpected series of events that lead to me earning two (2) AWS certifications in the process of becoming an AWS Academy Accredited Instructor of both Cloud Foundation and Cloud Architecture classes.

Around New Year's 2019, this author was asked (by a thesis committee member) to teach a graduate class in cloud computing, which I accepted. The offer to teach turned out to be a slow train comin'. As discovered after the start of class, at the end of January, the existing curriculum included 20 components of AWS Academy content which was not accessible by the >70 enrolled students (as well as by this instructor). Why this was, was in week 1 of the class a mystery to both parties.

It turns out that said content was deprecated content, and the brand new 2019 version of the AWS Academy Cloud Foundation (CF) was available, but only if certain pre-requisites were satisfied by the class instructor. To request an instance of the new AWS Academy CF class and labs, the person submitting that request had to be accredited by AWS Academy to teach their new CF class. At the end of January, that was news to me, and quickly became information that was shared with the students and faculty.

And, the plot thickens. As in most systems, there are processes, rules and regulations. No worries, it's all good. To be so accredited, that person has to pass through barriers and gates, i.e., sit the 20 hours of class, complete the 10 knowledge assessments and finish the ~9 hours of labs, and pass the CF certification exam. Now bear in mind, for the students in the graduate course, there were lectures on cloud architecture, Python software development on AWS, and in-depth presentation of AWS resources and services, etc., to be created by this instructor.

Cutting to the chase, this instructor jumped through all of the hoops and by week five the students had access to their online CF class (one week behind the initial course schedule). A special shot-out to the AWS Academy team for turning around my request for the CF class incredibly quickly!

AWS Certified Cloud Practitioner Validation Number# PN49EN3CDE411H30

AWS Certified Cloud Practitioner Issue Date: February 12, 2019

AWS Certified Cloud Practitioner Expiration Date: February 12, 2021

Please note that an AWS Academy Accredited CF Educator is not assigned a public validation number. The AWS Academy needs to be contacted directly.

AWS Academy Accredited Cloud Foundation Educator Certification Issue Date: February 12, 2019

AWS Academy Accredited Cloud Foundation Educator Certification Expiration Date: February 12, 2021

In mid-March, the author completed the AWS Academy Cloud Architecture (CA) class lectures, knowledge assessments and labs. On April 8, 2019 , the author sat and passed the AWS Solution Architect Associate certification exam. On May 7, 2019 the author earned accreditation to teach the AWS Academy CA class.

AWS Certified Solution Architect Associate Validation Number# WVWVCWPCJJ1EQRKH

AWS Certified Solution Architect Associate Issue Date: April 8, 2019

AWS Certified Solution Architect Associate Expiration Date: April 8, 2021

 Solutions Architect - Associate

AWS Academy Accredited Cloud Architecture Educator Certification Issue Date: May 7, 2019

AWS Academy Accredited Cloud Architecture Educator Certification Expiration Date: May 7, 2021

This manuscript was first published in Amazon Kindle at the end of May 2019.

The author can be reached at charles@thesolusgroupllc.com

Marketing materials describing the consulting services provided by my company are available at www.thesolusgroupllc.com